A compendium of

# Flower Essences

A beginners guide to the new essences from around the world

**By**

**Clare G. Harvey** **Peter Tadd** **Don Dennis**

Published by:

**International Flower Essence Repertoire**

The Living Tree, Milland, Nr Liphook, Hampshire, GU30 7JS

Tel: 01428 741 572
Fax: 01428 741 679

Email: flower@atlas.co.uk

Front cover photo:: Don Dennis
Back cover photo: Don Dennis



Printed in the United Kingdom

# Contents



N.B. For ease of identification, each essence product in this Compendium has a unique 'ifer' code reference number. This helps in differentiating between different sizes of a particular essence, as well as helping one to differentiate the 'same' essence made by different developers when ordering. You will see the codes within each chapter and also in the categories List, and the Index sections.

Colour Code Reference: For ease of reference the categories List and Index are colour coded by essence range. A key to the colours is printed on the inside of the back cover.

To the future generations,
in hope that their explorations of flower essences
will be as compelling and fruitful as our own,
yet lead on into further vistas which we at present
cannot imagine.

# Preface

Flowers are one of the most delightful expressions of nature, not only do they gladden our hearts but are able to lift our spirits and soothe our minds with their magical healing qualities.

Since the time of Dr Edward Bach, a Harley Street physician who reminded us that the essence of flowers was available to help us heal ourselves, the flower essence field has literally blossomed. The art of flower remedy making has been rediscovered, and by borrowing from ancient healing traditions such as that of the Aboriginies in Australia, and other indigenous peoples from around the world, revived.

These people had an instinctive relationship with plants and flowers and an intimate knowledge of their powerful life enhancing properties that we too can benefit from in this ever increasing stressful world.

By its very nature, life today has its pressures, not only at work, in the environment and home, but in the sheer speed of the pace of life in general.

It is in this climate that people are now making empowered choices about taking responsibility for their own health and well being by seeking new ways of managing stress creatively.

The question is: How can we manage our lives in the most balances and intelligent way possible, whilst still achieving all that we need to? This is where flower essences come into their own!

It is a great pleasure to be able to introduce you to the wonderful world of flower essences as presented in this beautifully illustrated and informative guide to the various ranges available today. Here you will find essences and combinations to help you chill out, aid sleep, boost energy and concentration, cope with any physiological and emotional upsets, with major life changes and a myriad of stresses that can be at the heart of physical ailments.

There are travel aids for jet lag, remedies to help stock smoking and spritzers to clear the office space and protect one from electromagnetic pollution, to mention but a few.

Essences have a multi-level approach and help to reach the root of a problem whilst dealing with presenting issues.

With these invaluable tools at our finger tips it is now possible to see how to manage our stress at whatever level it manifests, with positivity and therefore navigate our lives with energy, enthusiasm and in balance.

*Clare G Harvey is recognised as a world authority on Flower Essences and acts as a consultant at The Hale Clinic, London. A teacher and author of The Encyclopaedia of Flower Remedies and The Healing Spirit of Plants, she is co-director with Don Dennis of the International Flower Essence Repertoire and The International Federation for Vibrational Medicine.*

# Approaching the world of flower essences.

This compendium offers a wide range of flower essences representing IFER's intention and commitment to provide the consumer with the best remedies available in the UK and Europe. Each essence line is the result of the unique sensibilities and hard work of the 18 developers. Flower essences are made by floating the flowers on the surface of water or pouring water over the opened blooms into a bowl. The etheric energies of the plant are transferred into the water. The habitat as well as the people involved are also recorded in this process giving an added flavour to each essence line. IFER's repertoire now spans a large area of the world from Brazil to Alaska and Australia to the UK. The producers' personal relationship to the specific plant and to Nature is imparted as a vibrational input into these products. Indeed there can be a detectable difference between essences of the same plant species due to different procedures and individuals. Some bring a needed intensity whilst others are quieter and gentler in their approach. Some, as with Dr. Bach before them, have in the space of a few years brought the gift of their wonderful essence lines to the world. But many of these developers have spent fifteen or twenty years or more growing with their product line.

How is the consumer to determine which essence or essence line is right for them and their family? One may start by meeting the developers and their products, as well as the photos of the flowers themselves. In this book you can begin by taking a look at their flowers, and reading their personal experiences of Nature's healing intention. You may simply like a developers face, or the name, picture, or unique description of an essence. These first intuitive responses often prove correct as guidance pointing towards those essences which are most suitable for you at this moment in time. Another approach, in the form of an extensive and very helpful index, is to be found at the back of the book.

What is increasingly apparent from working with the intelligence of Nature is the three-fold benefit (physical, etheric, and spiritual) of including essences in your personal health care. While there are specific benefits associated with each plant, the experience of taking an essence goes beyond the medical model of symptom and remedy to one of attunement to our spiritual nature. This process of essence application reinforces the etheric layers of the aura. These layers are vital and highly refined, having a direct impact on both the cellular level and the mind. One can think of flower essences as genies in a bottle.These radiant forces suffuse our auras with a feeling of lightness, goodness and a reassurance of being at one with our natural environment. From this state of wellness, unhealthy or blocked emotions can be released with a new sense of security. So not only are particular issues addressed, but we are also helped in our general life goal of feeling happy and grateful to be alive.

Nature cleanses the aura every time we take time to go for a walk in the garden, park, field, woodland or sea side. What is it that works so magically and unconsciously, is it more than simply the fresh air, the exercise, the beauty of the landscape? Being in Nature is what we all need and miss. Flower essences are one way to imbibe that magic directly. If in the first few seconds of taking an essence, we take a moment to fully feel the essence, the experience in the body is palpable. Flower essences enter the accupuncture meridian system the same way the homeopathic do sublingually.

One of the two major meridians, the conceptual vessel, terminates at that point under the tongue, thus giving entry to the entire meridian and yogic chakra system. From there the essence finds paths to adjust to each persons energetic make up. I have clairvoyantly witnessed what happens in this process with awe and amazement when I have offered various flower essences to students on my courses over the last several years. Much of this information has been fed back to the IFER, helping them to gain further insight into the subtle workings of the essences.

Watching the light of the essence flow through the etheric body has given me the clear understanding that the essence "knows" what it is doing. An essence may target the same area of the body or energy centre or chakra but following different paths to reach its goal. In some cases an essence will travel to a weaker chakra than it is normally ascribed to, due to the inter-relationship of these two chakras. The inherent intelligence of flower essences reveals a clear difference between that which is encoded in flower essences and that of homeopathic remedies. With homeopathic remedies having a single vibrational tone and amplitude, the practitioner needs to match both the remedy and the potencies to the presenting symptoms. Flower essences take a little of the work out of this process by interacting intelligently with our own subtle bodies, whilst holding the etheric pattern of the plant, mineral or animal. At the same time it maintains a direct link to a more conscious and interactive force in each of us which it engages in a direct energetic 'dialogue'. This force is our spiritual link: the Devic.

The devic aspect of the flower essence is the key to a successful range of essences. The energetic imprints of a flower or plant is simple enough to make, and anyone can do it, even radionic machines are capable of this. To be able to reach into the "spiritual waters" in order to invite in the devic energy requires an evolved human soul and direct devic guidance. Whereas yellow white physical ether correlates to the past and the spiritual blue ether to the future, devic ether which is gold or silver or diamond colour has no relationship to time whatsoever. Devic presence is all pervasive and over-lighting.They are very much like Taoist immortals who have attained the wisdom of the ages. Yet for the Devas to manifest into our bodies or into trees or in animals they have to work through physical and spiritual ethers. These ethers are utilised as carrier wave forms which are naturally aligned to the earth and the sky. Carrier waves are an underlying wave form which can transport a second set of wave frequencies. The Devic manifests though these two primary etheric wave forms of the past and the future. The Devas, in doing so "want us to see the bigger picture", which directly connects to our deeper spiritual identity with the essential implication that this awareness manifests in everyday life. In fact the devic resides in an interior aspect of the heart chakra which in the ancient Indian texts is referred to as Devata, the inner angel and the Sanskrit root for our word Divine.

## Why do they work?

Flower essences began in the beginning of the twentieth century with the well known Medical Doctor Edward Bach, who later became a homeopath. His love of walking in nature lured him into tasting the morning dew on flower petals. To his surprise he discovered a level of information in these droplets of water which were very specific to each species of flower. Over time he acquainted himself with many plants and discovered that their subtle forces could indeed help cure the ills of his patients.

Is there any scientific evidence to back the idea that dewdrops or water in any form can store information? This is the shared area of understanding with homeopathy which in its higher potencies has no actual physical substance remaining and yet the water is still imprinted with the healing properties of that remedy. Over time the data base of those helped by homeopathy has grown and this is now true with flower essences. But the fact that people feel and are better does not explain just how or why these non-chemical substances work.

Sacred springs and wells are a part of our folk history not only in Europe but world wide. Some are still in use today. Water is water but why were our ancestors attracted to certain sites? Why are we still? Scientific experiments have been made in recent years which have no direct connection with flower essences but support the principles behind their production . To understand this phenomenon of water more closely a group of Japanese scientists began the study of water in a most unusual way; they froze water into snowflake-like crystals taken from various sources. Some from polluted rivers, others from springs high in the mountains where people maintained their folk traditions. The water was taken to a lab where it was frozen and photographed . The patterns which appeared from the same source were not random but uniquely identical in their crystalline patterns. Hundreds of samples from a single source showed common and distinguishable patterns which they call a "crystalline grid". Waters from different sources showed unique patterns; very beautiful ones were from the purest sources, whilst others not fully formed came from polluted lakes or streams, and even London tap water. Later experiments using sound, music and even written words placed on the bottles created verifiable and astounding results.

It is now understood that water has the ability to absorb information and is spatially affected by it, as well as having the ability to absorb and be transformed by ether. The fact that water can hold healing vibrations was known in America in the early 19th Century, and utilised by a New Englander, Phineus Parkhurst Quimby, who transmitted spiritual healing into water which he bottled and then posted to clients. In the 1980's The Mobius of Society in Santa Monica, California ran a number of trials of an experiment using nine different healers. These unrelated individuals transmitted healing "vibrations" into sealed bottles of water which were then sent to a laboratory for spectrographic analysis. In this double-blind study, there was a consistency in the degree of change in the spatial relationship of the water molecules. The greater the healing force, the greater the "space" in between the water molecules. This space is the etheric space which is the very sense of expansiveness that one has after a good meditation or walk in Nature. We "feel" lighter and, indeed, the water in our bodies is.

We consist mostly of water: between 65% for the oldest group and up to 85% for infants. The water in our bodies and our cells are re-encoded very readily by these essences. The above-mentioned study demonstrates that water encodes the energies of a place and even the sound of music or human thought, but it does not answer how. For this we need to take the quantum step into the "fifth element" ether. Ether is the subtle force which creates a bridge between the physical and the non-physical. It is geometric, self-luminous, and while there are various colours from yellow to violet, each layer or etheric dimension is itself monochromatic. Ether is also holographic, and goes beyond the spectrum of physical light. It is interactive while retaining properties which are related to time and to space. Water will hold the etheric encoded energy of the essence making process for a month or so. After that the etheric forces absorb other influences and begin to align to them weakening the initial imprint. If at least 20% cognac/brandy or vodka is added to the water, the pattern will be preserved for years.

These are very exciting times as those who are intuitive and sensitive to the subtle forces in Nature and their own bodies are finding a bridge with the latest advancements in science. An introduction to the world of flower, gem and animal essences can begin with this compendium or expand an already developed interest. IFER carries a great number of products, not to overwhelm, but to be able to offer the variety of essences which have been carefully monitored over the years through consumer feedback, practitioner support and our own quality control programme. This includes staff who love their work and respect their direct interaction with the products they handle, as well as their customers. Along with them I am using my refined clairvoyant ability to maintain close contact with the essence lines and with many of the developers, and examine any possible quality control questions that might arise (which I am pleased to say is rare). Please read on to see how one may directly approach this growing field of awareness and health.

*Peter Tadd is a clairvoyant healer and lecturer living in Co. Cork, Ireland with his wife Jennifer Corcoran and their three children. In 1978 Peter began to use his innate abilities to help guide others through their life challenges. As this gift grew in depth and scope he began to see and understand the chakra system, acupuncture meridians, and the aura in greater detail. Peter travels throughout the U.K., Europe, the United States and Canada offering private consultations and healing sessions, and offers seminars on healing and on how to feel and see "the finer things" in life.*

# Introduction

The most frequently heard comment made by visitors to our shop who are relatively new to flower essences, is "Where do I begin?" Surrounded by some 1,500 essences from 18 or more developers from around the world, it can certainly appear daunting, and perhaps wanting of an explanation! And now that these same products are beginning to be available in more and more health food and other shops around the U.K. and Europe (as well as elsewhere around the globe), the need for some manner of reasonably comprehensive guide and introduction to these new essences is increasingly apparent.

It would be good to be clear on one point at the outset: that this is a young and very rapidly developing and changing field. Ten years from now this Compendium you have in your hands will be primarily of historical interest I would wager, insofar as the various essence lines described herein are likely to have undergone momentous changes in the intervening years. In spite of the fact that Dr. Edward Bach in effect began the ball rolling in the 1930's, the modern development of flower and other vibrational essences is still in its early years, perhaps akin to where the field of Homeopathy was in the 1880's. Over the past 25 years there has been an enormous amount of research carried out by people around the world, drawn intuitively towards the healing energies of the flowers of their region.

For many decades after the death of Dr. Bach there was a view held in some quarters that the 38 flowers of his work were all the world might ever need from flower essences. Yet it is a widely held misconception that his 38 remedies were the only ones around, even in the 1930's. The making of flower essences has been a part of the folk healing tradition of southern Italy for at least the past century; there are reliable reports of essence making being carried out in the Austrian alps at the end of the 19th century and early 20th century. There is also the folk tradition in the German-speaking countries of walking barefoot through a wildflower meadow of a morning, to gain the benefit of the dew from the flowers. Dr. Bach was nevertheless a true pioneer, and one of the critical contributions he made to this field was a method of preserving the essences, i.e., with the use of brandy. Without this ability to both keep the liquid 'clean', and the energy of the flower retained within the bottle indefinitely , the world of essence making and use would by necessity always have remained locally based.

So there was an inevitability to the development of more essences beyond the original 38 of Dr. Bach's repertoire, and if not by reason of other traditions, then certainly at least by dint of curiousity.

Dr. Bach was in my view a true visionary though, and it has continually impressed me how so many of the new developments of this field were foreshadowed or implied in his work. For example, Rock Water could be said to prefigure the development of gem elixirs such as those made by the Alaskan Flower Essence Project. Crab Apple essence has been known for many years to have a cleansing action on the skin (and as the sixth component in the Five Flower Cream it serves marvellously in this capacity, for example helping to clear acne). This establishes the principle that in certain circumstances a flower essence may have an impact on the physical level, not simply (as Dr. Bach taught) on the underlying emotions of any given condition. And now in Australia there are flower essence creams for treating pain and arthritis which are being used in 18 hospitals. Again, Dr. Bach began the idea of combination essences, which are both very effective and may also be more accessible to the general public.

## Local vs. Global

One question that frequently gets asked is whether or not it might be best to take only flower essences that are made locally, or at least from within one's region or country. There are several elements to a sensible answer to this question in my mind, and the answer is certainly not either "yes" or "no". The first point is that Dr. Bach himself saw his own essences reaching out to "all the four quarters of the world to heal people who are ill" , and if it was good enough for Dr. Bach, then... Secondly I would raise a practical point: for a certain condition, there may be an essence made elsewhere in the world which is especially effective, so why not avail oneself of it? For example, there are many hundreds of cases of women who have struggled to conceive, who have been helped by the use of She Oak from the Australian Bush Flower Essence line. One must not underestimate the exceptional levels of research and intuitive skills, care and integrity that the essence makers who are described in this book have brought to the work they are doing.

At the same time it can be important to link with the flowers of nature around one. If you keep a garden, or even just a few house plants, it is likely to be the case that these flowers of your garden or house are already interacting with you energetically to some degree. Making essences with these plants can be a richly rewarding experience, and certainly not one to be discouraged! So in summary on this point, we advocate looking both globally and locally for the essences which most suit you.

## Our Selection

How does the IFER make its selection of essence ranges? There are a few elements and principles in our approach. We look first and foremost for essence lines which are vibrationally "good", harmonious and effective; and the line needs to be consistently so. No amount of research can make up for any disturbances or lack in an essence at the energetic level. Nevertheless we do also look for clarity of information, and in effect a 'pedigree' of case histories. The personal qualities of the developer are also important, for they are a part of what is referred to as the "co-creative process" of the essence making. One of the mysteries of essence making is that there is a life-long energetic connection between an essence maker and the essence, no matter the distance that separates them in the world. So integrity in the maker is vital. We also only carry lines which are made by the people known to us, for the same reasons.

There is a view, promoted especially by one medium, that an essence of a flower will be the same no matter who makes it or where it is made. In our view this is simply grossly incorrect. For example we have three Gorse essences from three different makers. A few years ago we examined these with Peter Tadd and Sandra Epstein (of the Ararêtama Essences of Brazil, who is also gifted with 'seeing'). It was quite clear that each essence went to distinct and different depths of the heart chakra. Within a therapeutic context these differences can be crucially important. One might liken this to a song being sung by a baritone, tenor, and an alto: it is the same song, but the effect on us in hearing it is different in each case.

In looking at a painting, one of course is able to appreciate it without meeting the artist. Yet if the opportunity arises to meet the painter, one does gain some further insight into the work. It is much the same with essences, and this is one important reason why we have brought the various essence makers to the UK over the years to teach weekend seminars. And while the research of the present generation will hopefully be built upon by those that follow, yet it will always be the case that the individual who makes the essence line plays a central role in determining elements of the energetic profile of their line. All of the essence makers whose products we carry understand and know the importance of this aspect of their work, and that in effect essence making is what I like to call a "temple activity". An inner tranquillity and calm is needed in order that the higher frequencies of the devic realm may come into the process.

We also have a bias towards those essences which are in need of being imported into the UK. There are simple commercial reasons why an importer/distributor needs to remain focused on those products which need their services to reach a given market. Nevertheless we also endeavour to support several of the best of the essence lines made here in the UK, and do what we can to assist these to reach further to more overseas markets and therapists. And while the IFER is a business, it is nevertheless made up of staff members who are primarily motivated by their love of the essences.

We also make one line of essences ourselves – the Living Tree Orchid Essences – but we submit these to the same scrutiny that we submit any other essences to, or even more. The making of these orchid essences came about as a surprise for me, and certainly was not a conscious intention when the IFER was founded in 1996. It is nevertheless a source of constant delight to both me and my essence-making partner Heather, and this involvement in the making process has deepened my understanding and appreciation of the rest of the essences we carry.

It must be emphasised that the selection of essences presented in this book (as well as those carried by the IFER) is not intended to be either exhaustive nor exclusive. There are a great many essence lines being produced now globally, probably something in excess of 200 makers, both large and small. IFER has not had the opportunity nor the resources to contact all of these and examine their products. So if a line is not represented here with which you are familiar, please be assured that we are not passing judgement on all the essences that are in existence! We are only stating that the essences which we carry and which are described in this book are of a very high standard, and are essences which we are proud to represent.

**How Essences are Made**

The fundamental intention of the essence making process is to gather and infuse into liquid the healing energies associated with a flowering plant. This intention can be carried out in two main ways :

1. The tradition begun by Dr. Bach involves cutting a few flowers from a healthy, unstressed plant, and placing these in a bowl of water for a few hours during a sunlit morning. The flowers are then removed, and brandy is added to the water in a 50/50 ratio . This is what is known as the "mother tincture".

2. Non-cutting methods: there are several of these. Vasudeva & Kadambii Barnao of the Living Essences of Australia pour water over the blooms of the plant in the wilderness. Shabd-sangeet Khalsa

of the Dancing Light Orchid Essences places a bowl of water underneath the blooms of the orchids for several hours or longer, but has no actual contact between the blooms and the water . The Living Tree Orchid Essences combine these two approaches. All three techniques work very well.

In each technique the resultant liquid is called the "mother tincture", and just a few drops of the mother tincture are added to what is known as a "stock" bottle. It is the stock essence which is normally sold, or the next dilution which is called "dosage" – it is in this form that most of the combinations are made available, as these are ready to use, straight out of the bottle.

Gem elixirs are made simply by placing a good 'clean' gemstone in the bowl of water, and leaving it in the morning sun.

Environmental essences are normally made within an environment of a certain exceptional and pristine quality, to 'hold' the energies of that place and time. Fuller understanding of these may be gleaned by reading the Alaskan essences book, The Essence of Healing.

**Animal Essences?**

These caught us entirely by surprise when we first encountered them several years ago. I would have to admit to extreme scepticism at the very idea when we were first contacted about them. But for us there has never been a clearer case of "the proof is in the pudding". These essences amazed us, for they appear to convey a clear energetic imprint from the devic level of the animals; and they work. I believe that these essences from Daniel Mapel are truly exceptional, and despite them challenging our beliefs perhaps, ought to be allowed for in one's exploration of the realm of the new vibrational essences.

**Aura Sprays**

Until a few years ago most people involved with flower essences were of the view that one should not mix a flower essence with an essential oil, for fear that the oil might interfere of even destroy the etheric energy of the essence. This was based on the supposition that essences were akin to homeopathic remedies in this regard. But in fact this is not the case, rather quite the contrary: the blending of the two types of substances in a spray can actually be synergistically powerful, each enhancing the other's action. Star Riparretti of the Star Essences of California was amongst the first to demonstrate this to a wide audience with her marvellous Angel Rejuvenation Spray; and in the last few years this has become the fastest growing area of essence development. In this book there are some 36 aura and space clearing sprays described, but four years ago we had only two!

**Safety & Combining**

One way to think of flower essences is as though they are music. This can be a helpful metaphor when thinking about combining essences. A string quartet, or a reggae band, can play wonderful music, with several instruments playing harmoniously together; so can flower essences. But it would not be very advisable to have both the quartet and the band playing in the same room at the same time! Think of a theme, and select a few essences which are each addressing that theme, and one is likely to have a harmonious blend. Combining essences from within one line of essences is somewhat akin to asking a number of musicians with the same training and background to play together: there is an inherent rapport already. Combining essences from different lines can be very rewarding, but also requires more care and attention if one is to have a harmonious blend. (One can easily think of instances of the musical equivalent, both positive and … well…) When I first encountered the new essences some eight years ago, in my enthusiasm I ended up creating a combination that was composed of 21 different essences from five different lines, many of which had no relationship in terms of theme to one another. One does not persist long with such an experiment, and it is not to be recommended. In musical terms, this was cacophony!

Flower essences are currently in daily use by perhaps a million people worldwide, and to date we have never heard of anyone coming to harm from their use. One would be hard-pressed to find another mode of therapy where one could say that.

Vibrational essences can safely be used with all other forms of treatment, and at all stages of one's life. Homeopaths are increasingly prescribing essences to their clients in conjunction with their homeopathic preparations; aromatherapists are blending essences with their oils; kinesiologists are muscle-testing for essences in ever-increasing numbers; and so on. Due to their innate intelligence, essences are flexible and very largely self-adjusting, and so are able to be incorporated with other forms of treatment quite readily, yet with very positive results.

These are indeed challenging times we live in, and the contrast between recent world events and the world of flower essences could hardly be overstated. Man's inhumanity to man continues unabated; and meanwhile the Earth herself cries out to both receive and to give healing. It is the music unheard, constantly playing softly amongst the trees and fields of flowers, a hum or a vibration which whispers of the Love at the ground of being. Nature offers this love to us in myriad ways, and not least through the astonishing variety and beauty and delicacy of the flowers. It is aspects of this Love from Nature's bounty that we find offered as well in the essences described herein.

# Alaskan Flower Essence Project

Region: Alaska

Founded: 1984

DEVELOPERS: Steve Johnson, Shabd-sangeet Khalsa, Janice Schofield, Jane Bell

In 1983 Steve Johnson ran a fire station in a a remote village on the northern shore of Lake Minchumina, located in the geographical centre of the state, with an imposing view of Denali, the tallest mountain on the North American continent. It was here that he began preparing the Alaskan Flower Essences. He founded the Alaskan Flower Essence Project (AFEP) with Shabd-sangeet Khalsa in 1984, preparing essences from many remote areas of Alaska, moving in 1991 to Homer in southern Alaska. He was joined in 1985 by Janice Schofield and in 1992 co-created the 48 Gem elxirs with Jane Bell.

THE ESSENCES: Prepared in several pristine and remote wildflower areas of Alaska, the flower essences have been collected from plants growing in an environment that is elementally intact, These essences teach us that it is possible to adapt and prosper in an environment that seems to be more challenging than supportive. They help us to respond better to our challenges to be used as opportunities for the transformation of our attitudes about struggle, conflict and difficulty.
There are three kits of flower essences, a set of Gems and a set of Environmental essences. Steve also produces 9 Combination essences and 3 Combination Feng Shui sprays.

## **Flower** essences

### Alder *7.5ml lfer 1026*

promotes clarity of perception on all levels; helps us integrate seeing with knowing so that we can recognize our highest truth in each life experience.

### Alpine Azalea *7.5ml lfer 1028*

helps us achieve unconditional self-acceptance through the release of self-doubt; opens our hearts to the spirit of love; teaches us compassion through understanding.

### Balsam Poplar *7.5ml lfer 1032*

for the release of physical and emotional tension associated with sexual trauma; balances the circulation of life force energy in the body; helps to ground and synchronize our sexual energy with planetary cycles and rhythms.

### Black Spruce *7.5ml lfer 1034*

promotes the integration of information from past lessons and experiences into present time awareness; helps us access eternal and archetypal wisdom from the collective consciousness of the Earth.

### Bladderwort *7.5ml lfer 1036*

helps us shatter illusion through clear inner knowing; promotes discernment when faced with dishonesty in others; strengthens our ability to perceive the truth regardless of the confusion that surrounds it.

### Blueberry Pollen *7.5ml lfer 1040*

helps us expand on all levels to accommodate abundance; facilitates the release of mental and emotional attachments that limit our ability to manifest higher purpose in physical form.

### Blue Elf Viola *7.5ml lfer 1038*

dissipates the protective energy that has been built up around our anger, rage and frustration; helps us understand the issues at the root of these emotions so they can be expressed in a clear and heart-centered way.

### Bog Blueberry *7.5ml lfer 1042*

for neutralizing the beliefs that limit the experience of abundance on all levels; encourages us to open to the abundance that is offered with acceptance and gratitude.

## Bog Rosemary *7.5ml Ifer 1044*

promotes the release of fear and resistance held deep in the heart; strengthens trust in Divine healing and support.

## Bunchberry *7.5ml Ifer 1046*

helps us become aware of and then release our attachment to distraction; promotes mental steadfastness and emotional clarity in demanding situations.

## Cassandra *7.5ml Ifer 1048*

calming; encourages stillness of mind; enables us to perceive life from a quiet inner perspective.

## Cattail Pollen *7.5ml Ifer 1050*

helps one connect with the personal truth that illuminates one's chosen life path, and with the inner strength to act in alignment with this truth.

## Chiming Bells *7.5ml Ifer 1052*

encourages the experience of joy, peace and stability at the physical level of our beings; helps us open our hearts to the loving energy of the Divine Mother.

## Columbine *7.5ml Ifer 1058*

helps us appreciate our own unique and personal beauty, regardless of how it differs from others; strengthens our sense of self and the ability to project ourselves out into the world for others to see.

## Comandra *7.5ml Ifer 1060*

helps us develop our potential to see the physical world from a higher perspective; brings support for maintaining the necessary perspective on both the seen and unseen worlds as we move through the current dimensional shift; opens the heart to be a bridge between the third and fourth dimensions.

## Cotton Grass *7.5ml Ifer 1066*

helps us come to an understanding of the core issues that led to an accident or injury so that we can release the physical, emotional and mental trauma associated with it.

## Cow Parsnip *7.5ml Ifer 1068*

promotes inner strength; assists with the process of adapting to a new environment; encourages peace of mind and contentment with present circumstances, even during times of intense transition and change.

## Dandelion *7.5ml Ifer 1074*

promotes awareness and release of emotional tension held in muscle tissue; increases body-mind communication so we are better able to identify the underlying issues and attitudes that lead to the creation of tension in our bodies.

## Fireweed *7.5ml Ifer 1082*

heals shock and trauma; strengthens our grounding connection to the Earth; helps break up and move out old energy patterns that are being held in the etheric body so that new cycles of revitalization and renewal can be initiated.

## Forget-Me-Not *7.5ml Ifer 1084*

facilitates the release of fear, guilt and pain held in the subconscious; enables us to regain respect and compassion for ourselves and for others.

## Foxglove *7.5ml Ifer 1086*

stimulates the release of fear and emotional tension; enables our perceptions to expand to connect with the truth of the situation.

## Golden Corydalis *7.5ml Ifer 1090*

supports the reintegration of identity after an experience of deep transformation; helps one establish and maintain a link with the higher self that facilitates the integration of life experience according to the needs of the soul.

## Grass of Parnassus *7.5ml Ifer 1092*

showers all levels of the energy system with the cleansing and nourishing benefits of Light; helps one bring past experiences to completion on all levels.

## Green Bells of Ireland *7.5ml Ifer 1094*

opens our awareness to the co-creative consciousness that is present in nature; helps the newly born greet the Earth; strengthens the energetic connection between the physical body and the Earth.

## Green Bog Orchid *7.5ml Ifer 1096*

stimulates the gentle release of pain and fear from deep levels of the heart; expands awareness of one's inner nature; supports the development of a deeper heart connection with others and with the nature kingdoms.

## Green Fairy Orchid *7.5ml Ifer 1098*

helps us create a level of honesty in the heart where nothing is hidden from the self; expands the heart so that it may contain the fullness of the inner male and inner female.

## Grove Sandwort *7.5ml Ifer 1100*

helps us establish clear energetic connections with the Earth; supports a nurturing relationship between the Earth and all living beings; strengthens physical and emotional bonds between mothers and children.

## Hairy Butterwort *7.5ml Ifer 1102*

helps us consciously access the support and guidance we need in order to move through transition, conflict, or difficulty with ease, grace and deep understanding, and without the creation of crisis or illness.

## Harebell *7.5ml Ifer 1104*

teaches us to look within to find the love we seek; helps us open all areas of our life to Universal Love and to the presence of the Divine.

## Horsetail *7.5ml Ifer 1106*

connectedness; opens and expands channels of communication between the conscious, subconscious and superconscious levels of our beings; improves inter-species communication.

## Icelandic Poppy *7.5ml Ifer 1108*

supports the gentle unfolding of spiritual receptivity; strengthens our capacity to integrate and radiate spiritual energy into all aspects of our lives.

## Jacob's Ladder *7.5ml Ifer 1112*

aligns intention and motivation with the wisdom of the Higher Self; helps us let go of the urge to try to figure things out and just open to receive what is available in each moment.

## Labrador Tea *7.5ml Ifer 1114*

centers energy-in the body-in the moment; relieves stress associated with the experience of extremes; helps us continually learn a new perspective of balance.

## Lace Flower *7.5ml Ifer 1116*

strengthens self-acceptance and our sense of self-worth; promotes the realization of how each person's unique contribution enriches the whole.

## Ladies' Tresses *7.5ml Ifer 1118*

promotes deep internal realignment with life purpose through the release of trauma held at the cellular level; helps us reconnect energetically with parts of the body that have been injured or traumatized.

## Lady's Slipper *7.5ml Ifer 1120*

regulates circulation in all of the major energy pathways; increases awareness of the flow of subtle energy in and around the body; helps us receive, focus and direct healing energy for ourselves and others.

## Lamb's Quarters *7.5ml Ifer 1122*

heals separation between the heart and the mind; balances the power of the mind with the joy of the heart.

## Monkshood *7.5ml Ifer 1130*

provides protection and support for getting in touch with the deepest levels of the inner self; strengthens our ability to interact with others by fostering a clear recognition of our own Divine identity.

## Moschatel *7.5ml Ifer 1132*

teaches us how to accomplish more by grounding our mental focus into the Earth; helps us learn how to co-create with nature through celebration and play.

## Mountain Wormwood *7.5ml Ifer 1134*

stimulates the release of resentment and the healing of old wounds; supports us in surrendering unforgiving areas within ourselves and in our relationships with others.

## Northern Lady's Slipper *7.5ml Ifer 1138*

provides nurturing energy for the healing of core traumas and wounds that have strongly impacted the physical and energetic structures of the body; helps us allow our bodies to be touched and healed by infinite gentleness.

## Northern Twayblade *7.5ml Ifer 1140*

helps us ground our sensitivity to the subtle realms more fully into our physical body and life experience; helps us enlighten our most basic needs, instincts and mundane realities with the finest aspects of our spiritual wisdom.

## One-Sided Wintergreen *7.5ml Ifer 1142*

helps sensitive people become aware of how they impact and are impacted by others; teaches us how to work in close proximity with others without losing our center; helps us create functional energy boundaries based on an awareness of our own sensitivities.

## Opium Poppy *7.5ml Ifer 1144*

for finding a balance between doing and being; helps us integrate previous experiences so we may live more fully in the present.

## Paper Birch *7.5ml lfer 1148*

encourages a gentle unveiling of the true and essential self that is present within; helps us gain a clearer perspective of our life purpose and how to live it.

## Pineapple Weed *7.5ml lfer 1150*

helps us maintain a calm awareness of ourselves and our surroundings so that we can remain free from injury and risk; promotes harmony between mothers and children, and between humans and the Earth.

## Prickly Wild Rose *7.5ml lfer 1156*

helps us remain openhearted when we are faced with conflict and struggle; builds trust; encourages openness and a courageous interest in life.

## River Beauty *7.5ml lfer 1168*

an essence of emotional recovery, reorientation and regeneration; helps us start over after emotionally devastating experiences; empowers us to use adverse circumstances as opportunities for cleansing and growth.

## Round-Leaved Sundew *7.5ml lfer 1172*

for surrendering attachment to the known and letting go of resistance to the unknown; helps us bring the strength of the ego into alignment with Divine Will.

## Shooting Star *7.5ml lfer 1176*

strengthens one's connection to inner spiritual guidance; brings a deeper understanding of cosmic origins and earthly purpose.

## Single Delight *7.5ml lfer 1178*

for those suffering from feelings of isolation; helps us open to and link energetically with other members of our soul family.

## Sitka Burnet *7.5ml lfer 1180*

for healing the past on all levels; helps one identify issues that are contributing to internal conflict; works with an individual to bring forth the full potential for healing that lies within a given process.

## Sitka Spruce Pollen *7.5ml lfer 1182*

balances the masculine and feminine expressions of power within an individual; supports right action in the present moment.

## Soapberry *7.5ml lfer 1184*

stimulates the release of tension from the heart associated with a fear of nature; helps us move through fear inducing situations with an open heart; supports us in channeling the expression of power through our hearts.

## Sphagnum Moss *7.5ml lfer 1186*

helps us release the need for harsh judgment or criticism of our healing processes; enables us to create a space of unconditional acceptance in the heart so that core issues can be brought there for healing.

## Spiraea *7.5ml lfer 1188*

encourages unconditional acceptance of support from all sources; teaches us how to nurture and be nurtured by life through openness and gratitude.

## Sticky Geranium *7.5ml lfer 1190*

for getting un-stuck; supports decisive and focused action; helps us move beyond previous stages of growth and self identity.

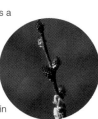

## Sunflower *7.5ml lfer 1200*

strengthens one's radiant expression of self; encourages a balanced expression of masculine energy in men and women; promotes a functional relationship with authority.

## Sweetgale *7.5ml lfer 1202*

helps us identify and release deep emotional pain and tension that undermines the quality of our communication and interactions with others, especially in male/female relationships.

## Sweetgrass *7.5ml lfer 1204*

cleanses and rejuvenates the etheric body; brings lessons and experiences to completion on the etheric level; removes disharmonious energies from our home and work environments.

## Tamarack *7.5ml lfer 1206*

promotes self-confidence by helping us reach a deeper understanding of our unique strengths and abilities; encourages the conscious development of one's individuality.

## Tundra Rose *7.5ml lfer 1208*

restores hope, courage and inspiration to those who have much to offer but are close to giving up; strengthens the ability to bring a larger expression of joy and enthusiasm to the fulfillment of one's responsibilities.

**Tundra Twayblade** *7.5ml lfer 1210*

opens the heart to allow unconditional love complete access to areas of the body that are in need of healing; supports the clearing of trauma held at the cellular level of one's being.

**Twinflower** *7.5ml lfer 1212*

promotes balance in communication; helps one learn to listen and speak to others from a place of inner calm and focused neutrality.

**White Fireweed** *7.5ml lfer 1216*

calms the emotional body after a shocking experience; clears emotionally painful experiences from the cellular memory and helps us release our identification with these experiences so that rejuvenation and renewal can begin.

**White Spruce** *7.5ml lfer 1218*

grounds spiritual wisdom into the body; helps one bring logic, intuition and emotion together into unified action in the present moment.

**White Violet** *7.5ml lfer 1220*

builds trust in the protection of the Higher Self and benevolent spiritual forces; helps those who are highly sensitive or acutely aware of their surroundings maintain a strong sense of self regardless of the dynamics of their environment.

**Wild Iris** *7.5ml lfer 1222*

opens awareness of our inherent creative potential; helps us recognize the beautiful expression of Divine creativity that we are; encourages us to share our inner beauty and creative energy freely with others.

**Wild Rhubarb** *7.5ml lfer 1224*

promotes mental flexibility; brings the mind into alignment with Divine Will through the heart; encourages a relaxation of inappropriate mental control; balances the rational and the intuitive.

**Willow** *7.5ml lfer 1228*

stimulates mental receptivity, flexibility and resilience; helps us remove our resistance to consciously creating our lives.

**Yarrow** *7.5ml lfer 1230*

seals energy breaks in the aura; strengthens the overall integrity of the energy field; helps us know and be the source of our own protection.

**Yellow Dryas** 7.5ml lfer 1232

support for those who are exploring the edge of the known; helps one maintain an energetic connection to one's soul family during dynamic cycles of growth and change.

# **Gem** essences

**Aquamarine** *7.5ml lfer 3184*

brings a calm, quiet clarity to an over-active mental body; increases the ability to achieve a neutral, serene state of mind; helps create a mental oasis of cool, clear receptivity.

**Aventurine** *7.5ml lfer 3185*

strengthens the central vertical axis which stabilizes us during expansion experiences; helps us move into and through new experiences with grace, stamina and perseverance; good for spiritual trailblazers and pioneers.

**Azurite** *7.5ml lfer 3186*

grounding communication; opens and strengthens the connection between the feminine Earth forces and the 5th chakra; helps us communicate with vitality, authenticity and gentleness.

**Black Tourmaline** *7.5ml lfer 3187*

helps us exchange old unwanted energies being held in the body for fresh, clean, neutral energy; a precision tool for the release of toxic energy from the mind, emotions and physical body.

**Bloodstone** *7.5ml lfer 3188*

strengthens one's connection to the Earth; brings a stronger flow of Earth energy into the 1st and 2nd chakras; stimulates the release of emotional energies that have been stuck in the lower chakras; rebalances these energy centers after trauma or emotional upset.

**Brazilian Amethyst** *7.5ml lfer 3189*

transmutes energy from lower to higher vibratory rates; helps to lift energy from an overly material state; helps one sense and experience one's unique spiritual identity.

**Brazilian Quartz** *7.5ml lfer 3190*

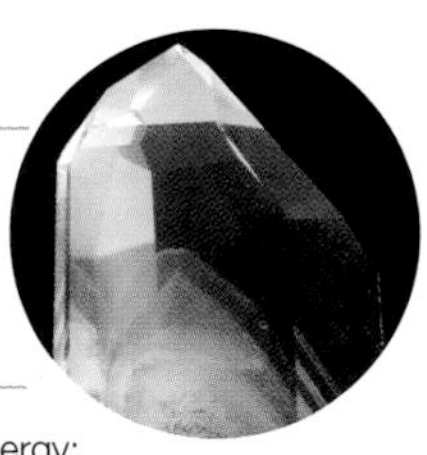

the essence of cleansing white light; energizes and synchronizes the auric field, the subtle bodies and the physical body with the Earth's natural vibration.

**Carnelian** *7.5ml lfer 3191*

increases the etheric body's ability to access pranic energy; energizes and clears the nadirs, (the energetic interface between the etheric body and the meridians), allowing a greater flow of energy to the meridians.

**Chrysocolla** *7.5ml lfer 3192*

opens, softens and expands the inner dimensions of the heart chakra; helps us release tension and armoring around giving and receiving love; increases flexibility in the mind and body to allow the vibration of love to flow.

**Chrysoprase** *7.5ml lfer 3193*

brings the heart chakra into harmonious union with the green energy frequency of the planet; synchronizes the subtle bodies with the heart energy of the Earth; helps us accept the Earth as our home.

**Citrine** *7.5ml lfer 3194*

harmonizes the mental body with higher spiritual laws; increases access to Divine intelligence; amplifies qualities of concentration, centering and rational mind.

**Covellite** *7.5ml lfer 3195*

brings strength, clarity and definition to the auric field; acts as a protective filter that encourages us to relax energetically, thereby enhancing our natural ability to receive love and support from the environment.

**Diamond** *7.5ml lfer 3196*

brings clarity to the 6th chakra; harmonizes Divine and personal will; helps us activate personal will in its highest form; strengthens our ability to act in alignment with Divine purpose.

**Emerald** *7.5ml lfer 3197*

a universal heart cleanser and balancer; helps us contact the energies of the Divine Mother and the Divine Feminine; gently coaxes the heart to open to a greater experience of love in the physical body.

**Fluorite** *7.5ml lfer 3198*

the "break up" elixir; increases the circulation of energy into the physical body by breaking up blockages in the etheric body.

**Fluorite Combo** *7.5ml lfer 3199*

synchronizes movement between the etheric and physical bodies; fine tunes our focus so that we can move through an issue or healing process with precision and balance.

**Gold** *7.5ml lfer 3200*

brings strength and balance to the 3rd chakra; for accessing and bringing forth the highest aspects of personal identity; helps us tap into our inner truth, joy and wisdom as a source of creative power.

**Green Jasper** *7.5ml lfer 3201*

reconnects body rhythms with the Earth's rhythms when there has been a disruption to the natural flow; helps us connect to the wild feminine; restores earthly sensuality and healthy sexuality.

**Hematite** *7.5ml lfer 3202*

strengthens energetic boundaries in the emotional body; promotes emotional independence rather than co-dependence; helps us maintain a state of compassionate detachment while witnessing intense emotions in others; helps us contain our own emotions in a responsible way.

**Herkimer Diamond** *7.5ml lfer 3203*

a highly developed transmitter of white light; promotes clarity of vision; stimulates healing on all levels; facilitates clarity during the dream state; brings balance and focus to the 6th chakra.

**Jadeite Jade** *7.5ml lfer 3204*

a vibration of peace, balance and timeless simplicity; helps us stay centered in the moment with an awareness and acceptance of our true essence.

**Kunzite** *7.5ml lfer 3205*

opens the heart to an awareness of one's angelic presence; helps one experience the spiritual love of the angelic kingdom and integrate it into the physical body.

**Lapis Lazuli** *7.5ml lfer 3206*

opens and clears channels of communication in the 5th chakra; amplifies the ability to hear information from physical and nonphysical sources; clears confusion between hearing and knowing.

**Malachite** *7.5ml lfer 3207*

grounding; helps align and harmonize the physical, emotional, mental and spiritual levels of being; supports the unity of one's being in all circumstances.

**Moldavite** *7.5ml lfer 3208*

connectedness; an energetic window into universal perspective; helps us stay present in the moment while accessing what we need to express our earthly potential.

**Montana Rhodochrosite** *7.5ml lfer 3209*

brings strength and solidity to the 4th chakra; clears confusion and chaos from the heart; clarifies intent and promotes courageous, heart centered action.

**Moonstone** *7.5ml lfer 3210*

cleanses and circulates energy in the emotional body; increases feminine energy aspects of receptivity and intuition in women and men; balances and focuses the psychic forces during menses.

**Opal** *7.5ml lfer 3211*

rejuvenates spent emotional and mental forces and counteracts the depletion of color frequencies in the aura; feeds the etheric and subtle bodies with a full spectrum of luminous colors; replenishes our creative energies.

**Orange Calcite** *7.5ml lfer 3212*

amplifies the body's ability to assimilate light at the cellular level; uplifting, energizing and warming; dispels darkness and grief.

## Pearl *7.5ml lfer 3213*

promotes the release of layers of irritation in the mental and emotional bodies which are seen in the physical body as hardness and inflexibility; helps one turn antagonism for oneself or one's illness into awareness and acceptance.

## Peridot *7.5ml lfer 3214*

the stone of new beginnings; stabilizes the subtle bodies during the incubation period of new ideas and creative projects; helps us initiate new cycles of learning and experience.

## Pyrite *7.5ml lfer 3215*

helps us build an energetic foundation in life based on our highest personal truth; strengthens sense of self, especially with regard to group dynamics and peer pressure; helps us solidify and honor our true values.

## Rhodochrosite *7.5ml lfer 3216*

increases energy, balance and stability in the heart chakra and in the physical body; brings a balance of nurturing Earth energy to the heart chakra after an experience of healing and transformation.

## Rhodolite Garnet *7.5ml lfer 3217*

increases our ability to inhabit the physical body; helps us reconnect energetically with parts of the body that have been injured or traumatized; rebuilds the web of etheric energy in areas disrupted by surgery.

## Rose Quartz *7.5ml lfer 3218*

opens, softens and soothes the heart; helps one connect to and nurture the inner child; harmonizes the heart forces so an individual is able to maintain intimacy with oneself and others.

## Ruby *7.5ml lfer 3219*

energizes and balances the 1st chakra and supports the ability to ground spiritual energy into the physical body; works with the lower chakras to awaken higher impersonal love.

## Rutilated Quartz *7.5ml lfer 3220*

promotes precision alignment with higher sources of energy and inspiration; helps us physically anchor the ability to access, synthesize and communicate information from other dimensions.

## Sapphire *7.5ml lfer 3221*

devotion to Divine purpose; helps synchronize the energy system with higher purpose; intensifies the qualities of loyalty and responsibility to one's true work on the planet.

## Sapphire/Ruby *7.5ml lfer 3222*

for balancing spirituality with physical ability; enables us to gently integrate higher purpose into physical reality and receive physical nurturing through the fulfillment of Divine responsibilities.

## Scepter Amethyst *7.5ml lfer 3223*

opens and prepares the 7th chakra to receive energy from the higher chakras; helps us activate our highest potential through the embodiment of a new core of spiritual identity, authority and leadership.

## Smoky Quartz *7.5ml lfer 3224*

grounding and calming; synchronizes body energy with Earth energy; regulates and stabilizes the detoxification of unwanted energies from the physical, emotional and mental bodies.

## Spectrolite *7.5ml lfer 3225*

bathes and nourishes the entire energy system with full spectrum light; renews and refreshes our perspective; helps us again see the magnificent in the mundane, and the Divine in the ordinary.

## Star Sapphire *7.5ml lfer 3226*

promotes trust in the universe; helps us focus our awareness on what is necessary for the soul's progression in life; supports the formation of energetic connections that support the realization of our life goals.

## Sugalite *7.5ml lfer 3227*

brings depth and a physical richness to our spiritual lives; helps us physically manifest a warmer, more feminine quality of spirituality; promotes an easy acceptance of, rather than a hard striving for the spiritual realm.

## Tiger's Eye *7.5ml lfer 3228*

self-empowerment; strengthens the energetic boundary between our true natures and our emotional experiences; helps us maintain a strong sense of self-identity when dealing with powerful emotions such as anger, fear and jealousy.

## Topaz *7.5ml lfer 3229*

clears energy blockages in the solar plexus; helps us tap into appropriate sources of universal energy; strengthens the ability to act decisively from a clear sense of personal identity.

## Turquoise *7.5ml lfer 3230*

attunes the energy field to the ancient wisdom and sacredness inherent in all of life; cleanses and deepens our connection to the soul of the Earth; helps us live a life of simplicity with gratitude and reverence for All.

## Watermelon Tourmaline *7.5ml lfer 3231*

balances the universal polarities of yin and yang; helps us establish equality between the magnetic and dynamic (giving and receiving) qualities of love; brings the green, physical, Earth frequency into harmony with the pink, spiritual, angelic qualities of love.

# **Environmental** essences

## Chalice Well *7.5ml lfer 1000*

Made at the Chalice Well Gardens, Glastonbury, UK. Connects us to the profoundly personal and eternal support that is constantly available from the angelic, elemental, plant and mineral kingdoms. It reminds us that we are not alone - we are a part of the entire web of life and All That Is, and we can draw upon this matrix of support whenever we are struggling and need help to take the next step on our life's path.

## Full Moon Reflection *7.5ml lfer 1004*

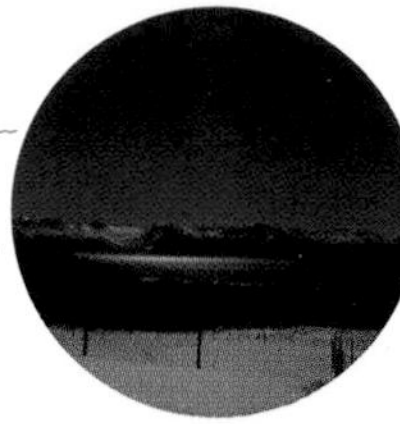

Penetrates deep into the subconscious to bring forth that which lies unresolved beneath the surface. It offers us an opportunity to let a piece of our shadow be illuminated by the light of our conscious awareness.

## Glacier River *7.5ml lfer 1006*

Prepared at the river flowing from the terminus of the Gulkana glacier in central Alaska. Embodies the process of perpetual release from form. It helps us release patterns of feeling, thinking and doing that have become rigid and unyielding.

## Greenland Icecap *7.5ml lfer 1008*

This essence helps us remain flexible and feel supported as we move through deep inner change. Limited Edition

## Liard Hot Springs *7.5ml lfer 1010*

Prepared from the water of Liard Hot Springs in B.C., Canada. An essence of cleansing, re-creation and renewal, that brings us back in touch with the innocent truth of who we really are - spiritual beings who have come to this Earth to learn.

## Northern Lights *7.5ml lfer 1012*

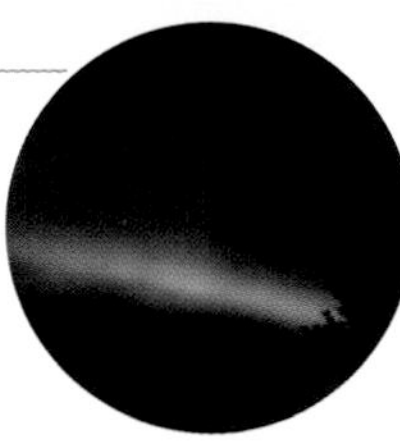

Made under a swirling green display of Northern Lights. This essence gives us the opportunity to liberate our earthbound perspective and join in a dance with the source of our creation. It's healing focus is to cleanse and prepare the heart for the creation of a new matrix of connection with others based on Universal Love.

## Polar Ice *7.5ml lfer 1014*

An essence of transition and the completion of cycles; for achieving a more patient understanding of the subtleties of time; helps us stay present in a place of pure waiting, with no anticipation of what is to come. Limited Edition

## Portage Glacier *7.5ml lfer 1016*

A powerful and catalytic energy that helps us release what is unnecessary and inappropriate in our lives from the mental, emotional and physical bodies. Helps revitalize and balance the entire energy system.

## Rainbow Glacier *7.5ml lfer 1018*

Made on Rainbow Mountain in the Alaska Range. A grounding and balancing energy for those manifesting resistance to fully connecting with the Earth plane. Helps physically anchor those who are strongly focused in the celestial or cosmic realms.

## Solstice Storm *7.5ml lfer 1020*

Made during a thunderstorm on summer solstice day, at Lake Minchumina in the central interior of Alaska. A powerfully charged essence for cleansing and release; helpful in stabilizing the human electrical system; discharges static energy being held in the body and in one's environment. Limited Edition

## Solstice Sun *7.5ml lfer 1022*

Made on the 'night' of June 21/22, as the midnight sun danced along the peaks of the Brooks Range in the northern interior of Alaska. Solstice Sun catalyzes one's ability to access and circulate a stronger current of light energy throughout the physical body. It opens the heart and the energy pathways of the body in preparation for a peak experience, and helps a person integrate such an experience after it has taken place.

## Tidal Forces *7.5ml lfer 1024*

An essence of rhythm and balance, of loss and gain, of adapting ourselves to the swiftly changing currents of life. Helps us release the old and receive the new with constant and unyielding fluidity. Limited Edition

# **Combination** Essences

## Calling All Angels™ *7.5ml lfer 4132 / 30ml lfer 4130*

**Angelica/Chalice Well/Chiming Bells/Kunzite**

Helps one to contact the love, guidance and protection of the angelic realm. It brings a very soft, loving and serene energy into your heart, physical body and environment.

## Fireweed Combo™ *7.5ml lfer 3166 / 30ml lfer 4127*

**Dwarf Fireweed/Fireweed/River Beauty/White Fireweed**

Supports the processes of transformation, transition and change. It can be used to prepare for a transformational experience of any kind, but it is especially useful when you are in the middle of an intense process and need extra support to get through it.

## Guardian™ *7.5ml lfer 4134 / 30ml lfer 4129*

**Covellite/Devilís Club/Round-Leaf Orchid/Stone Circle White Violet/Yarrow**

Helps one to create a powerful force-field of protection in the aura. It invokes positive, harmonious energies that help you claim your energetic space, maintain your grounding, and feel the protection of strong, healthy boundaries.

## Lighten Up™ *7.5ml lfer 4999 / 30ml lfer 5000*

**Carnelian/Grass of Parnassus/Orange Calcite/Solstice Sun**

Designed to increase your ability to embody light. Its overall effect is to uplift, energize, inspire and nourish. Specifically for people who suffer from light deprivation, also helpful for those who are depressed, caught in negative patterns or situations, or feel cut off in any way from their inner sources of light.

## Purification™ *7.5ml lfer 4133 / 30ml lfer 4128*

**Black Tourmaline/Fireweed/Portage Glacier/Sweetgrass**

Designed to cleanse and purify your home and work environments and your personal energy field. Can be utilized to break up and cleanse stagnant patterns of energy on any level.

## Soul Support™ *7.5ml lfer 3344 / 30ml lfer 4125*

**Cattail Pollen/Chalice Well/Cotton Grass/Fireweed/Labrador Tea/Malachite/River Beauty/Ruby/White Fireweed**

Brings strength and stability during emergencies, stress, trauma and transformation. Provides support to rejuvenate and restore balance on all levels.

## Travel Ease™ *7.5ml lfer 3793 / 30ml lfer 4126*

**Black Tourmaline/Covellite/Smoky Quartz/White Violet/Yarrow**

Specifically designed to ease the negative effects of air travel, including what is commonly referred to as jet lag. This formula supports the establishment and maintenance of functional energy boundaries. If you are environmentally sensitive and have difficulty being confined in small, constricted spaces for long periods of time, Travel Ease will help you feel as though you have all the personal space you need, even on a crowded flight.

One of the areas which Steve Johnson and Jane Bell of the AFEP have been pioneering has been in creating a bridge between the world of vibrational essences and that of Feng Shui. An example of their interest is found in their Sacred Space Sprays™ (Calling All Angels, Guardian, and Purification).

These mixtures of Alaskan flower essences, gem elixirs, and environmental essences, along with carefuly selected essential oils, may be used both for space clearing as well as for cleansing and harmonizing one's aura. Spraying Calling All Angels or Guardian in a child's bedroom at bedtime can help the child to feel more secure and sleep more easily.

Rooms and offices which have experienced arguements will retain some energetic elements from the altercation: the Sacred Space Sprays help to clear those etheric remnants away and invoke a higher light into the space.

# **Sacred Space** Sprays

## Calling All Angels™ spray *120ml lfer 5122*

Combination of essences as described above, with the addition of these essential oils: Rose Otto, Carnation, Alpine Lavender, and Pink Grapefruit. Helps one to contact the love, guidance, and protection of the angelic realm. Promotes the release of tension and helps us open our hearts to the love and peace of the angels.

## Guardian™ spray *120ml lfer 5121*

Combination of essences as described above, with the addition of these essential oils: Hyacinth, Litsea Cubaba, Tangerine, Lime, and Melissa. Helps one to create a powerful force-field of protection in the aura, and to claim one s energetic space, maintain one s grounding, and feel the protection of strong healthy boundaries.

## Purification™ spray *120ml lfer 5120*

Combination of essences as described above, with the addition of these essential oils: Peppermint, Lavender Mailette, Black Spruce, and Frankincense. Designed to cleanse and purify your home and work environments and your personal energy field. This spray transports the purity of the wilderness into our complex man-made environments, awakening our senses, and reminding us of our true natures.

# Aloha **Flower** Essences

Region: Hawaii

Founded: 1988

DEVELOPER: Penny Medieros started her life in England and her great love of the outdoors led her to live on the Island of Hawaii. The sub-tropical climate allows her to immerse herself in nature all year round. Her intimate involvement with the exquisite flowers led her to develop sensitivity and attunement to the messages of nature. From them she has gleaned essential information on how the flowers' energy (or 'mana') can support humans.

THE ESSENCES: The 70 Individual essences ,10 Combinations and Mists are designed to restore'the power of life' (or 'mana') that normally flows freely within us. When the smooth flow of life force is restricted or blocked, disharmony and ill-health ensue. The essences are made from a rich and spectacular array of exotic sub-tropical blooms. The ancient priests (known as 'Kahunas') made full use of the healing powers of the blooms to uplift and heal their spirits. These essences offer solutions to life's problems such as stress, lack of self-esteem, interrelationships, self-empowerment, life-direction and purpose

## **Flower** essences

### **A'ali'i** *15ml ifer 2789*

A heart essence which fosters states of care, concern and real joy in a disharmonious relationship wherein one feels innately cold, distant and unloving towards another, due to discordant interaction with this person at a prior time.

### **Akia** *15ml ifer 2790*

A liberating essence that strengthens the willpower and lends focus to those who experience frustration in fulfilling their higher purpose in life. Helps one to overcome constant pressures and disharmony of others and be calm and genial while fostering attunement to one's higher will and destiny path.

### **Amazon Swordplant** *15ml ifer 2728*

An essence to enhance free flowing emotional expression, which leads to improving one's relationships. Useful in past life therapy to focus on the source of emotional blocks.

### **Avocado** *15ml ifer 2729*

To alleviate fear of being touched by another - physically and psychologically - promoting relaxed acceptance, pleasure and sensitivity to being touched.

### **Awapuhi-melemele** (Yellow Ginger) *15ml ifer 2730*

To increase sensitivity, magnifying perceptions of sight, hearing, and touch. Bringing one into the "here and now" it aids relaxation and can be used with hypnotic regression to release repressed subconscious mind traumas.

### **Bamboo Orchid** *15ml ifer 2731*

To inspire self-reliance, faith and trust in oneself. Taken consistently to clear karmic blocks it gives clarity to one's higher destiny path.

### **Bougainvillea** *15ml ifer 2732*

Rekindles awareness to the magic, beauty and wonder of life. For mystical and higher inspiration, enthusiasm and purposefulness.

### **Chinese Violet** *15ml ifer 2733*

For restoring close family relations when differing opinions and belief systems between family members has created hostilities and alienation.

**Coffee** *15ml ifer 2734*

Taken consistently, Coffee flower essence aids one to overcome the psychological cravings for coffee.

**Cotton** *15ml ifer 2735*

For releasing fear and its accompanying stress. To sharpen one's visual perceptions and be able to face fearful life situations.

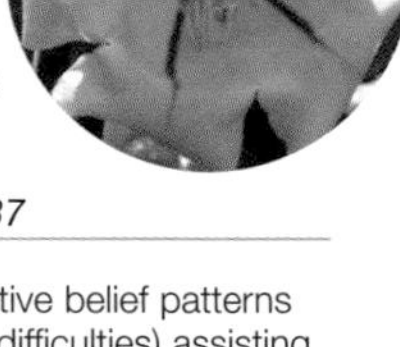

**Cup of Gold** *15ml ifer 2736*

A heart-centered essence for opening up and sharing one's abundance and knowledge with genuine warmth and love.

**Day-Blooming Waterlily** *15ml ifer 2737*

For releasing conscious and subconsciously held negative belief patterns (sourced in fear, guilt, feelings of inadequacy and past difficulties) assisting one to experience sexual fulfilment with one's partner.

**Hau** *15ml ifer 2738*

A calming, healing and balancing influence, which is helpful for those overcome by nervous stress.

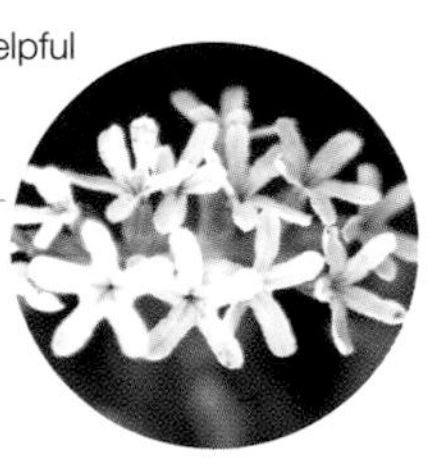

**Hinahina-ku-kahakai** *15ml ifer 2740*

To empower women to fulfil their own life's purpose, restoring willpower and direction, especially when confused or lost due to male domination.

**Ili'ahi** (Hawaiian Sandalwood)
*15ml ifer 2741*

For deepening receptivity to Aromatherapy oils and sensitivity to aromas. In meditation, this essence energizes the crown chakra and enhances an awareness of bliss.

**Ilima** *15ml ifer 2742*

To dispel deeply held material and intellectual illusions and become aware of higher spiritual truths.

**Impatiens** *15ml ifer 2743*

To alleviate impatience, restoring tolerance and acceptance of situations and circumstances beyond one's control.

**Jade Vine** *15ml ifer 2744*

For overcoming negativity and opening up to others. For developing deep, heart-centered communication and sincerity.

**Kamani** *15ml ifer 2745*

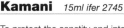

To protect the sanctity and integrity of a place from negative energies (use in spray bottle or bowl of water). Also heals trauma and disharmony by clearing the heart center of a person.

**Koa** 15ml ifer 2746

An essence that affects the crown chakra, to be used with meditation practices. Bringing deep peace and light from the higher realms, it promotes transformation and healing.

**Kou** *15ml ifer 2747*

Stimulates the brow chakra, promoting clarity of perception: for psychic and clairvoyant abilities. Taken consistently, it discourages astral possession due to excessive alcohol consumption.

**Kukui** (Candlenut Tree) *15ml ifer 2748*

For inspiring understanding and calmness and to promote emotionally 'opening up' to others. It helps one to overcome fears, anger and anxiety. To heal relationships, especially those carried over from past lives.

**La'au'-aila** (Castor Bean) *15ml ifer 2749*

A calming and strengthening essence for those who are overcome with deeply ingrained anxieties, fears and phobias.

**Lani Ali'I** *15ml ifer 2791*

An essence that strengthens the willpower, helping you to make 'right decisions' and take 'right action' based on higher guidance (excellent for parents and those in leadership positions).

**Lehua** *15ml ifer 2750*

Strengthens the female aspect, enhancing self esteem by increasing sensuality and joy in femininity. This liberating effect restores balance to the psyche by enhancing activity of the sexual chakra.

**Lotus** *15ml ifer 2751*

The Lotus flower has for thousands of years symbolized spiritual enlightenment. Indeed, this flower essence's purpose is to accelerate spiritual evolvement and enhance healing on every level within the human system.

**Macadamia** *15ml ifer 2752*

For those who feel trapped in a life situation, this essence dissolves negative reactionary patterns, bringing clarity for constructiveness and love.

## **Mai'a** (Banana) *15ml ifer 2755*

Brings balance and harmony primarily to the sexual energy of men. This leads to improvement in the quality of their relationships with women, and true sexual fulfilment. Additionally this essence seeks to balance the quality of an individual's energy drive in life when it is too aggressive or conversely too weak.

## **Mamaki** *15ml ifer 2793*

A liberating essence that calms and clears the 'busyness' of one's headspace, bringing the consciousness into the 'here and now'. A truer perception of reality is thus observed.

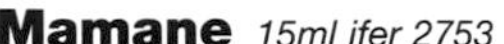

## **Mamane** *15ml ifer 2753*

To bring illumination for understanding of divine truth, dispelling erroneous, spiritual and religious beliefs that have governed one's life. Clarity and emotional well being ensues.

## **Mango** *15ml ifer 2754*

Increases one's ability to assimilate the higher frequencies of cosmic light energies, which assists spiritual growth, and aids in the reduction of need for denser physical foods.

## **Marica Iris** *15ml ifer 2792*

The essence inspires innovation and attunement to the healing needs of you and others. Excellent for health specialists and therapists.

## **Melastoma** *15ml ifer 2794*

This essence vitalizes the etheric (electromagnetic) body promoting well being in those who are stressed or weakened by illness.

## **Milo** *15ml ifer 3284*

An essence to restore personal power and drive to one who has been living in a restrictive environment, such as a prison, mental institution or hospital - or even a long-held job.

## **Naio** *15ml ifer 2756*

Strengthens the willpower to break the addiction of overeating.

## **Nana-honua'** (Angels' Trumpet) *15ml ifer 2757*

For attunement to the solar angelic realms. For soul level guidance, clarity of thought and sharpness of mind.

## **Nani-ahiahi'** *15ml ifer 2758*

To release deeply held overwhelming emotional issues that have been internally repressed.

## **Naupaka-kahakai** *15ml ifer 2788*

To connect to your inner knowingness and wisdoms acquired in past lives.

## **Night-Blooming Waterlily**
*15ml ifer 2760*

Inspires unconditional love in a relationship, mental attunement and enrichment of the lovemaking experience.

## **Niu** (Coconut) *15ml ifer 2761*

The flower essence stimulates a mother's breast-feeding instinct. It aids in balancing male and female energies. Influences clarity when there is confusion over sexual issues.

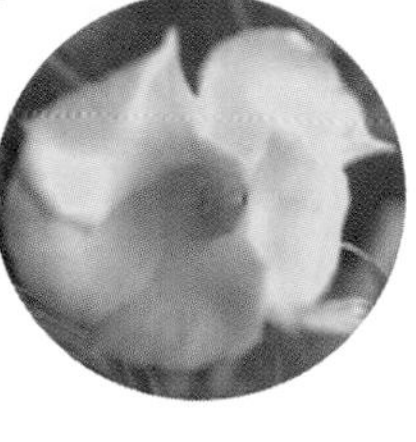

## **Noho-malie** (Be Still) *15ml ifer 2762*

Instills calmness and upliftment to those who feel agitation, unrest and inner conflict, especially if this stems from past life events.

## **Noni** *15ml ifer 2763*

To prepare women psychologically for childbearing and motherhood. Noni purifies and cleanses the emotions, aiding the body to detoxify. For attunement with the Earth Mother, awakening instincts of nurturing, caring and love. This essence is relevant for mothers-to-be, those that care for the welfare of others in different careers, and also for people who have been deprived of childhood love and care.

## **Ohai-Ali'i** *15ml ifer 2764*

For mental flexibility and openness to the thoughts and ideas of others.

## **Ohelo** *15ml ifer 2765*

To purify oneself of deep fears, darkness and isolation, which has engulfed a person who has been involved in extreme negativity in this and/or past lifetimes.

## **Ohi'a-'ai** (Mountain Apple)
*15ml ifer 2766*

Strengthens the mind's control over the immune system when it is weakened from disease, which has the effect of enhancing general vitality.

## Pakalana *15ml ifer 2795*

An essence to restore inner peace and true inner identity. Used as a meditation essence it is particularly beneficial for advanced lightworkers, healers and initiates on a spiritual path those who are finding their progress is hindered by the demands of life.

## Pa-nini-o-ka *15ml ifer 2768*

For restoring one's balance in the energies of day and night. To relieve deep-seated fears of lower astral entities and fearful dreams.

## Panini-awa'awa (Aloe) *15ml ifer 2767*

A speciality remedy for healing holes in the etheric body which can be caused by psychological stress.

## Papala Kepau *15ml ifer 2796*

An essence that promotes a holistic perspective, embracing higher truths and balance when dealing with the acquisition of money. Especially useful for those whose lives are immersed and focused on business and commerce, or conversely for those who deny themselves the idea of having money.

## Papaya (male & female) *15ml ifer 2769*

Enhances relationships by focusing on spiritual love between one another instead of looking at personality differences. Assists the clearing of mental confusion and tensions. Stimulates psychic abilities.

## Passion Flower *15ml ifer 2770*

Stimulates divine, unconditional love in the heart, which, brings healing and release of 'held in' negativity, psychological pain and trauma.

## Pa'u-o-Hi'iaka *15ml ifer 2771*

An essence for spiritual protection when encountering dark forces; for healing when so harmed, and for establishing higher solar and angelic contacts.

## Pleomele fragrans *15ml ifer 2772*

To bring positivity into one's mental framework and release depression, anxiety and irritability.

## Plumbago *15ml ifer 2773*

To restore love, caring and vitality to close interpersonal relationships within a family.

## Poha (Cape Gooseberry) *15ml ifer 2775*

An essence that promotes learning abilities in the young and those of all ages who suffer emotionally from relationship problems with family, close friends or childhood teachers. It promotes a vital and positive frame of mind and dissolves emotional blocks.

## Port St. Johns Creeper *15ml ifer 2797*

A soft, female essence which affects the mental body, softening it when there are tendencies of sarcasm or rigidity. Inspires sensitive, receptive communication.

## Pua-hoku-hihi *15ml ifer 3282*

Harmonizes and aligns one's individual will with that of the collective group or organization one is involved with; thus aiding a successful progression of its aims and activities.

## Pua kala *15ml ifer 2798*

An essence to stimulate the mind; for clarity and discernment between one's own ideas and those of others. The resulting open mindedness assists understanding and communication with others as one is able to embrace concepts and intellectual matters due to an improved mental balance. Telepathic abilities are also assisted.

## Pua-kenikeni *15ml ifer 2776*

Promotes clarity and purposefulness. Balances sexual promiscuity.

## Pua melia (Plumeria) *15ml ifer 2774*

Strengthens resolve and motivation to live life according to one's core beliefs - and/or practice ethnic spiritual traditions, which are often weakened or lost from the influence of others or the modern world at large.

## Pua-pilo *15ml ifer 2777*

For overcoming lethargy in order to become active and fulfilled in life. This essence can also liberate people with weight problems who do not overeat but have a negative self-image, are lethargic and need to break free from this inertia.

## Pukiawe *15ml ifer 2778*

A re-vitalizer emotionally and mentally - to overcome inertia and create care and interest in oneself and the environment. Promotes realization of our interconnectedness with all in life.

### **Spider Lily** *15ml ifer 2779*

Promotes a positive frame of mind and attitude. For men who feel alienation towards women this essence fosters loving attunement, respect and true equality with them.

### **Stenogyne caliminthoides** *15ml ifer 2780*

For those who are engaged in self-development, this essence assists a person to face their deep inner issues and/or past traumas when there is a tendency for avoidance. Assists integration and focus.

### **Streptocarpus** *15ml ifer 2799*

A transformational essence that clears the heart and conscience of those who suffer from being deceived by others. Also assists those who have deceived others to perceive in their heart and consciousness the results of their actions and align with their higher soul guidance.

### **Ti** (or Ki) *15ml ifer 2782*

An essence for relief of invasive thoughts and astral possession. Taken steadily it will rid the "grip" of an invading entity. Good to take in '"psychically stressed" environments, and for lifting a spell or curse put on a place. See Protection Blend

### **'Uala** *15ml ifer 2783*

An essence to restore communication in a young child who has suffered an accident or trauma and cannot express his/her feelings of shock, helplessness, frustration and anger. Thus healing is assisted. It is also appropriate for all ages of people who need to release deeply held negative thoughts and emotions associated with past trauma.

### **Ulei** *15ml ifer 2784*

An essence for communication and receptivity to others which improves the memory and facilitates past life recall. It promotes love and interest for others into balance with the logic of the mind. To connect diversely minded people, resolve hostilities and promote tranquility of mind.

### **Water Poppy** *15ml ifer 2785*

To promote a fluid balance between overactivity and lethargy. For releasing egocentric mental conflict so that a harmonic equilibrium with oneself and others may be experienced.

### **Wiliwili** *15ml ifer 2786*

Inspires positivity, courage and honesty to face major life issues. To re-evaluate belief systems and dissolve fears that can prevent clarity in relationships and dealings in life.

## **Aloha** mysts

### **Antitox Myst** *120ml ifer 5834*

For vitality that assists your immune system when you feel a little 'under the weather'.

### **Family Harmony Myst** *120ml ifer 5035*

For calming and dissolving fears, hurt and anger between family members, and dissipating rifts created by differences of opinion.
Available in drops: Family Relations *30ml ifer 4210*

### **Intimacy** *120ml ifer 5836*

For balanced and joyous sexual relations - releasing conscious and subconsciously held fears, guilt, feelings of inadequacy and past difficulties.
Available in drops: Sexual Relations *30ml ifer 4211*

As well as any essence line around, the Aloha essences demonstrate the principle that in effect all flower essences are also environmental essences, as the deep and powerful volcanic energies of the big island of Hawaii are the etheric context within which all of Penny's essences are made.

Having a unique power and purity, these therapeutic essences are now also available in the form of mysts, blended with a careful selection of essential oils.

Intimacy is a spray to help enhance loving relationships, and to help smooth out the tensions that may arise within a couple relationship. The action of the oils helps to ground the energy of the flower essences, whilst the action of the essences 'lifts' the action of the oils. This synergy helps one to understand just how effective these aura sprays from Hawaii are, with their delicate fragrances and healing energies which uplift, cleanse, and protect one's energy field.

### **Protection Myst** *120ml ifer 5838*

For clearing and keeping the integrity of your inner and outer space from invasive, negative thoughts and entities (within your consciousness or the atmosphere of your workplace, meditation area, therapy room, hotel room, etc.) Complements Feng Shui. Also for receptivity to inner guidance.
Available in drops: Protection *30ml ifer 3178*

### **Office Harmony Myst** *120ml ifer 5837*

For heart-mind communication - feeling part of and synchronised with the group/business aims - openness and sharing of skills.
Available in drops: Social & Business Relations *30ml ifer 4212*

### **Spiritual Awakening Myst** *120ml ifer 5839*

Assisting with meditation or spiritual practices. For aligning with Higher Self and experiencing the divine within. For knowing inner peace, bliss and integrating this into your life.
Available in drops: Spiritual Awakening 30ml ifer 4215

### **Stress Relief Myst** *120ml ifer 5840*

For calmness and being centered when you are overwhelmed by the demands of life and circumstances - for releasing anxiety, fear and anger.
Available in drops: Stress Relief *30ml ifer 3159*

## **Aloha** combinations

### **Aftershock** *30ml ifer 4217*

A calming influence to assist you through shock and trauma. Assists insight, the release of shock, for self-care and patience to heal.

### **Empowerment** *30ml ifer 4213*

To realise your own inner strengths and dynamic resourcefulness to define and MANAfest your own path in life and destiny

### **Self Esteem** *30ml ifer 4214*

For realizing your own self worth and gifts; dissipating negative emotions and attitudes towards yourself; overcoming self limitations and for self-acceptance.

**See also the listing at the end of each Myst's description.**

## **Aloha** - Mana *30ml ifer 5131*

Mana is an environmental essence made to embody the combined energies of the volcanic Fire Deva at Kilauea Volcano in Hawaii and the Overlighting Deva of this area. "Mana" means vital life force energy.

For vitalizing one's own "mana", lending strength and polarity to the body's natural electro-magnetic energy fields. Combats jet-lag, pollution from computers, fluorescent lights and electronic appliances. For creative inspiration and MANAfesting your reality. Acts as a catalyst in flower essence therapy and other healing work. Renews vitality.

NB: Store apart from other essences in a cool and dark place.

# Ararêtama **Rainforest** Essences

## Region: Brazil

Founded 1991

DEVELOPER: Sandra Epstein
Since childhood, Sandra has been fascinated with the natural world, and has had a particularly special communication and friendship with Brazil's Atlantic Rainforest. Her professional background, artistic education and therapy work are centred around a creative process which forms the basis for holistic healing. In later years, while researching a cure for a friend's illness, she was able to develop a system of vibrational essences which echo and link the rich biodiversity of this unique ecosystem.

THE ESSENCES: Araretama's vibrational essences contain the vibration of bromeliads, roots and lichens from the rainforest. They represent the force of communion, cleansing and regeneration among the species in this ecosystem. Whenever possible these essences are prepared without cutting or removing the resource from its original place, respecting the principle of preservation. Arar'tama, meaning 'place from which the light arises', invites you to participate on a journey through the awakening consciousness with the aid of vibrational essences. With respect for every living being and with the strength to support life's difficulties, it invites you to find your divinity; and taking the responsibility to face individual processes is the basic condition for this journey.



# **Flower** essences

### **Ararybá** *15ml ifer 2432*

Made from an *Aechmea carvalhoi* bromeliad, two *Araucaria sp.* trees, one male and one female and an *Araucaria* fruit.
Key word: Integration.
Benefits: Awakening of higher mind. Receptiveness to the divine. Organizes thought and affirms/promotes/stabilises conscious vision. Protection.
Symptoms: Hyper-sensitivity due to environmental stress. Lack of balance and centredness. Claustrophobia. Vulnerability.

### **Assá** *15ml ifer 2428*

Made from two *Philodendron imbe* roots and from the roots of a *Ybyapó* trees.
Key words: Gratitude, Compassion, Forgiveness.
Benefits: Balances love and power. Light, love and determination. Enables compassion. Helps one bo
Awakens gratitude.
Symptoms: Jealousy. Guilt. Sexual and emotional abuse. Co-dependency.

### **Bromelia One** *15ml ifer 2423*

Made from *Quesnelia testudo linud* bromeliad.
Key words: Receptivity, Openness.
Benefits: Works on the intuitive feminine aspect. Combats over-excitement. Promotes calm breathing. Flexibility.
Symptoms: Overload, feeling excessively tense. Mental and emotional rigidity. Fanaticism or excessive discipline. Fear.

### **Bromelia Two** *15ml ifer 2424*

Made from *Quesnelia testudo linud* bromeliad.
Key word: Unification.
Benefits: Integration of sexuality and spirituality. Awakening of the Kundalini. Peace, relief and humility. Resolves duality in the heart.
Symptoms: Ambivalence. Envy, jealousy and suspicion. Negative thoughts. Repressed aggressiveness.

### **Celebração** (Celebration) *15ml ifer 2425*

Made from *Nidularium seidelli* bromeliad.
Key words: Confidence, Joy.
Benefits: Helps expansion without fear during periods of transition. Celebrates the joy of living. Calms hyperactive minds. Develops self-expression.
Symptoms: Doubts and uncertainties. Insecurity. Lack of confidence. Submission

## Embó Rudá *15ml ifer 2426*

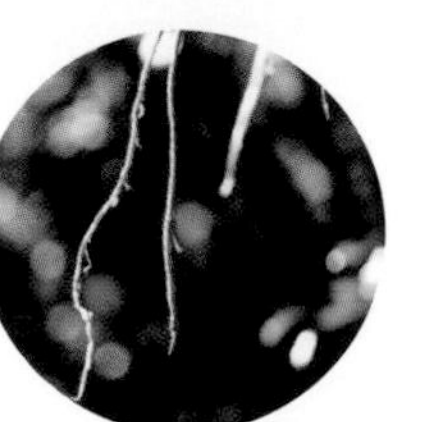

Made from an aerial root of *Philodendron imbe.*
Key words: Strengthening, Sensuality.
Benefits: Improves ability to flow with life. Communion with the Earth. Opens the sensorial channel. Sexuality, fertility.
Symptoms: Difficulty integrating sexuality and sensuality.
Disconnection. Congested menstrual flow. Pessimism.

## Imbe *15ml ifer 2422*

Made from a pendant root of *Philodendron imbe* looking for humidity.
Key words: Contact, Flowing.
Benefits: Encourages surrendering based on trust. Spiritual peace. Relief of muscular and nervous tension. Helps treat addiction.
Symptoms: Fear of intimacy. Conflicts in relationships. Obsessions. Anxiety.

## Indaiá *15ml ifer 5157*

Made from an *Ipomea sp*. flower.
Key word: Trust.
Benefits: Helps break up obsessive thoughts. Acceptance of one's inner creative nature. Heals pain from the loss of self-esteem.
Symptoms: Obsessive thoughts. Egocentricity. Autism. Fear of exposing oneself.

## Jumping Child *15ml ifer 2421*

Made from *Clauvinia cristata* mushroom.
Key words: Joy, Spontaneity.
Benefits: Hope based on connection with one's spiritual essence. Spontaneous self-expression. Brings vitality to verbal expression. Heals wounds (external use)
Symptoms: Emotional depression. Laziness, indolence. Discouragement. Stagnation.

## Kundalini *15ml ifer 4781*

Made from *Vriesia platynema* bromeliad.
Key words: Communion, Equilibrium.
Benefits: Confidence in one's potential. Opens the energy channels along the spine. Courage. Facilitates leadership.
Symptoms: Doubts. Vulnerability and hyper-sensitivity. Impulsiveness. The need to please others. Insecurity.

## Marupiara *15ml ifer 5159*

Made from Manacá tree flowers.
Key word: Joy.
Benefits: Global vision. Stimulates intuition. Develops a deep holistic perception. Abundance and emotional happiness.
Symptoms: Loss of focus. Excessive attention to detail. Redundant speech. Individualism.

## Moara *15ml ifer 2429*

Made from *Coegonium sp*. lichen.
Key words: Generosity. Expansion.
Benefits: Dissolves rigid patterns of behavior. Calms the overactive mind.Confidence in others. Altruism. Neutralizes excessive worries.
Symptoms: Authoritarianism. Criticism of others. Irritability. Envy. Impatience.

## Obaiti *15ml ifer 2435*

Made from an aerial root of *Philodendron gloriosum.*
Key words: Liberation from conditioned patterns. Focus.
Benefits: Removes psychological/emotional debris accumulated during life. Focus. Listening to others. Transforms old patterns.
Symptoms: Behavior obstructing growth. Repetitive mistakes. Difficulty studying. Lack of focus.

## Oribá *15ml ifer 3353*

Made from *Tillandsia usneoides* bromeliad, four different earth types (purple, ochre, pink and white) and a liana.
Key word: Healing. Capacity.
Benefits: Dissolves grief. Heals vulnerability. Accessing creative potential and discovering one's talents.
Symptoms: Denial of capacity to heal oneself. Lack of direction in life. Lack of goals. Fear of death.

## Oyamã *15ml ifer 5161*

Made from cacao tree (*Theobroma cacao*) flowers.
Key words: Confidence. Clarity.
Benefits: Confidence in one's inner knowledge. Provides conviction. Inspires confidence. Ability to say NO.
Symptoms: Low self-esteem. Depression. Doubt. Anxiety.

## Pyatã *15ml ifer 2427*

Made from two *Philodendron imbe* aerial roots: one connected to water and the other expanding through earth and a root sprout from a giant Ybiapó tree.
Key-words: Vitality, Creativity.
Benefits: Encourages sharing. Liberation and purification of vital blocks. Rebirth. Sexuality and fertility. Enables one to endure challenges (physical and emotional)
Symptoms: Convalescence. Panic. Disinterest in life. Excessive solitude. Impotence.

## Renascer (Rebirth) *15ml ifer 2434*

Made from *Tillandsia s. tricta* bromeliad.
Key words: Unification, Courage.
Benefits: Unites heart and mind. Integrates us with our deeper Life path..Teaches through experiences.
Symptoms: Difficulty beginning new cycles. Blocking our growth. Difficulty adjusting to changes. Nostalgia.

### **Revelação** (Revelation) *15ml ifer 2433*

Made from one *Ipomea sp*. plant, a white quartz and sea water.
Key-word: Release.
Benefits: Reveals blocks hindering spiritual development. Harmonizes the body's cycles. Self-expression. Self-acceptance .
Symptoms: Difficulty understanding patterns of behavior. Difficulty respecting internal rhythm. Dissatisfaction and frustration. Congested menstrual flow.

### **Rudá** - Compound essence *15ml ifer 5162*

Made from *Oribá, Thini-á, Moara, Assá, Bromeliad 2, Ararybá·* and *Kundalini* essences.
Key words: Harmony. Integrating experiences.
Benefits: Promotes peace. Protects. Helps assimilate experiences for our evolution. Assists with centering and focus.
Symptoms: Restlessness. Accidents. Difficulty studying or working. Feeling low.

### **Seiva** *15ml ifer 2430*

Made from the overflowing tree sap of a peach tree (*Prunus persica)*.
Key-word: Abundance.
Benefits: Releases emotional tension. Nutrition. Giving without sacrifice. Creativity and fertility.
Symptoms: Exhaustion and sensation of emptiness. Abandonment. Traumas. Neediness. Shame.

### **Tassi** *15ml ifer 5160*

Made from a liana *Ficus pumila*.
Key word: Protection.
Benefits: Strengthens incarnation. Builds confidence. Vitalizes the chakras; Protection
Symptoms: Addictions. Lack of vitality. Co-dependent relationships. Mental, emotional and physical vulnerability.

### **Thini-á** *15ml ifer 4107*

Made from *Tillandsia usneoides* bromeliad.
Key-word: Surrender.
Benefits: Feeling of lightness. Surrender to and connection with the essential light. Exalts inner brightness expressed as confidence. Perception and clarity.
Symptoms: Fear. Insecurity. Anger. Hyper-sensitivity. Excessive repetitive thoughts.

### **Yatê** *15ml ifer 5158*

Made from *Manacá* tree flowers and butterflies.
Key words: Consciousness, Transformation.
Benefits: Helps solve pragmatic questions. Stimulates teamwork. Detachment with responsibility. Sense of freedom.
Symptoms: Lack of balance. Difficulty with organization. Stagnation. Alienation.

### **Ybá** *15ml ifer 2431*

Made from *Aechmea carvalhoi* bromeliad.
Key word: Will.
Benefits: Inner permission to enjoy pleasure. Brings hope. Brings willingness, strength, vitality. Cleanses the aura.
Symptoms: Stress. Absence of the fire element - lack of will. Lack of sexual consciousness. Physical pain - external use.

## **New Flower** Essences

### **Caju** (Cashew) *15ml ifer 5786*

Made from cashew tree.
Key word: Fertility
Benefits: Good for transforming stagnated periods into rebirth. Supportive during pregnancy. Strengthens our vitality. Stimulates happiness.
Symptoms: Lack of energy and creativity. Infertility. Menopause and andropause.

### **Orquídea** (Orchid) *15ml ifer 5787*

Made from a wild yellow orchid with red center.
Key word: Motivation
Benefits: Helps us take responsibility for our own lives. Encourages us to accept all the cycles and stages of our life. Re-establishes optimism. To value life.
Symptoms: Depression. Lacking enthusiasm. Pessimism. Fearing death.

### **Soberania** (Sovereignty) - Compound essence *15ml ifer 5788*

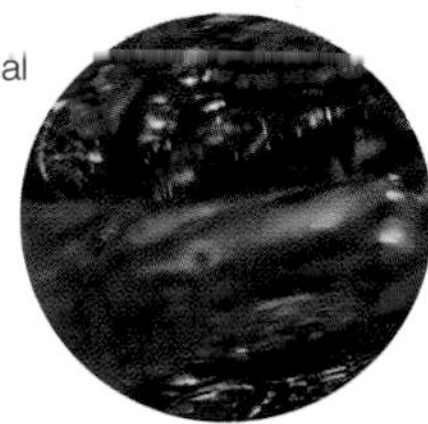

Made from environmental essences from the Atlantic Forest, elixir made of *lapis lazuli* minerals and vibrational essence of gold metal.
Key word: Self-value
Benefits: Works on self-esteem. Works on one's self-value. Strengthens our inherent qualities. Helps us recognise our more subtle personal qualities.
Symptoms: Insecurity. Low self-esteem. Fear of exposing oneself. Submission.

# **Aqua Ignea** essences

*Aqua Ignea* are products created with the intention of providing nourishment for the body and soul. The formula includes essential white rose oil, floral and Vibrational Atlantic Forest essences and regenerating oils related to chromotherapy. Each color corresponds to a frequency that needs to be harmonized.

## **Yellow:** Nutrition and Creativity *30 ml ifer 5169*

*'I have wisdom to nourish myself emotionally and I am able to reflect my intense and tender light within.'*

Vibrational Essences: Seiva, Celebração and Renascer
Application: Solar plexus, kidneys and hara (area below the bellybutton)

## **Orange:** Eros and Sexuality *30 ml ifer 5168*

*'With sexuality and pleasure, my desire ascends in love, taking me to the fountain of eternal and infinite youth.'*

Vibrational Essences: Kundalini, Embó-rudá and Ybá
Application: Groin

## **Red:** Vitality and Creativity *30 ml ifer 5167*

*'Through my vital balanced force, I manifest health and creativity within my life.'*

Vibrational Essences: Ybá, Pyatã and Seiva.
Application: Thyroid, thymus, kidneys and feet.

## **Pink:** Relationships and Love *30 ml ifer 5170*

*'Love is the Portal to supreme union between living beings and Affection is the Stars of this enormous constellation.'*

Vibrational Essences: Imbe, Moara and Bromélia 2.
Application: Chest

## **Blue:** Harmony *30 ml ifer 5173*

*'My being surrenders to happiness when in peace and resonance; it is with my interior and exterior universe, inside and beyond me.'*

Vibrational Essences: Thini-Á, Assá and Kundalini
Application: Temples, neck and hara.

## **Green:** Realization *30 ml ifer 5172*

*'Through the accomplishments of my projects, I embody confidence in my potential and become a participant in the evolution of the universe.'*

Vibrational Essences: Oribá, Embó-rudá and Ybá.
Application: Neck, thymus, hara and knees.

## **Magenta:** Insights and Solutions *30 ml ifer 5174*

*'I allow my greater will to manifest itself, illuminating my path with knowledge and clarity.'*

Vibrational Essences: Ararybá, Oribá, Revelação and Yatê.
Application: Sixth Chakra (forehead), nape of the neck, solar plexus and hara.

## **Violet:** Protection *30 ml ifer 5171*

*'I am a great cloth of light, aired and protected, in the cosmic web of life.'*

Vibrational Essences: Tassi, Ararybá and Thini-Á..
Application: Sixth Chakra (forehead), nape of the neck, solar plexus and hara

## **Clear:** Transformation *30 ml ifer 5166*

*'In the fusion of love and wisdom, I transmute obstacles and portals of light with humility and omnipresence.'*

Vibrational Essences: Oyamã, Jumping Child and Indaiá.
Application: Whole body

## **Virtude** (Virtue) *30 ml ifer 5849*

A composition of green and magenta colors. Works on transformations at a cellular level, bringing our virtues to the surface.

## **Visão** (Vision) *30 ml ifer 5850*

A composition of violet, pink and blue colors. Works on our virtues, which are expand and radiate through the subtle bodies, enlarging our vision of the world.

## **Emergenciel** (Emergency) Gel *60 ml ifer 5180*

Useful for topical application in all stresses and emergency situations.

# Australian **Bush Flower** Essences

Region: Australia

Year founded: 1987

DEVELOPER: Ian White

For the last 20 years, Ian has been practising as a naturopath and homoeopath from which he was in an ideal position to observe the results of using the Bush essences on his patients. A fifth generation Australian herbalist, Ian is a pioneer in researching the rare remedial qualities of the Australian Bush.

THE ESSENCES: Australia has many of the oldest and most varied species of flowering plants in the world. The native flowers used for these essences are gathered in unpolluted and naturally occurring regions of the vast Australian landscape. There are 68 individual stock essences that can be used singly or combined to treat any specific application. There is a range of combination essences and specially formulated mists and creams combining flower essences and essential oils. The Bush essences promote healing and balance through the release of negative beliefs and thoughts and not only help to give clarity to one's life purpose but also the courage, strength and enthusiasm to follow and pursue one's goals and dreams.

## Alpine Mint Bush *15ml ifer 1342*

- − Mental & emotional exhaustion; lack of joy and weight of responsibility of care givers.
- + Revitalisation; joy; renewal.

## Angelsword *15ml ifer 1343*

- − Interference with true spiritual connection to Higher Self; spiritually possessed.
- + Spiritual discernment; accessing gifts from past lifetimes; releases negative psychic energy; clear spiritual communication.

## Banksia Robur *15ml ifer 1344*

- − Loss of drive and enthusiasm.
- + Enjoyment of and interest in life.

## Bauhinia *15ml ifer 1345*

- − Resistance to change; rigidity; annoyance.
- + Acceptance and open mindedness; embracing new concepts and ideas.

## Billy Goat Plum *15ml ifer 1346*

- − Shame; sexual revulsion; dislike, even disgust of part of one's body.
- + Sexual pleasure and enjoyment; acceptance of one's physical body.

## Black-eyed Susan *15ml ifer 1347*

- − Rushing; always on the go; impatience; always striving.
- + Slowing down; ability to turn inward and be still; inner peace.

## Bluebell *15ml ifer 1348*

- − Cut off from feelings; fear of "lack"; greed
- + Opens the heart; joy; sharing.

## Boab *15ml ifer 1349*

- − Enmeshment in negative family patterns; for recipients of abuse and prejudice.
- + Personal freedom by releasing family patterns; clearing of other non-family negative karmic connections.

## Boronia *15ml ifer 1350*

- − Obsessive thoughts; infatuation; pining for recently ended relationships.
- + Serenity; clarity of mind and thought; creative visualisation.

## Bottlebrush *15ml ifer 1351*

- − Hoarding and holding on emotionally; overwhelmed by life changes.
- + Letting go; serenity whilst adjusting to change; bonding between mother and child.

## Bush Fuchsia *15ml ifer 1352*

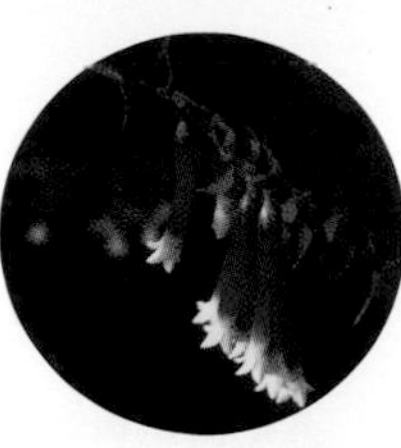

- ⊖ Inability to balance the logical and rational with the intuitive and creative; ignoring gut feelings.
- ⊕ Allows one to integrate information; develops intuition; trusting and following one's intuition.

## Bush Gardenia *15ml ifer 1353*

- ⊖ Taking loved ones for granted; unaware of others.
- ⊕ Renews interest in others; improves communication; passion.

## Bush Iris *15ml ifer 1354*

- ⊖ Fear of death; materialism; atheism.
- ⊕ Spiritual insight; awareness and understanding beyond the material/physical plane.

## Christmas Bell *15ml ifer 5785*

- ⊖ Sense of lack.
- ⊕ Manifest one's desired outcomes.

## Crowea *15ml ifer 1355*

- ⊖ Worrying; out of balance; feeling "not quite right".
- ⊕ Balances and centres the individual; in touch with one's feelings.

## Dagger Hakea *15ml ifer 1356*

- ⊖ Resentment; bitterness towards close family, friends and lovers.
- ⊕ Forgiveness; open expression of feelings.

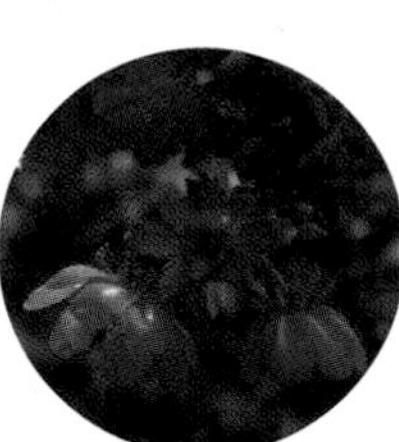

## Dog Rose *15ml ifer 1357*

- ⊖ Fearful; shy; insecure; apprehensive of others; niggling fears.
- ⊕ Confidence; courage; belief in self; ability to embrace life more fully.

## Dog Rose of the Wild Forces *15ml ifer 1358*

- ⊖ Fear of losing control; hysteria; pain with no apparent cause.
- ⊕ Calm and centred in times of inner or outer turmoil; emotional balance.

## Five Corners *15ml ifer 1359*

- ⊖ Lack of confidence; low self esteem; dislike of self; held in personality; self sabotage.
- ⊕ Love and acceptance of self; celebration of own beauty; letting true self stand out.

## Flannel Flower *15ml ifer 1360*

- ⊖ Dislike of being touched; difficulty verbalising feelings; uncomfortable with physical & emotional intimacy.
- ⊕ Gentleness; enjoyment of all physical expression and touch; trust to express and reveal self; sensuality; healthy boundaries.

## Freshwater Mangrove
*15ml ifer 3147*

- ⊖ Heart closed due to expectations or prejudices which have been taught, not personally experienced.
- ⊕ Openness to new experiences, people and perceptual shifts; healthy questioning of traditional standards and beliefs.

## Fringed Violet *15ml ifer 1361*

- ⊖ Distress; damage to aura; drained by others/situations.
- ⊕ Removes effects of past or present distress; psychic protection.

## Green Spider Orchid *15ml ifer 1362*

- ⊖ Nightmares and phobias from past life experiences; intense negative reactions to the sight of blood.
- ⊕ Telepathic communication; ability to withhold information until timing is appropriate; attunement.

## Grey Spider Flower *15ml ifer 1363*

- ⊖ Terror; panic; nightmares from unknown causes; fear of the supernatural and of psychic attack.
- ⊕ Faith; courage; calmness.

## Gymea Lily *15ml ifer 1364*

- ⊖ Arrogant; attention seeking; craving status and glamour; dominating and over-riding personality.
- ⊕ Humility; allowing others to express themselves and contribute; awareness; appreciation and taking notice of others.

## Hibbertia *15ml ifer 1365*

- ⊖ Rigid personality; fanaticism about self improvement; excessive self discipline.
- ⊕ Acceptance of self and own innate knowledge; integration of knowledge and philosophies.

## Illawarra Flame Tree *15ml ifer 1366*

- ⊖ Sense of rejection; being left out; fear of responsibility.
- ⊕ Self approval; self reliance; inner strength.

## Isopogon *15ml ifer 1367*

- ⊖ Unable to learn from past experience; stubborn and controlling personality.
- ⊕ Able to learn from past experiences; remember the past; retrieval of forgotten skills.

## Jacaranda *15ml ifer 1368*

- ⊖ Scattered; changeable; dithering; unfocused; rushing.
- ⊕ Decisiveness; clear mindedness; focused attention.

## Kangaroo Paw *15ml ifer 1369*

- ⊖ Unaware of appropriate social behaviour; insensitive to others' needs; self centred; awkward; clumsy.
- ⊕ Relaxed; sensitivity; saviore faire; enjoyment of people.

## Kapok Bush *15ml ifer 1370*

- ⊖ Easily discouraged; resignation, apathy.
- ⊕ Persistence; willingness to "give it a go"; application.

## Little Flannel Flower *15ml ifer 1371*

- ⊖ Denial of the "child" in the personality; too serious.
- ⊕ Playfulness; joyful; ability to have fun; spontaneity.

## Macrocarpa *15ml ifer 1372*

- ⊖ Personally drained.
- ⊕ Renews enthusiasm.

## Mint Bush *15ml ifer 1373*

- ⊖ Perturbation; confusion; spiritual emergence; initial turmoil and void of spiritual initiation.
- ⊕ Smooth spiritual initiation; clarity; calmness; ability to cope.

## Monga Waratah *15ml ifer 4554*

- ⊖ Neediness; inability to do things alone; disempowerment; addictive personality.
- ⊕ Strengthening of one's will; reclaiming of ones spirit; belief that one can break the dependency on any behavior, substance or person; self empowerment.

## Mountain Devil *15ml ifer 1374*

- ⊖ Hatred; anger; jealousy; holding of grudges; suspiciousness.
- ⊕ Unconditional love; forgiveness; happiness; inner peace.

## Mulla Mulla *15ml ifer 1375*

- ⊖ Distress associated with exposure to fire, heat and sun.
- ⊕ Reduces the negative effects of fire and the sun's rays.

## Old Man Banksia *15ml ifer 1376*

- ⊖ Disheartened; weary; phlegmatic personality.
- ⊕ Ability to cope with whatever life brings.

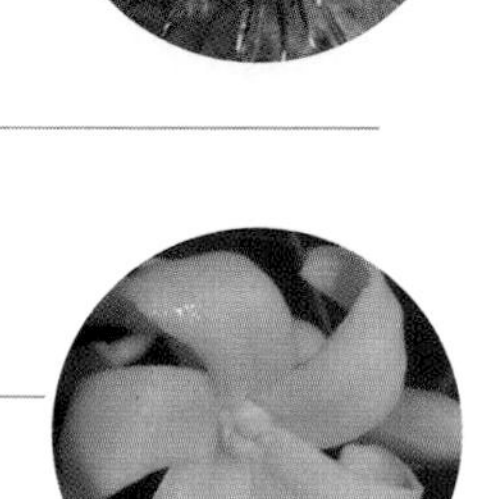

## Paw Paw *15ml ifer 1377*

- ⊖ Overwhelm; burdened by decision.
- ⊕ Focus and clarity.

## Peach-flowered Tea-tree *15ml ifer 1378*

- ⊖ Mood swings; hypochondria; easily bored and loses interest in projects.
- ⊕ Balance; responsibility for own health; completion of projects.

## Philotheca *15ml ifer 1379*

- ⊖ Excessive generosity; inability to accept acknowledgement.
- ⊕ Ability to accept praise; acknowledgement and love; open to abundance.

## Pink Mulla Mulla *15ml ifer 1380*

- ⊖ Deep psychic wounds; guarded and prickly persona to keep people away and prevent being hurt.
- ⊕ Deep spiritual healing; trusting and opening up.

## Red Grevillea *15ml ifer 1381*

- ⊖ Feeling stuck; affected by criticism; reliant on others.
- ⊕ Strength to leave unpleasant situations; boldness; indifferent to judgement of others.

## Red Helmet Orchid *15ml ifer 1382*

- ⊖ Unresolved father issues; rebelliousness; problems with authority.
- ⊕ Helps father/child bonding; sensitivity; respect.

## Red Lily *15ml ifer 1383*

- ⊖ Spiritually ungrounded; vagueness; indecisiveness; daydreaming.
- ⊕ Grounded; focused; living in the present; opens crown chakra; enhances spiritual evolvement.

## Red Suva Frangipani *15ml ifer 1384*

- Initial grief, turmoil, rawness and emotional upset of a rocky or just ended relationship.
+ Feeling calm and nurtured; inner peace and strength to cope.

## Rough Bluebell *15ml ifer 1385*

- Deliberately hurtful, manipulative, exploitive or malicious.
+ Compassion; release of one's inherent love vibration; sensitivity.

## She Oak *15ml ifer 1386*

- Distress associated with infertility.
+ Overcomes imbalances in females.

## Silver Princess *15ml ifer 1387*

- Aimless; despondent; lacking life direction.
+ Life purpose and direction; motivation.

## Slender Rice Flower *15ml ifer 1388*

- Racism formed from personal experiences; narrow mindedness; comparison with others.
+ Co-operation and group harmony; humility; perception of beauty in and acceptance of others.

## Southern Cross *15ml ifer 1389*

- "Poor me" mentality; poverty consciousness; feeling a victim; blaming others.
+ Personal power; positive attitude; taking responsibility for self.

## Spinifex *15ml ifer 1390*

- Sense of being a victim to illness.
+ Empowers through understanding and awareness of the emotional causes of illness.

## Sturt Desert Pea *15ml ifer 1391*

- Deep hurt; sadness; emotional pain.
+ Diffuses sad memories; allows one to let go; motivates.

## Sturt Desert Rose *15ml ifer 1392*

- Guilt; feeling bad about self because of previous action; easily led.
+ Allows one to follow own inner convictions and morality; personal integrity.

## Sundew *15ml ifer 1393*

- Procrastination; disconnected; spaced out; lack of focus.
+ Practical; attention to detail; grounded; focused.

## Sunshine Wattle *15ml ifer 1394*

- Struggle; stuck in the past; expectation of a grim future.
+ Optimism; hope; acceptance of the beauty and joy in the present; joyful expectation.

## Sydney Rose *15ml ifer 4766*

- Feeling separate, deserted, unloved, or morbid.
+ Realising we are all one; feeling safe and at peace; heartfelt communication.

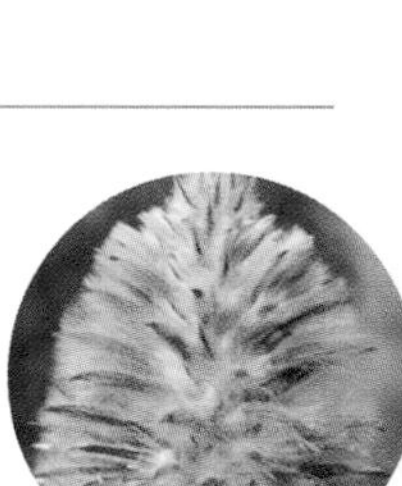

## Tall Mulla Mulla *15ml ifer 1395*

- Ill at ease; fear of circulating and mixing; loner; distressed by and avoids confrontation.
+ Feeling relaxed and secure with other people; encourages social interaction.

## Tall Yellow Top *15ml ifer 1396*

- Alienation; lonely; isolated.
+ Sense of belonging.

## Turkey Bush *15ml ifer 1397*

- Creative block; disbelief in own creative ability.
+ Inspired creativity; renews artistic confidence.

## Waratah *15ml ifer 1398*

- Black despair; hopelessness; inability to respond to crisis.
+ Courage; tenacity; faith; adaptability; survival skills.

## Wedding Bush *15ml ifer 1399*

- Difficulty with commitment.
+ Commitment to relationships and goals; dedication to life purpose.

## Wild Potato Bush *15ml ifer 1400*

- Sense of being weighed down and encumbered.
+ Freedom to move on in life.

## **Wisteria** *15ml ifer 1401*

- ⊖ Women who feel uncomfortable about their sexuality; fear arising from sexual abuse.
- ⊕ Trust; fulfilment and enjoyment of sexuality; allowing warm sensuous feelings in the body.

## **Yellow Cowslip Orchid** *15ml ifer 1402*

- ⊖ Critical; judgemental; bureaucratic.
- ⊕ Humanitarian concern; impartiality; can see both the detail and the big picture; objective analysis.

# **Companion** essences

## **Autumn Leaves** *15ml ifer 3306*

- ⊖ Difficulties in the transition of passing over from the physical plane to the sprirtual world.
- ⊕ Letting go; in one's last days before passing over it increases awareness and communication with loved ones in the spiritual world.

## **Lichen** *15ml ifer 3305*

- ⊖ Not knowing to look for and move into the Light when passing over; earth bound in the astral plane.
- ⊕ Eases one's transition into the light; assists separation between the physical and etheric body; releases earth bound energies.

## **Green** *15ml ifer 3337*

- ⊖ Emotional distress associated with intestinal and skin disorders.
- ⊕ Harmonise the vibration of any yeast mould or parasite to one's own vibration; purifying.

# **Combination** essences

## **Abund essence** *30ml ifer 3168*

- ⊖ Pessimistic, Closed to receiving, Fear of lack, Poverty consciousness
- ⊕ Joyful sharing, Belief in abundance, Clears sabotage, Universal trust

Releases negative beliefs, family patterns, sabotage and fear of lack. In so doing it allows you to be open to fully receiving great riches on all levels, not just financial.

*Essences:* Bluebell, Boab, Five Corners, Philotheca, Southern Cross, Sunshine Wattle.

## **Calm & Clear essence/cream/mist**

*30ml ifer 4812 / 50ml ifer 4823 / 50ml ifer 4813*

- ⊖ Always over committed, No time for self, Always last priority
- ⊕ Encourages own time & space, Healthy contemplation & relaxation

Helps to find time for one's self, to relax without external pressures & demands, to wind down & enjoy relaxing pursuits.

*Essences:* Black-eyed Susan, Boronia, Bottlebrush, Crowea, Bush Fuchsia, Jacaranda, Little Flannel Flower, Paw Paw.

## **Cognis essence** *30ml ifer 2228*

- ⊖ Day-dreaming, Confusion, Overwhelm
- ⊕ Clarity and focus

Gives focus and clarity when studying, speaking or reading . It assists problem solving by improving access to the Higher Self, which stores all past knowledge and experiences. It balances the intuitive and cognitive processes and helps integrate ideas and information.

*Essences:* Bush Fuchsia, Isopogon, Jacaranda, Paw Paw, Sundew.

## **Confid essence** *30ml ifer 2226*

- ⊖ Low Self Esteem, Guilt, Shyness, Lack of Conviction, Victim Mentality
- ⊕ Confidence, Integrity, Taking responsibility for one's life, Personal power, True to oneself

Brings out the positive qualities of self esteem & confidence. It allows us to feel comfortable around other people & be true to ourselves. It resolves negative subconscious beliefs we may hold about ourselves as well as any guilt we may harbour from past actions.

*Essences:* Boab, Dog Rose, Five Corners, Southern Cross, Sturt Desert Rose.

## Creative essence *30ml ifer 2236*

⊖ Creative blocks and inhibitions

⊕ Enhances singing, Creative expression, Clarity of voice, Public speaking

Frees your voice and opens your heart. Inspires creative and emotional expression in a gentle and calm way and gives courage and clarity in public speaking and singing.

*Essences:* Bush Fuchsia, Turkey Bush, Red Grevillea, Crowea, Flannel Flower, Five Corners, Tall Mulla Mulla.

## Dynamis essence *30ml ifer 2227*

⊖ Temporary loss of drive, enthusiasm and excitement

⊕ Renews passion and enthusiasm for life, Centres and harmonises your vital forces

Renews enthusiasm and joy for life. It is for those who feel 'not quite right', drained, jaded, disheartened or burdened by their physical body. It also helps with feelings of physical restriction and limitation.

*Essences:* Old Man Banksia, Macrocarpa, Crowea, Banksia Robur, Illawarra Flame Tree, Yellow Cowslip Orchid.

## Electro essence *30ml ifer 4811*

⊖ Negate or reduce Earth radiation, electrical radiation, flourescent lights, solar radiation and radiation therapy used to treat cancer.

⊕ stops storage of radiation in the body and helps emit radiation already stored, keeps body's energies intact.

*Essences:* Bush Fuchsia, Crowea, Fringed Violet, Mulla Mulla, Paw Paw, Waratah.

## Emergency essence/cream/mist

*30ml ifer 2230 / 50ml ifer 4820 / 50ml ifer 4814*

⊖ Panic, Distress, Fear

⊕ Ability to cope

Helps ease distress, fear, panic, etc. If a person needs specialised medical help, this Essence will provide comfort until treatment is available. Administer this remedy every hour or more frequently if necessary until the person feels better.

*Essences:* Angelsword, Dog Rose of the Wild Forces, Fringed Violet, Grey Spider Flower, Sundew, Waratah, Crowea.(plus Spinifex & Slender Rice flower in cream only)

## Face Hand & Body cream *50ml ifer 4821*

⊖ Dislike of physical self, body, skin texture & touch

⊕ Acceptance of physical body, Love & nurturing of self

Encourages acceptance of physical body, love & nurturing of self, feel, touch & self massage. Helps to deal with the dislike & non acceptance of body, skin texture & touch.

*Essences:* Billy Goat Plum, Five Corners, Flannel Flower, Little Flannel Flower, Wisteria.

## Meditation essence *30ml ifer 2229*

⊖ Psychic attack, Damaged aura, Tense and uptight, Psychically drained

⊕ Awaken spirituality, Enhanced intuition, Inner guidance, Access Higher Self, Deeper Meditation

Awakens one's spirituality and allows one to go deeper into any religious or spiritual practice. Enhances access to the Higher Self whilst providing psychic protection and healing of the aura. Highly recommended for anyone practising meditation.

*Essences:* Fringed Violet, Bush Fuchsia, Bush Iris, Angelsword, Red Lily, Boronia, Green Spider Orchid.

## Purifying essence *30ml ifer 4810*

⊖ Emotional waste, feeling encumbered, emotional baggage

⊕ Sense of release and relief, spring cleaned

To release and clear emotional waste and residual by-products, to clear built-up emotional baggage.

*Essences:* Bauhinia, Bush Iris, Bottlebrush, Dagger Hakea, Dog Rose, Wild Potato Bush.

## Relationship essence *30ml ifer 2231*

⊖ Confusion, Resentment, Emotional pain and turmoil, Blocked emotions, Inability to relate

⊕ Expressing feelings, Communication, Forgiveness, Breaks family conditioning, Renews interest

Enhances the quality of all relationships, especially intimate ones. Clears and releases resentment, blocked emotions and the confusion, emotional pain & turmoil of a rocky relationship. Helps one verbalise, express feelings & improve communication. Breaks the early family conditioning & patterns which effect us in our current adult relationships. For intimate relationships a perfect remedy to follow this combination is Sexuality Essence.

*Essences:* Bluebell, Bush Gardenia, Dagger Hakea, Mint Bush, Red Suva Frangipani, Boab, Flannel Flower, Wedding Bush, Red Helmet Orchid, Bottlebrush.

## Sensuality mist *50ml ifer 4816*

⊖ Fear of emotional & physical intimacy

⊕ Encourages intimacy, passion & sensual fulfilment.

Encourages the ability to enjoy physical and emotional intimacy, passion and sensual fulfilment.

*Essences:* Bush Gardenia, Billy Goat Plum, Flannel Flower, Little Flannel Flower, Macrocarpa, Wisteria.

## Sexuality essence *30ml ifer 2232*

⊖ Shame, Uptight about sexuality, Fear of intimacy, Lack of sensitivity, Emotional effects of sexual abuse

⊕ Renews passion, Sensuality, Enjoy touch and intimacy, Self acceptance, Fulfilment

Helpful for releasing shame and the effects of sexual abuse. It allows one to feel comfortable with and to fully accept one's body. It enables the individual to be open to sensuality and touch and to enjoy physical and emotional intimacy. Sexuality Essence renews passion and interest in relationships.

*Essences:* Billy Goat Plum, Bush Gardenia, Flannel Flower, Fringed Violet, Little Flannel Flower, Sturt Desert Rose,Wisteria.

## Solaris essence *30ml ifer 2233*

⊖ Fear and distress associated with fire

⊕ Reduces the negative effects of fire and the sun's rays

Relieves the fear and distress associated with fire, heat and sun.

*Essences:* Mulla Mulla (found in the desert of Central Australia, the hottest part of the continent), She Oak, Spinifex.

## Space Clearing mist *50ml ifer 4817 / 100ml ifer 4819*

⊖ Negative mental, emotional & psychic energies

⊕ Clears negative environments, Creates safe harmonious environments.

Creates sacred, safe and harmonious environments. Clears & releases environments with built up negative emotional, mental & psychic energies. Great for clearing tense situations & environments and restoring balance.

*Essences:* Angelsword, Boab, Fringed Violet, Lichen, Red Lily.

## Travel essence/cream/mist

*30ml ifer 2235 / 50ml ifer 4825 / 50ml ifer 4815*

⊖ Personally depleted and drained, Disorientated

⊕ Centres, Refreshes, Maintains sense of personal space

Beneficial for distress associated with all forms of travel, although it particularly addresses the problems encountered with jet travel. It enables a person to arrive at their destination feeling balanced and ready to go.

*Essences:* Banksia Robur, Bush Iris, Bottlebrush, Bush Fuchsia, Crowea, Fringed Violet, Macrocarpa, Mulla Mulla, Paw Paw, Red Lily, She Oak, Silver Princess, Sundew, Tall Mulla Mulla.

## Woman essence/cream *30ml ifer 3169 / 50ml ifer 4822*

⊖ Mood swings, Weary, Physical dislike

⊕ Female balance, Calm and stable,Coping with change

To encourage a woman's own innate strength and beauty through life's cycles and seasons of change. Remaining calm & stable, discovering & feeling good about self, beauty and body whilst coping with change. Harmonises any imbalances and emotions through puberty, menstruation, pregnancy and menopause.

*Essences:* Billy Goat Plum, Bottlebrush, Bush Fuchsia, Crowea, Five Corners, Mulla Mulla, Old Man Banksia, Peach-flowered Tea-tree, She Oak.

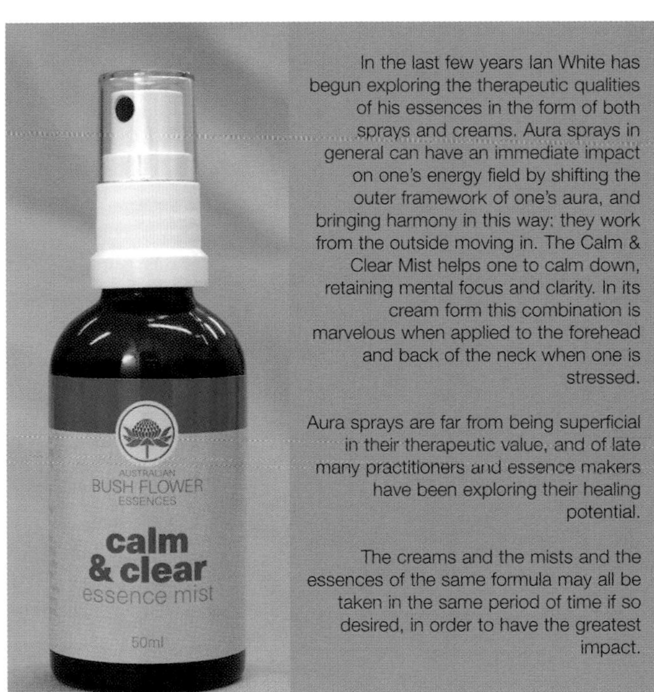


In the last few years Ian White has begun exploring the therapeutic qualities of his essences in the form of both sprays and creams. Aura sprays in general can have an immediate impact on one's energy field by shifting the outer framework of one's aura, and bringing harmony in this way: they work from the outside moving in. The Calm & Clear Mist helps one to calm down, retaining mental focus and clarity. In its cream form this combination is marvelous when applied to the forehead and back of the neck when one is stressed.

Aura sprays are far from being superficial in their therapeutic value, and of late many practitioners and essence makers have been exploring their healing potential.

The creams and the mists and the essences of the same formula may all be taken in the same period of time if so desired, in order to have the greatest impact.

# Bach **Combination Remedies** of France

Region: France

Founded: 1999

DEVELOPER: Gerard Wolf.
Gerard is French and is a Bach Practitioner and distributor of flower essences of many years' standing. In his work, he found that it was usually necessary to select several Bach flower essences in order to personalise remedies and relate them to present day issues. He also found that some of his clients were unable to choose the appropriate remedy when they were distressed. This led him to simplify the choice of Bach remedies and create a line that was 'themed', designed specifically for easy choice, quick assistance and positive support.

THE ESSENCES: To make this inspirational line of Combination Remedies, Gerard makes each individual flower essence himself using the traditional methods of Dr Edward Bach. The individual essences are made from flowers grown wild and picked at full bloom. It is from these essences that the 10 Combinations are formulated, helping to harmonise and balance the well-being of the whole family. They are not intended to substitute the use of Bach remedies, but offer to make the choice and use easier.

## Confidence *20ml ifer 5031*

**(Cerato, Elm, Larch, Gentian, Scleranthus, Wild Oat and Centaury)**

For those who lack self confidence and battle with a sense of failure. Assistance for those feeling withdrawn. Lack of self worth. This essence fosters greater self confidence and assertiveness. Can be taken prior to challenging situations such as public speaking, or attempting new activities.

## Courage (Faith) *20ml ifer 5036*

**(Aspen, Cherry Plum, Red Chestnut, Agrimony, Heather, Mimulus and Rock Rose)**

Heartens and restores faith in self and in life, so you can move on. For fear of the future, and fearing the worst. Negativity. Take when required or when anguished.

## **Energy** *20ml ifer 5035*

**(Centaury, Oak, Olive, Hornbeam and Wild Rose.)**

Mentally, emotionally and physically drained. Helps regain a sense of balance and enthusiasm.

## **Focus** *20ml ifer 5033*

**(Chestnut Bud, Clematis, Honeysuckle, White Chestnut, Scleranthus, Hornbeam and Wild Rose)**

For excessive day dreaming, listlessness, absent-mindedness, feeling scattered, or lack of focus. This combination is beneficial for those who find themselves falling back into old patterns of behaviour. Helps one stay attentive in the present moment.

## **Freedom** *20ml ifer 5032*

**(Agrimony, Crab Apple, Walnut, Centaury, Cherry Plum, Chestnut Bud and Chicory)**

Helps support and stabilise whilst the person is undergoing healing of dependency on substances. Assists "will power" for undertaking major changes, helps break co-dependent relationships with people, substances and life situations.

## **Harmony** (Dissolve Aggression) *20ml ifer 5030*

**(Chicory, Vine, Vervain, Impatiens, Beech, Willow and Holly)**

Calms and harmonises strong emotional states, such as anger, jealousy and resentment. Will assist those experiencing intolerance, irritation and possessiveness. Especially recommended for turbulent teenagers and sibling jealousy, to help bring about greater group or family harmony.

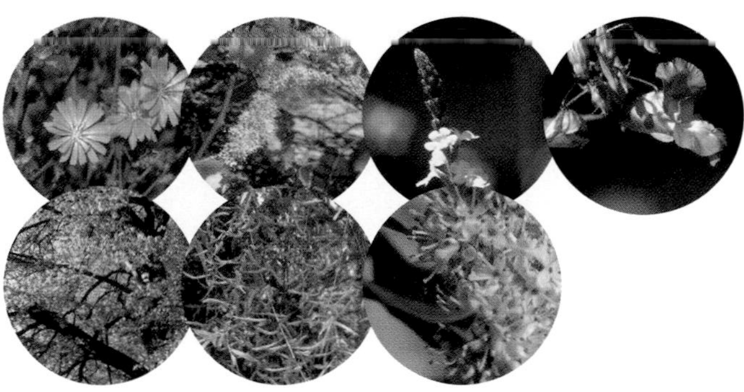

## **Joy** *20ml ifer 5037*

**(Wild Rose, Gorse, Gentian, Mustard, Sweet Chestnut, Star of Bethlehem and Willow)**

Helps lift gloom, dissatisfaction and unhappiness. When feeling disheartened, depressed and over sensitive. This combination will help bring about interest in self and one's environment.

## **Relief Remedy** *20ml ifer 5034*

**(Rock Rose, Impatiens, Clematis, Cherry Plum, Star of Bethlehem, Crab Apple and Scleranthus)**

Help is at hand, for self and others during times of crisis, shock, panic and emotional upheaval. Also recommended for anxious or upset animals, for plants needing help after re-potting or re-planting.

## **Serenity** (Relaxation) *20ml ifer 5039*

**(Vervain, Oak, Impatiens, Agrimony, White Chestnut, Pine and Crab Apple)**

For times of excessive activity, personal or professional stress, tension, or anxiety.
When burdened by life's pressures which can lead to insomnia, mental over-activity. Use of this combination helps bring peace of mind and relaxation.

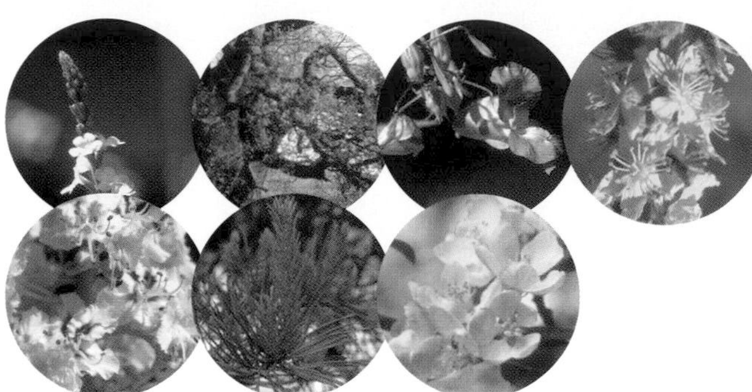

## **Sexual Passion** *20ml ifer 5038*

**(Crab Apple, Wild Rose, Larch, Pine, Hornbeam, Gentian and Impatiens)**

Can be used with concerns regarding lack of sexual desire and difficulties. Harmonising for relationship partners. Beneficial for greater expression of, and enjoyment of sexuality.

# Bailey Essences

Region: England

(Yorkshire Dales & Ilkley Moor)

Founded: 1967

DEVELOPER: Arthur Bailey

Arthur Bailey has a rigorous scientific background and has always had a love of nature. He has been involved in healing and meditation for most of his life. He understood that there is a direct interaction between the mind and body. An uneasy mind leads to an uneasy body and it is this uneasiness that is often the origin of illness. From this understanding and background Arthur was drawn to creating flower essences.

THE ESSENCES: The Bailey Flower essences act as catalysts for change and transformation. They are excellent for working on our states of mind and belief systems to help release the past to bring us up to date so that we can move forward. Only when old conditioning and beliefs dissolve can we truly 'come into the present moment'. There are now 48 individual essences and 12 Composites. All are hand-made by members of his family using pure water and vodka as a base.

## **Composite** essences

### Anger & Frustration *10ml ifer 5493*

To balance and stabilise our fire energies so that we can take proper control of our lives.

### Childhood *10ml ifer 3330*

Helps to free energies that have been blocked since childhood. For those locked in childhood patterns.

### Confusion *10ml ifer 5492*

For when our lives are confused and we feel unable to see clearly what we should be doing.

### Depression & Despair *10ml ifer 3902*

For those times when we become locked in negative thought patterns, including the depths of despair

### Fears *10ml ifer 3493*

Fears can constrict much of our lives. This essence helps us to let go of fears so that we can live in greater freedom.

### Grief *10ml ifer 1308*

This is very helpful for all cases of grief and anguish where there is deep distress.

### Liberation *10ml ifer 3482*

To dissolve our emotional attachment to objects, events and people.

### Obsession *10ml ifer 1321*

For when a particular thought just keeps going round and round and will not go away. The "mouse on the treadmill" type of feeling.

### Sadness & Loneliness *10ml ifer 5494*

For those times when we need comfort, love and reassurance. Encourages new beginnings.

### Self Esteem *10ml ifer 5468*

For those who feel disempowered, often dominated by others, and are unable to assert themselves in the world. Blocked-off self-love.

### Shock & Trauma *10ml ifer 5461*

Essence of choice for sudden or long-term shock and trauma.

## Stuck in a Rut *10ml ifer 5491*

For use when we feel stagnated or trapped by the circumstances surrounding us.

## Tranquillity *10ml ifer 1335*

Brings peace to the over-active mind. It helps to empower us by bringing us into the present moment.

## Transition *10ml ifer 3526*

For when there are major changes in life, when the past needs to make way for the new.

## Yang *10ml ifer 3339*

Helps to build the outgoing "male" power whilst bringing stronger links with the intuitive "Yin" aspects of the personality.

## Yin *10ml ifer 3340*

The counterpart of the Yang essence, this builds the intuitive wisdom aspects of the personality whilst keeping both feet firmly on the ground.

# Single essences

## Almond *10ml ifer 4970*

The supportive inner teacher, the guide. Forms links with our souls and encourages intuition.

## Arizona Fir *10ml ifer 3885*

To help us to celebrate life and existence as spiritually based beings.

## Bistort *10ml ifer 1294*

To provide loving support at times of major change in our lives.

## Black Locust *10ml ifer 5587*

For protection against the negative influences of other people, including psychic attack.

## Blue Pimpernel *10ml ifer 3904*

Rediscovering our spiritual nature whilst growing up in a superficially material world.

## Bog Asphodel *10ml ifer 1297*

For the "willing slave" - those who help others yet frequently ignore their own needs.

## Bracken (Aqueous) *10ml ifer 1299*

For when intuitive sensitivity was blocked in childhood, resulting in a fear of the intuitive side of one's nature.

## Buttercup *10ml ifer 1301*

For those who find it difficult to let the "sunshine" into their lives. Helps one to let go of embittered feelings.

## Cymbidium Orchid *10ml ifer 4971*

Relates to the hidden side of our nature, brings peace and harmony to the subconscious parts of our mind.

## Early Purple Orchid *10ml ifer 1304*

For unblocking the energy centres in the body and protecting any vulnerable spaces so created.

## Hairy Sedge *10ml ifer 1309*

For those who worry and find it difficult to keep their minds in the present moment. This inattention can result in poor memory.

## Himalayan Blue Poppy *10ml ifer 5588*

The essence of spiritual lineage. To fulfill our potential in this lifetime, we need to build on strengths gained in the past. Furthers insight and psychic skills.

## **Leopardsbane** *10ml ifer 1311*

For those who are at a major change point in their lives. They may feel as if they are living on a knife-edge.

## **Lilac** *10ml Ifer 1313*

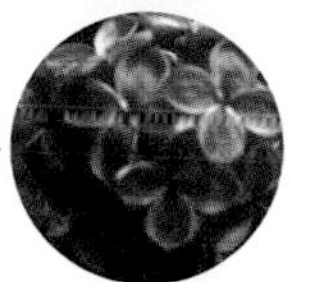

For those whose personal development has been stunted by dominant influences, usually in childhood or adolescence.

## **Lily of the Valley** *10ml ifer 1314*

For yearning. For those who have become blocked by desiring the unattainable.

## **Magnolia** *10ml ifer 4973*

For unconditional love. This essence helps to bring and awaken within us the energies of love and compassion.

## **Mediterranean Sage** *10ml ifer 3505*

For the "Earth" qualities of warmth, comfort and wisdom. Helps to catalyze insight from a firm earthed base.

## **Milk Thistle** *10ml ifer 1317*

This remedy is for those who do not love themselves. Often they try to make up for this by trying to please others.

## **Monk's Hood** *10ml ifer 1318*

For difficulties of long standing that have their roots in the distant past. Helps to bring one up-to-date.

## **Oxalis** *10ml ifer 1322*

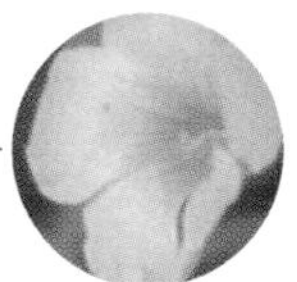

For things that "have you by the throat" and seem so overpowering that there appears to be no way out.

## **Red Frangipani** *10ml ifer 4972*

The essence of awakening. Re-unites us with the true source of our being which lies beyond the spiritual dimension. Brings joy and new levels of perception and confidence.

## **Sea Campion** *10ml ifer 3352*

For separation in early childhood and its consequent insecurity and fears. Stimulates loving, protective energies.

## **Single Snowdrop** *10ml ifer 1329*

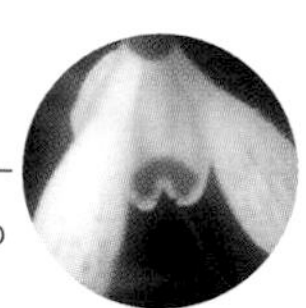

For breaking through to new levels of consciousness. Helps to bring insight and support during such times.

## **Solomon's Seal** *10ml ifer 1331*

For the busy mind. This remedy helps bring quietness and detachment.

## **Speedwell** *10ml ifer 5797*

Increases powers of insight, whilst preventing us from becoming emotionally entangled with what we perceive.

## **Spotted Orchid** *10ml ifer 4989*

To help us overcome difficulties and blocks on our path of personal growth.

## **Spring Squill** *10ml ifer 1332*

For freedom after breakthrough. Helps us to soar like a bird, finding our own true path in limitless space.

## **Thrift** *10ml ifer 1334*

For helping to open up the psychic sensitivity but keeping the person firmly grounded at the same time.

## Tufted Vetch *10ml ifer 1336*

For sexual difficulties caused by an incorrect sexual self-image - usually due to childhood conditioning.

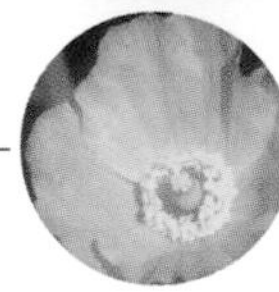

## Welsh Poppy *10ml ifer 1338*

For those who have lost their fire and inspiration and become day-dreamers.

## White Lotus *10ml ifer 4974*

For bringing peace and unification to body, mind, spirit and soul.

## Wood Anemone *10ml ifer 1340*

For use where there are very old difficulties - genetic or Karmic.

# **Flower Essences** of the **Netherlands**

Region: The Netherlands
Founded: 1986
Developers: Bram and Miep Zaalberg

THE ESSENCES: The essences are made nearly exclusively with plants and flowers growing in Bram and Miep's large organic garden, which allows them to become familiar with all the cycles of the plants growth and characteristics. This close, affectionate relationship with the plants and flowers is one of the hallmarks of their line of essences, as is their care and attention to all the energetic aspects of their work. Due to increasing demand they released these essences to a broader public in 1990. The essences possess a great purity and are very powerful in their action. Organic brandy is used for preserving them and to assure the highest possible standard of purity.

This range comprises 28 individual stock essence and four combinations.

## **Standard** set 1

### **Bosrank - Clematis** - *Clematis vitalba*

*10ml ifer 2363*

For awakening and giving a clearer picture of your actions. Clarifies thought processes. Helps obtain a more conscious insight into the handling of our affairs. Assists in the forming process. Gives more insight and an overview of the cause and effect process. Gives clarity to the unconscious. Aids working to express the light.

### **Engelwortel - Angelica** - *Angelica archangelica.*

*10ml ifer 2364*

Provides protection from the spiritual worlds with help from loving forces on high planes. Provides spiritual protection for infants and spiritual development of consciousness. Strengthens ability to experience loving spiritual forces in daily life and work. Promotes spiritual insight, encouraging growth and protecting the consciousness. Increases trust in the leadership of the Higher Self when confronted with unknown areas - a "Godly" trust with a good earth-bound feeling without doubting your personal Wisdom.

### **Judaspenning - Money Plant** - *Lunaria annua*

*10ml ifer 2365*

For those who find material earthly business more important than the unity with their own Being, the Universe and Nature. Lusting after material things resulting in the "handing in" of intuitive strength. Lack of balance in connection with spiritual development through too much striving after worldly possessions and power.

### **Klaproos - Red Poppy** - *Papaver rhoeas*

*10ml ifer 2366*

Strengthens the inner woman, a warming and empowering essence for feeling vulnerable and unable to transform their vulnerabilities. Gives power to work with vulnerabilities. Increases the inner quality of love. Calms extreme sexuality in men and women; helpful also for men and children, especially when they cannot sleep after a busy day.

### **Mycena** - *Mycena polygramma*

*10ml ifer 2367*

Mushroom-remedy. For a strong connection with the earth, developing a sense of belong on earth through choice without feeling one has to. Being able to carry on in difficult situations and uncertainties, especially when everything around you seems to be in ruins. As well as purifying, mushrooms help nature eliminate hard-to-digest elements such as wood or radioactivity. "Gnome" energy and the influence of Pluto.

### Paarse Dovenetel - Red Henbit

*- Lamium purpureum*

*10ml ifer 2368*

Strong earthly bonds and joy in physical activity. Gives clarity in chaotic activity; stimulating the organising process - very useful when moving house. Purifies one's energies providing a strong flow of earthy life force through the body, soul and spirit, which will ease confrontational situations. Apply topically for blockages in the wrists and joints. Enables self expression which stimulates a stronger love for the earth. A positive catalyst promiting love for the environment and a joyful life.

### Regenboog - Rainbow *- development combination*

*10ml ifer 2369 / 30ml ifer 4981*

The bridge between Heaven and Earth; a combination essence for personal development, made from the flowers of Borage, Impatiens, Moneyplant, Red Henbit and Red Poppy. Brings creativity and development. Works horizontally to bring expansion and new impulses; stimulates new activities; opens all chakras and helps break barriers that block our development; brings awareness to the process of development.

### Reuzenbalsemien - Impatiens - *Impatiens glandulifera*

*10ml ifer 2370*

Patience and calm; understanding; knowing that all life continues in its own unique time; spontaneity; recognizing your inner and outer chaos and helps to integrate this within consciousness; clears actions out of one's deepest inner self. Development of oneís own inner timing; becoming aware of disturbances by others; helping to express oneself clearly towards others.

### Rode Bosvogeltje - Orchid *- Cephalanthera rubra*

*10ml ifer 2371*

Unity of being in all circumstances. Being able to continue all actions from one's own source without self sacrifice, so one is able to follow one's own path. Softens hardness and aids circulation. Seeing the reflection of yourself in the outside world. Opening you to "higher" energies. Helps healers when short of energy not maintaining a strong connection with their Higher Selves. Gives more power for the healing of others and allows the life force to stream out of the Higher Self into the world.

### Terra *- An emergency combination*

*10ml ifer 2372 / 30ml ifer 2385*

A combination of Angelica, Clematis, Mycena, Rode Bosvogeltje and Yellow Star Tulip,
A first aid remedy for all kinds of complaints. Clears the blockages and then aids quick recovery. Brings peace and calm in tense situations. Opens the solar plexus. Gives strength in difficult times. Recommended use: 2-5 drops straight from the stock bottle under the tongue and/or to hold the bottle during prolonged periods of tension. Can be applied locally.

### Teunisbloem - Evening Primrose

*- Oenothera lamarckiana*

*10ml ifer 2373*

Night blooming flower. Strengthens the creative forces of the moon. Helps us to (re)discover and connect with a sense of self-confidence and the inner feminine. Brings insight into old patterns of incest, rape and problems in the area of sexuality, giving support and help for discussing such problems, and bringing everything out into the open.

### Yellow Star Tulip

*- Calochortus monophyllus*

*10ml ifer 2374*

For sensitive people who are not sure of where they are going. Allows us to reveal our sensitivity and make use of it. Excellent aid for bringing into being what our heart tells us to be true, and to start on projects that have been signaled inwardly for some time but have remained hidden deep within. Gives us trust in all changes and stimulates us to act.

## **Standard** set 2

### Beemdkroon - Field Scabious

*- Knautia arvensis*

*10ml ifer 2375*

Brings transformation and wisdom. Quiets the thinking and purifies unnecessary thoughts through the earth. Positive thinking. Helps us to handle things better, to be more perceptive and open to others and the environment. Connects us to the higher spheres, allowing them to reflect out into our surroundings.

### Boerenwormkrulid - Tansy

*- Tanacetum vulgare.*

*10ml ifer 2376*

For doubt and inability to make decisions. Helps to take direct action and gives insight into the process that if you are not making decisions nothing will happen. When you are stuck in a web of hesitation, the Tansy will give trust and help to connect you with your higher self. Strengthens the heart and gives insight into the deepest core of doubts on all levels of your being.

## Kleine Viltinktzwam - Little Inky Cap

*- Coprinus xanthotrix*

*10ml ifer 2377*

Helps us let go of emotions; when vulnerable, brings emotional strength and universal trust. Helps one rise above emotions and promotes the letting go of old anger quickly and easily. Helps you resist pressure by others and stand strong for yourself.

## Komkommerkruid - Borage

*- Borago officinalis*

*10ml ifer 2378*

Strengthens the heart in difficult circumstances and brings gladness and joy. Allows you to resist difficulties or discouragement and go on despite adversity. When losing faith, brings back joyfulness and strength to one's heart.

## Kruidje Roer Me Niet - Sensitive Weed

*- Mimosa pudica*

*10ml ifer 2379*

Brings stability, clarity and strength to the soul and mind. For choosing and maintaining your path with certainty. To create space, undisturbed by others and pursue self-development under all circumstances. To feel protected and supported by the environment.
A quick recovery aid.

## Papegaaieblad - Alternanthera

*- Alternanthera dentata*

*10ml ifer 2380*

Centered feelings, without fear of expression; staying centred. Undisturbed by people or their issues. To do the work you believe in and bring your Higher truth into reality and expand it. To give full expression to what is. To love the earth from the deepest core of your being.

## Purple Flower - *Centratherum punctatum*

*10ml ifer 2381*

Brings light to energy around the head, allowing the mind to relax. Heightens awareness in healing; trusting in our work as healers and ability to bring this out into the world. To reflect the light of our being into the different kingdoms (animal, mineral, plant and human); open up to the power of nature; insight and awareness of our environment.

## Sneeuwklokje - Snowdrop

*- Galanthus nivalis*

*10ml ifer 2382*

Releases deep pain, tears and old traumas especially those that originate from not being true to yourself. Doing everything for others and forgetting oneself. To recover oneís own beauty and importance. To feel free to please oneself. Brings a strong sense of trust deep down.
Joyful refreshing energy after the long and dark (emotional) winter.

## Vingerhoedskruid - Foxglove - *Digitalis purpurea*

*10ml ifer 2383*

To go beyond thinking. Eases the mental processes, to be able to contact the heart again. Helps let go of mental structures and patterns of how to behave, especially patterns from past lives, eg. the monastic life. Accepting the connection with the higher self as the center and source of a higher quality of love in our lives. Brings a playful nature. Gives joy and pleasure in sexuality and life generally. Helps gain insight into a problem or difficult situation. Balances the polarity of the higher self with the polarity of the earth.

## Wijnruit - Rue - *Ruta graveolens*

*10ml ifer 2384*

For spiritual protection, especially the psychic realms; gives insight when somebody is absorb oneís energies through spiritual influence or disturbance, especially focused around the crown chakra and the line of connection with the higher self. Gives insight into old deep hidden fears and more strength to act out of feeling. If somebody is too precise, this essence helps them to see things more easily, thereby cleansing old physical problems which have been held in the body.

# **Research** essences

## Greater Celandine - *Stinkende Gouwe - ChelidÛnium m·jus*

*10ml ifer 4204*

The cherry on the cake; the finishing touch, making life more complete; promotes decisiveness. Integrates the inner masculine and feminine, For men and woman. Combines right and left hemispheres of the brain, masculine and feminine. Improves relationships, especially when a wall has been built up between people.

## Ground Ivy

*- Hondsdraf - GlechÛma heder·cea*

*10ml ifer 4205*

Clears away old emotions, making one aware of unseen behaviour patterns. For abundance, strength and expansion; helps with personal development and finer attunement, brings out the finer qualities of your being.

## Smooth Hawksbeard - *Klein Streepzaad - CrÈpis capill·ris*

*10ml ifer 4206*

Brings balance between action and repose: brings new energy and vitality, softens rigid structures. Helps one connect with one's own base, to feel at ease with others. Helps clear emotional issues related to childhood as well as those of today. Helps recharge energy and store it in the bones, giving of Love and warmth.

**Sneezewort** - *Wilde Bertram - Achillea ptarmica*
*10ml ifer 4207*

Provides protection on the spiritual path. For aspiring to pure standards and values which previously eluded. Helps one express clear thoughts and visions without having to lean on others; gives self-confidence.

**Protection** - *Bescherming - A combination of the Sneezewort, Greater Celandine, Rue and the Sensitive weed.*
*10ml ifer 4208 / 30ml ifer 4980*

Gives protection. Brings calms to the deepest centre of one's being in times of tension from the outer world. Surrounds and protects with a mantle of light. Brings awareness of emotions and energies one may be absorbing.

**Love** - *Liefde - A combination of Borage, Foxglove, Greater Celandine, (red) Poppy, Red Henbit, Snowdrop and Yellow Star Tulip.*
*10ml ifer 4209 / 30ml ifer 4979*

Awakens Love for oneself, others and the earth. Helps connection to the earth and opens the heart to self love. Enables one to give this Love out to others, without self-denial. A powerful catalyst which connects you to the higher light and your Angel of Love.

**Goldenrod**
*-Guldenroede - Solidago officinalis*
*10ml ifer 4962*

Keywords: Individuality and the Other Person. Inability to open oneself to others. Unable to let go of ego or direct oneself to higher qualities. Brings self-trust and self-confidence, helps develop open-heartedness and hospitality. Gives strength, opening your being with love towards your environment, bringing enthusiasm, abundance and cooperation as a result of a better connection to your higher self.

**Ground Elder** - *Zevenblad - Aegopodium podagraria*
*10ml ifer 4963*

Helps manifest self growth through better connection with one's true self. Helps one let go and open to the higher self. For difficulty resolving old restrictions and emotions which prevent growth. To work on earth for the higher goal and integrate to the higher development of the earth: the expression of your heart. Brings integration and cooperation from the environment through the expression of the heart,

**Giant Stropharia** - *Reuzenstropharia*
*- Stropharia rugoso-annulata*
*10ml ifer 4964*

Brings new insight into activities. Helps direct oneís consciousness from difficulties to pleasure and fun. Helps one to get on with life. Connects one to the earth and releases energies and tensions that are stuck behind the eyes back into the ground.

# New **research** essences

**California Poppy** - *Het Slaapmutsje - Eschscholzia Californica*
*10ml ifer 5867*

Helps one trust and listen to oneís own heart. Brings inner calm and protection from the outside world. To go beyond the superficial surface and search for inner wisdom. Helps when you are too open to the ideas and thoughts of other people. Reveals the ancient, universal knowledge found in the Akashic records and in the depths of your being. Helps sleep problems and addictions. Establishes a balance between light and dark, integrating spirituality with the energy of mother earth.

**Trumpet Vine**
*- De Trompetklimmer - Campsis radicans*
*10ml ifer 5868*

Relieves mental processes and allows one to listen to the heart.. Breaks through communication barriers in a gentle way, helping you express your deeper emotions, without conflict. Helps one express freely what is in your heart and mind. Has given good results for people who stutter.

**Peppermint** - *De Pepermunt - Mentha piperita*
*10ml ifer 5869*

For times of difficulty and challenge. Helps process difficulties in one's life and in the world. Deals with deep emotions and problems in the world around one. Strengthens and prepares one for many eventualities and problems, bringing insight into behaviour patterns and structures held since birth, Helps let go of unseen patterns. Particularly helpful for emotions and energy which have accumulated in the area of the stomach and the digestive system.

**Star of Bethlehem** - *Vogelmelk - Ornithogalum umbellatum*
*10ml ifer 5870*

Opens one to universal strength and connection with one's Higher Self. Helps one remain undisturbed by influences from surroundings. Clears away blocks to one's connection to the Higher Self. This can vary from viruses to sorrows to everything which has accumulated throughout one's life. Opens one to regenerating energies and recovery of strength in one's own time. Allows one to listen to their Higher Self, refusing the influence of others. A truly universal flower and essence which helps one believe in one's own beauty and brings awareness of the next level of higher energy.

# Dancing Light **Orchid** Essences

Region: California/Alaska

Founded: 1995/1980

DEVELOPER: Shabd-sangeet Khalsa (SSK) had been making flower essences for over 20 years (co-founding the Alaskan Flower Essence Project with Steve Johnson). She had no intention of making any more essences but because of her magical connection with the devic energy of orchids, she was compelled to comply with the strong 'directives' from the orchids as she was tending the flowers, 'hearing' the healing message presented to her in prose!

ESSENCES: Orchids are considered to be the queens of the plant kingdom and have an exceptionally high rate of vibrational frequency. Their blossoms often take on the shape of angels and are said to create a link between the higher spiritual levels and mankind. This range of essences is unique in the flower essence world because of their growing habitat. They are made in lovingly cultivated greenhouses, something which surprised SSK, having previously made essences from wild flowers located outdoors in the pristine environment of Alaska.

The Dancing Light essences comprise five sets of seven essences each, seven Sister Moon Oils and a Birch Tree Deva Oil.

These orchid essences intend to work with our own blueprints and act as internal guides bringing us back into alignment so that we are able to fulfill our destinies. The human experience is very demanding and often times damaging to the original blueprints we designed. There is no oasis to go to for realignment so the overlighting beings assist in this way with the strong intentions and focus of the Dancing Light Orchid Essences.

Imagine a multi-dimensional blueprint which overlights and infuses our circuitry with our original blueprints. It takes the struggle out of transformation when one's own intact blueprints are once again accessible and in fact functioning as overlays or rather inner lays. Suddenly we can simply realign instead of struggling for ideals of perfection lost.

## Set 1

**Wise Action** *Cattleya loddogessi var. coerulea*

*7.5ml ifer 3421*

This essence offers a blueprint of embodying the infinite wisdom in all action. Actions embodying the spark of infinite intention = wisdom in action.

**Wonderous Heart** *Vanda javerii* *7.5ml ifer 3422*

"If you can feel the wonder, you can proceed"

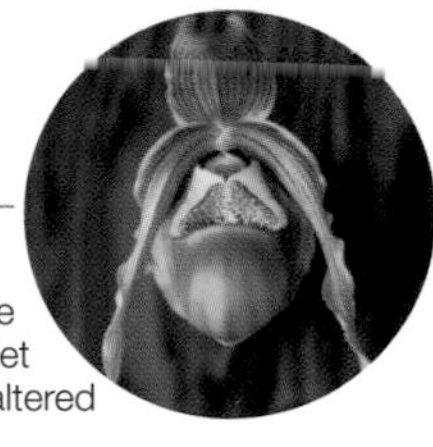

**Purpose Flows**

*Phragmipedium ecuadorense*

*7.5ml ifer 3423*

In the heart one finds the well spring of life purpose up-welling, bubbling, spilling over and trickling with the fluidity of water. Let your purpose well up within you, let it be your sustaining pool. This essence inlays the unaltered blueprint of purpose flowing freely.

**New Perceptions** *Ansellia gigantea* *7.5ml ifer 3424*

Keen focus takes place with this essence. It is about shifting paradigms with effortless ease, it is imprinted for perceptual expansion. See, feel, sense, find and utilize abundance and opportunity where it hasn't been expected and is not obvious.

### **Vibrant Humour** (formerly Idiot Glee)

*Vanda roeblingiana 7.5ml ifer 3425*

I am the brash youngster, I am the fits of giggles, I am the aches in the face from smiling, I am the tears of laughter. I bring you the most intense, senseless joy that you shall have the good fortune to endure.

### Balancing Extremes

*Paphiopedilum lowii*

*7.5ml ifer 3426*

Renewed Balance comes full circle excluding the wide swings of pendulum-like motion; instead "be" the balance from within. Express the truth and radiance of yourself in balance. Why did you go so far out of balance? What did you lose sight of? Time to honour you, time to regain balance within.

### **Dance of Creation** *Vanda coerulea 7.5ml ifer 3427*

I am the soothing essence of exquisite awareness. My purpose is to tickle your mind and the pathways into your heart so you will join in the merry dance of creation.

## Set 2

### Clearing Inner Pathways

*Aeranthes henrici*

*7.5ml ifer 3428*

My subtle light penetrates and prepares the internal communication paths for enlightenment. Consider this essence to be like a vibrational rotorooter, clearing the passages for clearer images, imaginings, for light to travel on the internal pathways.

### **Clearing Blockages** *Phragmipedium caudatum*

*7.5ml ifer 3429*

This essence brings a blueprint, a fresh example to the body of how the energy is supposed to move. Overall theme fluidity and flexibility.

### **Radiant Strength** *Phragmipedium besseae*

*7.5ml ifer 3430*

This essence supplies the blueprint for radiance. For those who are so good at hiding their radiance that now that it is time to be so, they cannot completely do so. The stronger you radiate, glow the safer you are as you strengthen your energy field by your radiance of your boundless self.

### **Centered Love** *Bollea coelestis*

*7.5ml ifer 3431*

This essence embodies the blueprint for heart centered love. A good essence to use when you want communications to come through the heart. This essence will facilitate shifts in the heart which may open one to exploring new relationships.

### **Reading Energy Fields** *Angreceum sesquipedale*

*7.5ml ifer 3432*

When auras blend information is exchanged; you can use this essence to read your own energy field. Whatever others have been expressing or holding onto, you have picked it up. It will increase your ability to interpret the information you pick up in your energy field.

### Reveals Mystery Within

*Aeranthes grandiflora*

*7.5ml ifer 3433*

An invitation to explore the inner mysteries of the self so that greater integration takes place and instead of ego being left behind it is brought along on the journey of the spirit, soul, ego. Invite the daily self into the night, to the places of mystery that lie within.

### Walking out of Patterns

*Rhyncholaelia digbyana*

*7.5ml ifer 3434*

This essence is for walking out of the rhythms of old emotional patterning. Feel with the heart, and come into alignment with the soul's purpose.

## Set 3

### Essence of the Edge

*(Environmental Essence)*

*7.5ml ifer 3497*

The Essence of the Edge is for those who are doing their work at the cutting edge. It is for comprehending the purpose of the edge in their lives at present. It is a safety net for those who are pushed to the edge...

## Defining Edges *Brassia arcuigera*
*7.5ml ifer 3794*

This essence is a blueprint for being in form with definition without creating separation. In form it is good to know your edges as this leads to clarity.

## Unveiling Self *Oeonia volucris* *7.5ml ifer 3795*

True Self in form recognizing Self beyond and within form and still in oneness, not caught in illusion of ego senses. Ego bows, is not separate yet feels in awe of its own true Self.

## Gossamer Steel/Enduring Love
*Phalaenopsis Texas star x P. Brother delight*
*7.5ml ifer 3796*

This essence will open the heart to higher octaves of love. Touch the fine threads of love, let their music resound within. Exquisitely fine love, its essence embodies the strength to endure, and is more resilient than circumstance. Love needs the opportunity to bud, blossom, and flourish. Love is sustainable.

## My Own Pure Light
*Paphiopedilum Eagle peak x Paphiopedilum Niveum* *7.5ml ifer 3797*

Purification is being the light without restricting the flow. Embrace the darkness as it screams to be released from the body's cells... Life has had its traumas; the light embraces all that is and never is diminished. The struggle is gone and I am light.

## My Heart Knows *Paphiopedilum tonsum*
*7.5ml ifer 3798*

Grace is the quality of fitting actions to the circumstances of the moment: knowing in your heart what to do, and when.

## Heart Wings *Psychopsis papilio* *7.5ml ifer 3799*

Let your heart fly with the energies of this essence, let the wings of your heart lift you. Perspectives of spirit are unburdened. We must feel free, think free, break free and fly free, and then create anew...

# Set 4

## Dancing Light Spirit *Calypso bulbosa var. occidentalis*
*7.5ml ifer 3922*

Spirits of nature take & relinquish form with the same effort as we do breath. Form is but one representation of who & what we are. This essence is a gateway for us to call forth the spirits of nature.

## Lucid Dreaming
*Angraecum eburneum var. typicum*
*7.5ml ifer 3923*

I am your companion for exploring forgotten places and those yet to be explored. The vast unknown is larger than you can ever know and yet you may go exploring there. Take my essence when you sleep, when you journey, when you want to awaken evermore.

## Earth Mother Nurtures *(Environmental essence)*
*7.5ml ifer 3924*

Earth Mother Nurtures essence was made on a hill above the Pacific Ocean. The hill slopes gradually toward the ocean; a spring meadow giggling with dwarf wild flowers and grasses that carpet the earth. Earth Mother is a collective of beings with a capacity for compassion that is unfathomable. They do so with infinite compassion and love to assist us in our journey towards enlightenment. This essence is an invitation; a welcoming into the heart of the earth.

## Manifesting Thought Forms
*Paphiopedilum Leanum superbum* *7.5ml ifer 3925*

We have imprinted this water with the thought forms of the creative process. Intentions manifest gradually at first as they move through the ethers to where you can notice their formation and then their form, and at some point formation is crystallized. When you are in tune with the devic realm all things manifest; they do so in time, and in degrees.

## My Song Calls Me Home
*Phragmipedium amazonica* *7.5ml ifer 3926*

When using this essence you are sending out a call for self location. Devic intentions direct the songs outward from your manifest self traveling the light paths that trail you, just as light from stars travels, so does your own, leaving behind a trail to be followed. The light path you have left behind will lead to your "lost" facets of self. You can always trace yourself, no part of you is ever lost.

## Graceful Transformations

*Masdevallia coccinea v. harryana*

*7.5ml ifer 3927*

A caterpillar makes a cocoon wherein it transforms into a butterfly. You, in essence do the same; we assist you in dis-carding the disused energies, thought forms, emotional patterns etc., we help to fit you with the new forms of self you are manifesting.

## I am In my Body / Expansive Embodiement

*Masdevallia ignea 7.5ml ifer 3928*

I am the blue print for light embodiment. I assist with the process of full incarnation bright with lightness of spirit being. This essence is about establishing a new basis of experience and understanding of spirit-body relationship - a new level of the functioning of who & what we are in the experiencing of the physical body. Imagine your body full of tiny spaces so the light within you shines outwardly like the sun's rays through clouds. Imagine seeing your light rays shining outwardly in every direction. The source is the infinite within you...

# Set 5

## Internal Marriage *combination essence*

*7.5ml ifer 3807*

This essence is like taking a walk hand in hand with someone and that someone is yourself, it is about integrating duality's, complementary opposites, female and male energies within; internal marriage. Feel the energy of this combination, it's so delightful; imagine the joy of falling in love and the experience of the coming together of your energies like this.

## Infinite Patience *Paphiopedilum rothchildianum*

*7.5ml ifer 4722*

A pattern of consciousness directly accessing the gaps between thoughts; drawing on the limitless creative intelligence a deeper level of patience than is generally experienced in life. This is patience to carry one through great or lasting challenges.This is deeper than the patience of the mind, this is like breathing in the infinite.

## Higher Levels *Paphiopedilum parishii 7.5ml ifer 4723*

Higher Levels essence supports transformative growth by helping one to release the present form which one has become accustomed to and moving towards the newly forming next higher level. It takes courage and trust in the truth of one's heart, soul and limitless being to release the known and move to a higher level. Experience creates trust in the process of one's own evolution, the more one does this the easier the process becomes.

## I Like Being Me *Restrepia guttulata & a Piece of a Mountain*

*7.5ml ifer 4936*

I Like Being Me flower & rock essence: I am the embodiment of self love and acceptance. I look to nothing outside of myself for reference as to my worth, acceptability, love ability, inner wealth, and inner health. I like being me. I am unique among all possibilities.

## Devic Awareness *Miltonia hybrid Jean Sabourin 'Vulcain'*

*7.5ml ifer 4937*

Devic Awareness essence is touching into the fundamental elemental awareness of the life force all around you, within you. All aspects of life are intelligent; gleaming; shimmering; vibrating with life force energy and creative cosmic intelligence. At what level do you wish to be aware? Turn your focus there. Elemental light. Elemental sound. Elemental motion. Elemental breath. Much of this awareness is purely experiential, far beyond thoughts the mind can capture.

## Stepping Ahead Now *Combination essence*

*7.5ml ifer 4938*

You've done the work; now it is time to go forth into that which you have newly created, that which you along with
Creation, have prepared. The elements are in place, the atoms and molecules are arranged correctly; in alignment with your intentions. The canvas is prepared, ready to receive your brush strokes. The mud is perfect, ready to receive your foot prints. Step ahead now.

## Heart to Heart *Combination essence*

*7.5ml ifer 4939*

This essence assists in attuning to one's truest source of navigation, the heart. There is an energy that emanates from the heart that another heart recognizes as true. Let your heart be your guide is an expression based in truth of experience and being. Get to the heart of the matter. Let this essence assist you in going deeper within, through the gateway of the heart to the heart of the Self. Herein dwells not words, simply being, herein lies peacefulness and the essence of love.

## Meditative Mind *Mexipedium xerophyticum*

*7.5ml ifer 5435*

Meditative Mind Orchid Essence is truly a gift to behold.
A quiet mind is like a rare flower, like an unusual day of calm, flat on the ocean, no waves, just glassy smooth water. A quiet mind is a gateway to pass through.
Be still, this essence is an invitation to commune, to assist with diving into the deeper levels of the mind and beyond, to explore self in deeper meditative states, where the true treasures of life reside. Have you felt an inkling of this bliss? Do you want more?
This vibration supports developing the meditative practice and experience.

# Sister Moon Flower Essence Oils

(For External Use Only)

Sister Moon Flower Essences Oils are Anointing Oils created to enhance and help expand your most important relationship; the one with yourself. The value of these flower essences lies within each woman who opens the bottle and is carried by its vibration.

## Celebrating Women's Beauty *10ml ifer 3800*

Offers vibrational support and inspiration for exploring your inner beauty, self expression and a strong sense of self belief.

## Sisterhood of the Rose *10ml ifer 3801*

Assists you in accessing the heart; your innermost being. The heart is the balance point where you can transmute or transcend your experiences of heaven and earth. The Rose energy helps connect your head with your heart.

## Women's Healing Lodge *10ml ifer 3802*

Lends you undying strength and a gateway into the safe, warm womb of the sacred healing places within you.

## Star Sisters of the Lilac Rays *10ml ifer 3803*

Calls out to the infinite within you with a resonance beyond physical hearing, expressing cosmic joy and laughter. This essence encourages stillness within so that you may listen to the silence.

## Sisters of the White Crystals *10ml ifer 3881*

Assists you in developing self clarity. Let this essence help activate you in remembering who you truly are so that you may know and honor yourself.

## Sisters of the Moon Time *10ml ifer 3805*

Stirs you to ask how you want to empower yourself. What rite of passage do you need? Allow this essence to assist you in drawing the creative energies from within your womb. Choose your creation, gestate its development and bring forth its new life with all the care and nurturing a mother gives her new born child. You embody all the powers of creation.

## Sisterhood of the Golden Rays *10ml ifer 3806*

Celebrates the strength and hearts of women. This essence assists you in accessing your ancient roots and abilities. Earth Mother is the source for our physical life; she offers her resources in form for your spiritual journey as you walk the earth. You are not captive in form, you are a deeply bonded explorer challenged to bring the formless into form on this bountiful sphere.

## Birch Tree Deva Oil *60ml ifer 3506 / 120ml ifer 4117*

An inspired creation blending the sacred with the scentual.
Supports the steady progress of becoming aware of one's life purpose while cultivating the undying force of souls' purpose to be acknowledged and acted upon.
Birch Tree Deva Oil is a living oil that embodies the life force of the Alaskan Birch forest as well as containing Birch & other pure essential oils, two Birch Tree flower essences and Birch Tree Spirit Essence of Other Realms.

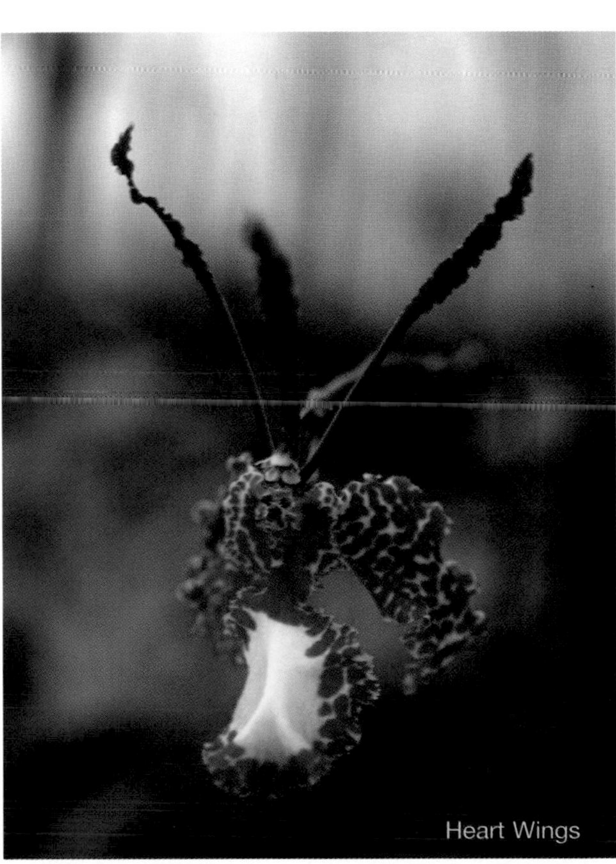

Heart Wings

# Dancing Light Orchid Essence Mists

## **Focus** *120ml ifer 5635*

Focussed awareness. Strongly and pointedly focuses one's energies so that one is able to devote oneself completely to tasks, studies, projects and/or intentions. Has a strong affect mentally, but it is not limited to mental focus. Creates a holistic alignment of chakras and subtle bodies; the surrounding energies, to also create a supportive atmosphere so that one is able to embrace that which one desires to focus upon.

## **Meditative Mind** *120ml ifer 5634*

A quiet mind is like a rare day of calm; flat on the ocean, no waves, just glassy smooth water. A quiet mind is a gateway to pass through. Dive into the deeper levels of the mind; beyond the mind. Explore the self in deeper meditative states, where the true treasures of life reside.

## **Opening The Heart** *120ml ifer 5636*

It is simple! Allow, feel the joy that is the open heart. Pass through into infinity within.

## **Sacred Space/Sacred Sphere** *120ml ifer 5633*

A sphere of light to 'be' within. It is protective yet allows one to interact. 'Be' sensitive within this sphere, 'be' so as you walk through the world in your sphere of what is sacred to you.

# **Findhorn** Essences

Region: Scotland

Founded: 1992

DEVELOPER: Marion Leigh originally trained as a homeopath in her native Australia where she also studied with Ian White (originator of the Australian Bush Flower Essences). Marion's experience is that the flowers tend to find her when they are ready to be made. Her refined communication and co-operation with the angelic/devic kingdoms gave birth to the development of the Findhorn Flower Essences. Her co-operation with the forces of nature harnesses the elements of earth, air, fire and water into the remedy with these being considered the blue print for all existence.

THE ESSENCES: The magic of the Findhorn Garden is world renowned, and it is in this place dedicated to the Divine Spirit within us and within nature that the Findhorn Flower Essences were developed. They are made using wildflowers from Scotland with pure water collected from the sacred healing wells. These essences restore equilibrium throughout the different levels of one's being by enhancing our awareness and spiritual growth. There are 38 individual stock essences plus a collection of combinations and a spray.

## **Apple** *(Malus sylvestris) 15ml ifer 2215*

Keynote: HIGHER PURPOSE

Apple helps us to realise positively our goals and visions. In contacting and clarifying our higher purpose and aspirations and freed from distractions, we focus our willpower and channel our energies into right action.

## **Balsam** *(Impatiens glandulifera) 15ml ifer 3508*

Keynote: TENDERNESS

Balsam facilitates love and acceptance of our physical bodies and our sexuality. Illusions of separateness are dissolved when we open to love and nurturing. We experience feelings of warmth, sensitivity and tenderness towards ourselves and others, and feel safe and present in our world.

## **Bell Heather** *(Erica cinerea) 15ml ifer 2211*

Keynote: SELF CONFIDENCE

Bell Heather helps to access inner strength and resolve to stand one's ground. We become resilient to stress, setback or disappointment when we remain flexible, consolidate our energies and stand firmly grounded and confident in ourselves.

## **Birch** *(Betula pendula) 15ml ifer 2219*

Keynote: VISION

Birch helps us to broaden our perceptions and transcend mental limitations. Through expanding our consciousness and seeing 'the bigger picture' we gain understanding and peace of mind. Birch frees our imagination and gives us hope for the future.

## **Broom** *(Cytisus scoparius) 15ml ifer 2210*

Keynote: CLARITY

Broom stimulates mental clarity and concentration. When our thinking is clouded or distracted, we may be hindered in our communication and expression. Broom illuminates the mind and from this brightness frees our intuition and thinking.

## **Daisy** *(Bellis perennis) 15ml ifer 2205*

Keynote: PROTECTION

Daisy helps us to remain calm and centred amid the turbulance of life when we feel overwhelmed. With true feelings of trust and of being protected, we are able to maintain our focus with openness and sensitivity and stay on purpose and on course.

## Elder *(Sambucus nigra) 15ml ifer 2220*

Keynote: BEAUTY

Elder stimulates the body's natural powers of regeneration and renewal. By resonating with the source of our own inner beauty and eternal youthfulness, we connect with true feelings of wellbeing and the circulation of those vital energies that may rejuvenate us.

## Globe-thistle *(Echinops sphaerocephalus) 15ml ifer 3509*

Keynote: AT-ONE-MENT

Globe-thistle helps us willingly and joyfully make sacrifices that will liberate us on our path. When we reconnect with our inner strength and resilience to do what we must, we can surrender the non-essentials in our lives and discover that letting go and serving the highest good brings us the deepest peace and joy.

## Gorse *(Ulex europaeus) 15ml ifer 2206*

Keynote: JOY

Gorse stimulates vitality, enthusiasm and motivation. When we feel run down or low, we risk withholding ourselves from fully participating in life by trying to conserve our energies. By reconnecting with the quality of joy and giving ourselves passionately to life, our hearts are uplifted and we are refreshed and renewed.

## Grass of Parnassus *(Parnassia palustris) 15ml ifer 3510*

Keynote: OPENNESS

Grass of Parnassus opens the heart to the healing power of love. Strong emotions, fear or vulnerability may cause us to create protective barriers which can cut us off from our true feelings. When we allow these powerful emotions to be, and transform them within the heart through love, our soul qualities of peace, joy and serenity can shine through.

## Harebell *(Campanula rotundifolia) 15ml ifer 2203*

Keynote: PROSPERITY

Harebell aligns us to the living of a prosperous life. When we feel lacking, or lose faith in ourselves or abilities, we may block the flow of vital energies. We re-align our awareness to the spirit of abundance and become open to receiving the limitless energy supply from the Universal Source.

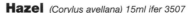

## Hazel *(Corylus avellana) 15ml ifer 3507*

Keynote: FREEDOM

Hazel can help free us to let go of all limitations which restrict growth, advancement and potential unfolding. Liberated of the need to be in control of the direction and flow of our lives, we find joy and freedom in movement and spontaneity.

## Holy-thorn *(Cratageus sp.) 15ml ifer 2216*

Keynote: ACCEPTANCE

Holy-Thorn awakens us to the presence of love in our hearts. When we are open and accepting of ourselves and others, we remove barriers to friendship and love, and free our creative expression.

## Iona Pennywort *(Umbilicus rupestris) 15ml ifer 3511*

Keynote: TRANSPARENCY

Iona Pennywort brings light into the darkest corners of our souls whereby we can let go of deep fears held in the psyche which help to create delusions, self-deception and judgement of ourselves and others. By bringing in the pure light of truth, we can move forward with a new awareness and purity of aspiration.

## Japanese Cherry *('Sakura' (Prunus serrulata)) 15ml ifer 4856*

Keynote: EQUANIMITY

Cherry helps us to open the heart to love and to transcend limitations of karmic and social heritage which bind us to past patterns of behaviour. When we let the heart guide us in all our relationships, notions of separativeness dissolve as we identify with the divine essence in everyone and everything. We feel empowered to act with compassion and in the spirit of goodwil

## Lady's-Mantle *(Alchemilla vulgaris) 15ml ifer 3512*

Keynote: AWARENESS

Lady's-Mantle helps us to access deeper resources of the mind. When we are unable or unwilling to be conscious on all levels, our awareness and understanding become limited. We can call on and bring to light all the power and intelligence which is inherently ours.

## Laurel *(Prunus lusitanica) 15ml ifer 2224*

Keynote: RESOURCEFULNESS

Laurel can assist us in manifesting our vision, and in empowering ourselves to find the resources to bring our ideas and ideals into form. When we bring a plan to fruition, we must be able to hold and synthesise many diverse energies. Wise in heart, we trust the spiritual worlds and Universal Source to support all plans which are for the good of all.

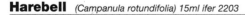

## Lime *(Tilia platyphyllos) 15ml ifer 2222*

Keynote: UNIVERSALITY

Lime brings an awareness of our relationship and interdependence with all life on Earth. When we open to and anchor universal love in our hearts, feelings of separateness are transformed and we create harmonious relationships in our lives.

## Mallow *(Malva Sylvestris) 15ml ifer 3513*

Keynote: ALIGNMENT

Mallow helps us to 'think in our hearts'. Separation in our thinking and feeling impedes us on all levels. Mallow activates our will to live in right relationship.

## Monkey Flower *(Mimulus guttatus) 15ml ifer 3514*

Keynote: PERSONAL POWER

Monkey Flower helps raise our vibrational energy from the lower self, empowering us to celebrate and be who we truly ARE. When we are not fully in our power, we may fear power in others or ourselves. With Monkey Flower we access the source of true power from the Higher Self and find the confidence to act NOW.

## Ragged Robin *(Lychnis flos-cuculi) 15ml ifer 2213*

Keynote: PURITY

Ragged Robin aids us in the processes of purification. We allow the free flow of life force and energies on all levels when we remove the obstacles to realising health and wellbeing.

## Rose Alba *(Rosa alba) 15ml ifer 3515*

Keynote: LOVE-IN-ACTION

Rose Alba represents the positive, outgoing, creative Principle. It assists in connecting the mind and the intuition to bring forth deeper insight. When we positively follow our intuitions, right speech and right action follow.

## Rose Water Lily *(Nymphaea sp.) 15ml ifer 3516*

Keynote: PRESENCE

Rose Water Lily helps us to rise above the pressures and demands of daily life which draw us into the depths of the material world. When we lose sight of our spiritual connections, by our aspiration we re-connect with Spirit and draw strength from this source deep within.

## Rowan *(Sorbus aucuparia) 15ml ifer 2225*

Keynote: FORGIVENESS

Rowan helps us to learn to forgive ourselves and others and to heal the past. By opening the heart to unconditional healing love we can release our attachments to habitual, inherited or karmically acquired patterns of behaviour and emotions, and live peacefully with ourselves and others.

## Scots Pine *(Pinus sylvestris) 15ml ifer 2218*

Keynote: WISDOM

Scots Pine helps us to find directions in our search for truth and understanding. When we open ourselves to listening truly, we can access our own inner source of wisdom, and feel guided on our way.

## Scottish Primrose *(Primula scotica) 15ml ifer 2208*

Keynote: PEACE

Scottish Primrose brings inner peace and stillness when we are confronted by fear, anxiety, conflict or crisis and helps to restore natural rhythms. When we are at peace in our hearts, unconditional love flows through us and harmony prevails.

## Sea Pink *(Armeria maritima) 15ml ifer 2217*

Keynote: HARMONY

Sea Pink helps to balance the energy centres. When we feel disconnected, or split off from our higher or divine nature, the inflowing life and consciousness energy streams may not be grounded in the material world. Sea Pink assists the flow of conscious vital energies throughout the body.

## Sea Rocket *(Cakile maritima) 15ml ifer 3517*

Keynote: REGENERATION

Sea Rocket helps us to open to the experience of abundance in all its forms. When we find our resources drying up, or swinging from 'feast to famine', our insecurities may cause us to accumulate or hoard. We cut ourselves off from the Universal Source. With purity of purpose we can again receive and give freely, trusting all our needs will be perfectly met.

**Silverweed** *(Potentilla anserina) 15ml ifer 2204*

Keynote: SIMPLICITY

Silverweed helps us to live lightly in our bodies and on Earth, through moderation and self-awareness. When we become caught up in material concerns, we may lose contact with our higher purpose. We can lift our awareness through deep contact with the forces of nature and life to break through into higher levels of self-realisation.

**Snowdrop** *(Galanthus nivalis) 15ml ifer 2214*

Keynote: SURRENDER

Snowdrop allows us to access deep inner stillness and to surrender to the processes through which we can release the past. We find hope - and seeing the light at the end of the tunnel - move towards it. Even in our darkest hours we find hope in the revelation of light, the flame of eternal life within.

**Spotted Orchid** *(Dactylorhiza fuchsii) 15ml ifer 2207*

Keynote: CREATIVITY

Spotted Orchid helps us rise above our narrow views or insularity to look beyond the imperfections we see. When we are too introspective, we risk becoming pessimistic and our outlook on life reflects these limitations. Spotted Orchid allows us to see freshly, to find the beauty and perfection in everything. With a positive attitude, our vision is broadened and we find our own perfect expression.

**Stonecrop** *(Sedum anglicum) 15ml ifer 2202*

Keynote: TRANSITION

Stonecrop aids in times of profound personal transformation. We realise change is happening around us and within us at the deepest levels. But this process has its own timing, and we may feel stuck, unable to push through the barriers which hold us back. Stonecrop allows us to release our frustrations and attachments to the past, embrace change and find the point of stillness and peace within.

**Sycamore** *(Acer pseudoplatanus) 15ml ifer 2221*

Keynote: REVITALISATION

Sycamore recharges and uplifts body and soul when we are stressed or worn down. Sycamore helps us to tap into the unlimited energy source of the life force which radiates, illuminates and energises our whole being. We can then experience the smooth flow of the energies in ourselves and in our lives.

**Thistle** *(Cirsium vulgare) 15ml ifer 2212*

Keynote: COURAGE

Thistle helps us to find true courage in times of adversity and to respond with positive action. When we encounter fear, our performance can be crippled. Thistle encourages us to access inner strength and to take appropriate action with confidence and certainty.

**Valerian** *(Valeriana officinalis) 15ml ifer 2223*

Keynotes: DELIGHT

Valerian is uplifting to our mind, body and spirit and helps us to rediscover delight and happiness in living. When we are weighed down in our busy lives by our responsibilities, we may miss the simple joys in life that bring us happiness. Through Valerian we may become more responsive in the moment, lighten up and have fun.

**Watercress** *(Rorippa nasturtium aquaticum) 15ml ifer 3518*

Keynote: WELLBEING

Watercress sounds a vibrational note of purification in our bodies. It can act as a powerful cleanser, stimulating our immune systems to clear stagnant energies and overcome disease, by refining, transforming and releasing all that is toxic to our health and harmful to our wellbeing.

**Wild Pansy** *(Viola tricolor) 15ml ifer 3519*

Keynote: RESONANCE

Wild Pansy helps clear and illuminate the head and heart channels when the energies they carry have become blocked or diverted. As receptivity, sensitivity and contact are re-established, these connections enable the life energies to flow freely and radiate throughout the whole being.

**Willowherb** *(Chamaenerion angustifolium) 15ml ifer 2209*

Keynote: SELF-MASTERY

Willowherb helps to balance the personality expressing authoritarian or overbearing behaviour by tempering force of personality with true power. Responsible integration of will and power issues is brought forth through love and humility, and the correct use of the will.

# **Combination** Essences

## Clear Light *25ml ifer 2415*

For bringing about a peaceful state of mind. By stilling and focussing the mind, Clear Light can assist in attuning to higher wisdom and inspiration, and influence mental clarity and brightness. An excellent aid to meditation and study.
(Findhorn Flower Essences of Rose Alba, Birch, Broom, Scots Pine and Water Element Essence)

## Eros *25ml ifer 4795 / 75ml gel ifer 4913*

To nurture love, sensitivity and intimacy. Without self acceptance it is difficult to be a loving partner. Cultivate healing love, sexual harmony and playfulness. Explore your erotic potential.
(Findhorn Flower Essences of Gorse, Elder, Sea Pink, Balsam, Holy Thorn, Sycamore and Rose Alba)
Also available in Aloe Vera Gel for external application

## Femininity *25ml ifer 4998*

Providing support for women's issues and cycles. During times of changing rhythms or mood swings, Femininity can help to release tension and restore emotional balance and wellbeing.
(Findhorn Flower Essences of Balsam, Lady's Mantle, Holy Thorn, Scottish Primrose, Rowan and Sea Rocket)

## First Aid *25ml ifer 2411 / 75ml gel ifer 4914*

A soothing remedy offering immediate relief in any crisis. In times of stress or trauma on the physical or emotional level, First Aid can help to relieve associated fear and ease pain and tension.
(Findhorn Flower Essences of Thistle, Scottish Primrose, Bell Heather and Daisy)
Also available in Aloe Vera Gel for external application

## Heart Support *25ml ifer 4996*

To heal the heart when affected by trauma or grief. For all issues connected with the heart, on the emotional or etheric level. Also supportive during times of major life changes.
(Findhorn Flower Essences of Scottish Primrose, Stonecrop, Rowan, Grass of Parnassus, Holy Thorn, Wild Pansy and Gorse)

## Holy Grail *25ml ifer 2361*

To integrate and harmonise the physical, emotional, mental and spiritual bodies. Bring balance and harmony into all aspects of your life through alignment and synthesis of body, mind and soul. Embody and express your full creative potential.
(Findhorn Flower Essences of Lady's Mantle, Balsam, Globe Thistle and Rose Alba)

## Jetstream *25ml ifer 4794*

To offset the negative effects of travel stress or fatigue. Travel can upset and disturb natural rhythms. Find balance to cope with motion and calm to overcome claustrophia or fear and arrive feeling 'ready to go'.
(Findhorn Flower Essences of Scottish Primrose, Sea Rocket, Wild Pansy, Daisy, Scots Pine and Sycamore)

## Karma Clear *25ml ifer 2414*

To release the tensions that bring pain, suffering and unhappiness. Heal the past through compassion and forgiveness, and by awareness and understanding of the karmic causes of life's predicaments and ailments.
(Findhorn Flower Essences of Birch, Snowdrop, Holy Thorn and Rowan)

## Life Force *25ml ifer 2096*

To overcome tiredness, low energy or burnout. Activating the vital life force and stimulating the body's powers of renewal, Life Force can help to uplift body and soul when fatigued.
(Findhorn Flower Essences of Gorse, Valerian, Grass of Parnassus, Elder and Sycamore)

## Prosperity *25ml ifer 5767*

Manifesting an abundance of wellbeing. Foster a sense of inner security and faith in yourself. Align with the Source of universal, limitless supply and manifest your dreams and goals.
(Findhorn Flower Essences of Harebell, Bell Heather, Elder, Laurel and Sea Rocket)

## Psychic Protection *25ml ifer 4997*

For protecting the emotional body against negative forces. Feel centred by creating a safe space within yourself. In crowded or overwhelming situations, Psychic Protection can help in detaching from other's negative thoughtforms or energies.
(Findhorn Flower Essences of Thistle, Iona Pennywort, Rose Alba, Watercress and Daisy)

## Revelation *25ml ifer 2412*

For transcending limitations and resistances which hold us back. By facilitating surrender to the highest personal unfolding of the vision of who you truly are, the inner inspiration needed to move forward is revealed.
(Findhorn Flower Essences of Stonecrop, Holy Thorn, Snowdrop and Hazel)

## Spiritual Marriage *25ml ifer 2413*

To integrate and harmonise the masculine and feminine qualities. Balancing the pairs of opposites creates a vital partnership between intuitive/creative self and intelligent/logical self. Dynamic union of our emotions and vision, with reason and action will maximise productivity and happiness.
(Findhorn Flower Essences of Apple, Holy Thorn, Mallow and Sea Pink)

## Sweet Dreams *25ml ifer 5792*

Good night Sleep well. Relaxing into deep sleep can be difficult when stuck thoughts, emotions, worry, anxiety, or tension agitate or overwhelm us. As we still and calm our energies and as natural rhythms are restored, we find balance and peace of mind.
(Findhorn Flower Essences of Birch, Grass of Parnassus, Lady's Mantle, Scottish Primrose and Valerian)

## Transformation *25ml ifer 5768*

Supporting personal growth and transformation. Choosing transformation means 'shining the light' on what needs to be reformed or changed. We can harmonise and transform seemingly opposing parts of ourselves, cultivate inner strength to persevere and stay on course, and willingly make sacrifices which will serve our highest good.
(Findhorn Flower Essences of Apple, Grass of Parnassus, Globe Thistle, Iona Pennywort, Sea Pink, Stonecrop and Watercress)

# Spray

## Sanctuary Spray *50ml spray iifer 5163 / 100ml spray ifer 5822*

A spray mist to help clear and transmute negative energies. Neutralise disharmony in the home, room and personal aura and bring in light, clarity and serenity.
(Findhorn Element Essences of Earth, Water, Fire, Air and Ether and also contains pure organic essential oils of Rose Alba and Frankincense)

# Flower Essences of **Fox Mountain**

Region:
Massachsetts, USA
Founded: 1994

DEVELOPER: Kathrin Woodlyn Bateman. Deep in the heart of rural western Massachusetts, USA, on Fox mountain, a small homestead in the Berkshire hills, Kathrin has developed her range of wildflower essences. Making essences was a natural development from her work with the land and her deep-felt connection with nature. This fulfilled her childhood knowing-ness that healing would become her major direction in life

ESSENCES: Based on 10 years of research, Kathrin has a full range of individual essences, 12 combinations and several kits including her Children's Kit , Goddess Kit, Trauma Kit, Meditational Trilogy and Goddess Collection. Surrounding Kathrin's homestead is 2,000 acres of state wildlife management area, a natural sacred site of incredible heart energy and beauty. The essences are made from plants grown organically in the lovely gardens and in the surrounding wild land

For a full list of the botanical names of this range, please visit the Fox Mountain website.

**Agrimony** *(yellow) 7.5ml ifer 5200*

Supports letting down defenses, allowing others to become closer to you. Helps one to more accurately embody one's self. Being able to be in relationship with one's self is the key to being able to be in a relationship and love others and the world around you.

**Angelica** *(green) 7.5ml ifer 5202*

For connecting to higher realms. Supports the ability to undertake with consciousness one's karmic lessons, and to open with love at each place of difficulty in one's life. Powerful healing essence.

**Blackberry** *(white) 7.5ml ifer 5203*

For manifesting will into action. Useful for procrastination. Good for tackling overwhelming tasks. Supports the ability to visualize a project and manifest vision into action. Tonic for body systems.

**Bloodroot** *(white with yellow center) 7.5ml ifer 5204*

Enhances connecting to the natural world and to one's spiritual foundation. Restoring energy pathways related to endocrine system. An effective aid to meditation. Focus through purification. Brings peacefulness.

**Blue Star** *(steel blue) 7.5ml ifer 5205*

Enhances ability to use meditative states to seek information from other dimensions. Lifts spirit into a dreamlike state transporting one beyond the perceptions of this dimension. Opens the wealth of dreams and subconscious.

**Borage** *(blue) 7.5ml ifer 5206*

For the courage that comes from centering down to one's core: knowing that no outer circumstance can truly harm the spark that is you.

**Buttercup** *(yellow) 7.5ml ifer 5207*

For improving self esteem. For knowing that we are each a special gift to the world. Keywords: Self-esteem, sense of self

**California Poppy** *(yellow/orange) 7.5ml ifer 5208*

Emotionally cleansing. Encourages the individual to look within for spiritual meaning. For those who look for external experiences to calm their restlessness. Helps one to stay in balance during times of learning and evolving.

**Chamomile** *(white/yellow center) 7.5ml ifer 5209*

Helps return of balanced calmness and aids in relief of nervousness due to tension and worries.

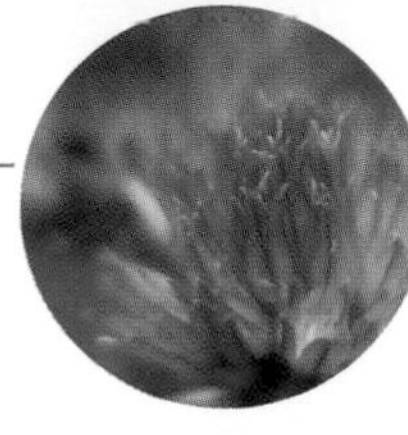

**Chive** *(purple) 7.5ml ifer 5210*

Creating healthy balances on many levels: male/female, left/right, yin/yang.. and realizing the energy that comes from being in that state of balance. Promotes inner harmony and compassion rather than co-dependency.

**Clary Sage** *(lavender and white) 7.5ml ifer 5211*

A centered, grounded connection to one's "gut" or primal self. Being connected to one's primal strength, animality, sensuality and sexuality. Feeling the power of the earth in one's solar plexus. Good for those fearful of this side of themselves.

**Clematis** "Ernest Markham" *(fuchsia) 7.5ml ifer 5212*

For reattaching to your life, overcoming indifference: brings energy back when it's been squeezed out by fear and tension. For being present in the NOW. Use along with other essences to redirect a life after a traumatic time.

**Comfrey** *(purple) 7.5ml ifer 5213*

A toner for nerves, helps heal nerve mis-function. Helps heal traumas from present or past lifetimes. A master healer and grounding force.

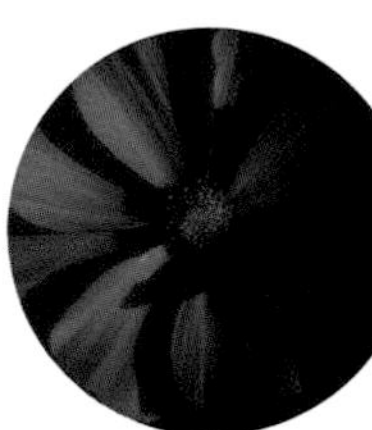

**Cosmos** *(dark pink) 7.5ml ifer 5214*

Helps to link the heart and throat chakras so that one can speak one's heart through one's throat. Clarity in expressing one's self.

**Crested Iris** *(purple with white) 7.5ml ifer 5215*

Carries the loving, healing energies of the great Mother and Father. Connects root chakra to crown chakra, survival mode to spiritual mode. Soothes inner child and teaches unconditional love.

**Dandelion** *(yellow) 7.5ml ifer 5216*

Helps the individual release tightness/tension from the body, especially when the cause is emotional stress. Helps eliminate negativity.

**Dill** *(yellow) 7.5ml ifer 5217*

Helps prevent loss of power that happens when one is unable to integrate information. Supports healthy connection to one's personal power.

**Forget-Me-Not** *(blue) 7.5ml ifer 5218*

For connection to one's spiritual guides. May also stimulate dreams and visions. Promotes utilizing one's brain in different ways.

**Garlic** *(white or soft lavender) 7.5ml ifer 5219*

For fear and pain held in the solar plexus. Supports strengthening of forces to prevent illness.

**Ginseng** *(green) 7.5ml ifer 5220*

Balanced and vital person power and a healthy connection to that power. Harmonious blending of male and female power, fully grounded within one's power. Nourishes health of immune, digestive and endocrine systems.

**Horseradish** *(white) 7.5ml ifer 5221*

Strengthening and empowering. Accepting the bitterness of life and moving on. Helps one release one's emotional baggage and accept and embody their strength.

**House Leek** *(rose-pink) 7.5ml ifer 5222*

Cleanses and revitalizes energy of the reproductive organs; supports the source the life-energy. Healthy outward expression of feminine aspects of self.

**Hyssop** *(purple) 7.5ml ifer 5223*

Helps to alleviate guilt, foster self-forgiveness, and in this role releases tension throughout the body.

**Iris** "Flight of the Butterflies"
*(purple with white, yellow and brown)*
*7.5ml ifer 5224*

Assists you in bringing lightness and beauty into your life by using your creative forces to consciously change your environment. Seeing and feeling joy and beauty. Nourishes circulatory, digestive and nervous systems.

**Ivory Hollyhock** *(ivory) 7.5ml ifer 5225*

Faith in the divinity of the Universe. Trust that everything is as it should be and that all happens with a greater purpose behind it.

**Lady's Mantle** *(chartreuse) 7.5ml ifer 5226*

Useful for both inner child work and support of mothering skills. Use for women in labour who do not already feel that archetype within themselves. Promotes kindness.

**Lavender** *(violet) 7.5ml ifer 5227*

A master healer balancing and aligning the nervous system. Aligning and stabilizing the alignment with one's divine self. For those feeling that their nerves are stretched to the breaking point. Soothing and calming for disease caused by overwrought condition of nerves.

**Lovage** *(chartreuse) 7.5ml ifer 5228*

Helps release physical and emotional toxins, feeling of awkwardness and discomfort. Reconnects child-nature and physical wholeness. Opens heart and releases grief.

**Malva Zebrina** *(lavender with maroon) 7.5ml ifer 5229*

Integration of body, mind, and soul; accepting these three aspects of self as one. Who are you, why are you here, where are you going. Purpose and destiny. Stimulates clairvoyant functions.

**Mauve Mullein** *(mauve) 7.5ml ifer 5230*

Healthy functioning of 6th, 7th and upper chakras. Ability to receive energy and access information through those chakras. Connections to divine wisdom and collective consciousnesses.

**Money Plant** *(purple) 7.5ml ifer 5231*

Lifts off blocks to believing that you deserve good fortune in your life. Relieves fear of success, releases energy, allowing the natural flow of giving and receiving. Good essence for self-esteem issues.

**Money Plant-White** *(white) 7.5ml ifer 5232*

A healthy balanced sense of one's worth and one's right to be present in the world. Use when deep emotional trauma leaves one feeling they don't deserve happiness.

**Monkshood** *(dark purple) 7.5ml ifer 5233*

Improves relationship with one's self through introspection and meditation. Calming, peaceful influence on the heart chakra. Connection to authentic self. Links one to multi-dimensional realities.

**Moonshine Yarrow** *(lemon yellow) 7.5ml ifer 5234*

Protection from becoming overwhelmed...from a sense of building panic. When small things loom large. Good for repair of extreme trauma. For survivors of holocaust, ritual abuse, war, black magic. Also useful for those coming off anti-depressants.

**Mugwort** *(green) 7.5ml ifer 5235*

Sense of being-ness and ability to open and integrate intense sacred knowledge. Very strong essence for use when seeking great depth of knowledge. Use with awareness and adequate psychic protection such as Yarrow.

**Pale Corydalis** *(pink & yellow) 7.5ml ifer 5236*

Surrendering to the power and intensity of process when facing changes or new experiences in life. Good during transition stage of a woman's labour.

**Penstemon** *(purple) 7.5ml ifer 5237*

Brings strength to help you move through exhaustion, overwork and personal trials. (Please don't use Penstemon essence to enable you to continue to overwork; seek to balance your life with relaxation and nurturing.)

**Pink Yarrow** *(pink) 7.5ml ifer 5238*

For someone who identifies with the emotions of those around them to an uncomfortable extent and lacks the boundaries to separate themselves from the energy of other people.

**Purple Bee Balm** *(purple) 7.5ml ifer 5239*

For enhancing the ability to envision your path more clearly Opens the throat chakra to speak the truth. Living self-responsibly in truth. Inner versus outer reliance. Good for vision quests.

**Purple Loosestrife** *(purple shade of pink) 7.5ml ifer 5240*

To release strife and relax. Helps keep events in perspective. For knowing that as opportunities close, new ones open. Good after traumas.

**Purple Mullein** *(purple) 7.5ml ifer 5241*

Opens the crown chakra and helps to integrate the knowledge that flows in. Full integration of spirituality into everyday life, more by "being" than by "doing".

**Queen of the Meadow** *(ivory white) 7.5ml ifer 5242*

A sense of wholeness and safety from being aligned with the maternal heartbeat of the mother earth. Heals trauma from childhood that lasts in spite of changed circumstances. Good for children who are sick.

**Red Hollyhock** *(red) 7.5ml ifer 5243*

Assists the return of good humor. Be fully present with joy now! Brings in buoyant energy and renewal of faith and hope.

**Rose Campion** *(fuchsia) 7.5ml ifer 5244*

Opens the heart chakra in a spiral; cleansing and releasing hurt. Balances heart and root chakra. Release of deep emotions without losing centeredness.

**Saint John's Wort** *(yellow) 7.5ml ifer 5245*

For angelic protection for when vulnerable due to spiritual expansion, trauma, illness or death. Also useful when chaotic dreams leave one feeling tired in the morning.

**Scarlet Pimpernel** *(peach pink) 7.5ml ifer 5246*

Stimulates the crown, heart and pituitary chakras, re-awakening and re-affirming love.

**Self Heal** *(purple) 7.5ml ifer 5247*

Helps one to take responsibility for one's own healing process. Helps you connect to your own wellspring of health and vitality. Useful to jump start the healing process. Try with Horseradish essence for long term illnesses.

**Shasta Daisy** *(white/yellow center) 7.5ml ifer 5248*

Helps one to integrate many diverse ideas into an understanding of the whole "picture".

**Snow Queen Iris** *(white) 7.5ml ifer 5249*

Awakening to and expressing divine love and grace. Helps you center in the purity of your self when caught up in the small concerns of everyday life. To remember your life's purpose.

**Spiderwort** *(white with blue) 7.5ml ifer 5250*

Releases negative thought patterns regarding one's purpose or immediate path in life. Allows one to accept limitations; calls for honesty and clarity, awareness of one's affect upon the world. Healing of self-esteem.

**Star Chickweed** *(white) 7.5ml ifer 5251*

For dissolving boundaries between your physical and spiritual selves. Helps you embody divine compassion and tolerance for those around you.

**Sunflower** *(yellow/brown centre) 7.5ml ifer 5252*

To treat either extreme of shyness or over aggressiveness. Or for those who have trouble in their relationship to their own maleness or males in their family.

**Sweet Pea** *(mixed colors of pink and purple) 7.5ml ifer 5253*

Helps you to sleep. Nurturing for babies and inner child. Alleviates fear of connection with spirit, others, and community. Good for those experiencing night terrors or nightmares.

**Tomato** *(yellow) 7.5ml ifer 5254*

Provides cleansing action for the body and helps in dissolving blockages and throwing off sources of disease. Use whenever an energy flow is blocked, whether it is physical, emotional, or mental.

**Tree Peony** *(dusky pink) 7.5ml ifer 5255*

Brings in so much unconditional love that one feels complete, preventing one from looking outside one's self for it. Also for those who feel unsafe being fully present in their physical body due to past trauma or abuse.

**Valerian** *(white shaded pink) 7.5ml ifer 5256*

Healing to the nervous system. Use for over-stretched nerves. Consider using with Moonshine Yarrow and Chamomile.

**Waterlily** *(pink) 7.5ml ifer 5257*

Allows you to open to new experiences, energies, and life phases in a gentle way, petal by petal. To let things unfold as they will with serenity.

**White Bleeding Heart** *(white) 7.5ml ifer 5258*

For deep emotional pain, for fear of lack or loss of love. For pain held in heart and throat chakras. For hopelessness. Heals and seals emotional wounds. Useful for inner child or for those who are grieving.

**White Foxglove** *(white with maroon spots) 7.5ml ifer 5259*

Helps heal grief, connects to and releases terror. Helps heal the heart by opening and letting memories flow through and release.

**White Mullein** *(white) 7.5ml ifer 5260*

For total integrity of self and actions. For bringing spirituality into life through one's actions. Use with Purple Mullein.

**Wild Ginger** *(maroon) 7.5ml ifer 5261*

For building closeness with natural world. Helps you release worldly concerns and be quietly content with your own light.

**Wood Betony** *(rosy purple) 7.5ml ifer 5262*

Balances the flow of sexual energy, bringing a tantric serenity to sexual connection.

**Yarrow** *(white) 7.5ml ifer 5263*

For protection against negative energies and emotions in your environment. Useful for practitioners of many healing modalities to prevent the absorption of their client's energy and imbalances.

# **Combination** Essences/ **Combination** Collections

### Creative Flow *7.5ml ifer 5300 / 30ml ifer 5551*

To dissolve blocks and to foster connections with your soul's inspiration. Used by many artists, composers, and even for creative problem solving.

### Exaltation of Flowers *7.5ml ifer 5301*

An amazing transformational essence bringing joy and balance. After taking for 5 nights I awakened to the realization that I felt an inner crystalline clearness, greater independence and a confidence in my ability to handle whatever life might bring with strength and integrity of spirit.

### Grieving *7.5ml ifer 5302 / 30ml ifer 5554*

For those facing loss or sadness. Releases a lifetime reservoir of grief, painlessly through the heart. Enveloping and soothing, may bring the release of needed tears.

### Healer *7.5ml ifer 5303*

For survivors of abuse, to cleanse and feel safe in one's body. Cleanses pain, guilt, and shame. Supports living in the present and feeling one deserves more positive interactions in one's life.

### Interesting Times/Life's Transitions

*7.5ml ifer 5304*

For when all that is safe and familiar starts to dissolve, for transitions. Brings strength and protection to move through to new opportunities.

### Lunar Intuition *7.5ml ifer 5305*

For times when one is feeling emotionally vulnerable: useful for a woman's moontimes.

### Master Yarrow *7.5ml ifer 5306*

A master healer of the auric shield. Creates protection and appropriate boundaries. Helpful for hyperactive individuals, stressful work or home situations or those undergoing chemo or radiation therapies.

### Motivation *7.5ml ifer 5307 / 30ml ifer 5556*

Brings focus and will to move forward and accomplish. Helps to remove blocks at the root of procrastination. Use for a day to work on a particular project or for a longer cycle for more generalized stagnation.

### Relaxation *7.5ml ifer 5308 / 30ml ifer 5557*

To bring ease to jangling nerves and emotional frazzle. Good for when too many words are running through the mind in hobnailed boots.

### Summer Solstice *7.5ml ifer 5309*

Made on Summer Solstice this essence deals with peak experiences and putting your "all" out into the world without holding back reserves. Good for performances or a day or night of high energy.

### Vision Quest *7.5ml ifer 5310*

To connect to inner guidance and manifest one's next step, to welcome and interpret visions. Use for meditation or for vision quests.

### Vital Balance *7.5ml ifer 5311 / 30ml ifer 5560*

Protecting your auric shield, bringing clarity and sharpness to the soul's vibration, fostering the connection to earth energy, and clearing away blocks that prevent healing.

# **Miscellaneous** Combination Essences

### Loved and Welcomed *7.5ml ifer 5871*

Formulated for children being adopted from situations of fear, poverty, uncertainty, and lack of love and safety. It's essential for shifting from fearful, lonely survival mode to being able to trust, feel connected and nurtured, safe and unconditionally loved. Useful for emptiness, hollowness and broken hearts. Shifts one from fear of loss or lack of love to being able to experience fully feeling loved, lovable, and loving.

### Sweet Sleep *7.5ml ifer 5872*

For those who find bed time and sleep to be frightening and lonely times. Fears, abandonment issues, trauma, vulnerability, grief and loss can all be enhanced by the darkness and physical separation from care givers. This essence supports safe and healthy sleep by providing protection of the soul during dreams, by helping one feel whole and safe, connected and nurtured, fully and joyfully present, trusting that needs will be met.

### Trauma Kit *7.5ml ifer 5391*

### Pre-Trauma *7.5ml ifer 5312*

To stabilize and maintain protection and balance for upcoming situation, whether a visit from difficult family, surgery or travel.

### Emergency Relief *7.5ml ifer 5313 / 30ml ifer 5552*

For acute crisis situations, this essences heals trauma on all levels. Supports emotional balance, awakens the soul's own healing incentive. Brings courage, encourages the soul to remain in the body and protects it from negative energies if it has separated. Facilitates soul/body fusion if needed.

## Trauma Ease *7.5ml ifer 5314*

For support during traumatic incidents and for chronic physical or emotional trauma. For long term situations....excellent for care givers or for those experiencing a long illness.

## Re-Enter Life *7.5ml ifer 5315*

To re-direct a life after a traumatic experience. Pulls your energy and focus back into the "NOW". Helps you get back into what you were doing when your life was interrupted by the traumatic event.

## Release Trauma *7.5ml ifer 5316*

To release the residues of trauma, to be taken for a few days at 3 months, 6 months and 12 months after the trauma, to cleanse the system of the unresolved feelings that cause "after shocks". For severe trauma you may need to take it on the 2nd and 3rd year anniversaries as well.

## Childbearing Kit *7.5ml ifer 5393*

## Conception *7.5ml ifer 5317*

A combination to help connect with the new soul, to feel your fertility and understand how to open your heart and body to a baby.

## Pre-natal Heal *7.5ml ifer 5318*

To heal fears and traumas of previous or your own birth, as well as feelings of inadequacy of mothering ability. Helps you to visualize motherhood.

## Pregnancy Tonic *7.5ml ifer 5319*

Use during pregnancy to help with the added strains of childbearing. Encourages optimum efficiency in the body's systems.

## Labor of Love *7.5ml ifer 5320*

Let this essence combination assist your labor's efficiency by encouraging you to let go and surrender to the power and intensity of the process. Helps you clear away old blocks, let go of pregnancy and accept motherhood.

## Mother and Child *7.5ml ifer 5321*

Body/soul fusion for the baby; helps the baby maintain conscious awareness during birth and stabilize the soul and body.

## New Family *7.5ml ifer 5322*

Helps integrate all members of the family into a cohesive unit. Take once a day in water, preferably all at the same time, perhaps with a family wish spoken out loud....an affirmation.

## Children's/Inner Child Kit *7.5ml ifer 5394*

## Boundaries *7.5ml ifer 5323*

To aid in recognizing and respecting boundaries; one's own and others. Strengthens one's protective shield to shut out excessive stimuli from the surrounding world.

## Calm Time *7.5ml ifer 5324*

Calming and relaxing after an exciting day or for stress and rush relief. To lose that scattered feeling and calm frayed nerves.

## Child Glow *7.5ml ifer 5325*

To support the gaiety, innocence and journey of discovery that life is all about. Brings cheer and lightness. Useful late in the afternoon or at the end of the day or for a longer time if a child is experiencing a general lack of these qualities.

## Initiative *7.5ml ifer 5326*

Independence, self reliance. To encourage exploration of the surrounding world; supports the joy of learning. Useful for someone disinterested in their surroundings. Very popular with some healers for their clients.

## Trauma Relief *7.5ml ifer 5327*

For pre or post-birth trauma. To heal wounds from current or past lifetimes. If trauma is known or suspected this trauma will likely provide relief.

## Worthiness *7.5ml ife1 5328 / 30ml ifer 5561*

To encourage healthy self-esteem, balance and sense of one's worth. Very popular with adults and children alike! Used at some point in many healing journeys.

## Goddess Collection Kit *7.5ml ifer 5335*

## Artemis *7.5ml ifer 5330*

Goddess of the hunt and moon. For support of being an independent spirit, intact within one's self. Use this essence to support you standing tall within your power as you meet your challenge alone. This essence has brought many women through tragic and shattering times they feel they might not have survived without it.

## Athena *7.5ml ifer 5332*

The beautiful, stately Goddess warrioress known for her ability to come up with brilliant strategies and logical solutions. She is the woman ruled by her head instead of her heart. Use this essence when you need to stay centered and pragmatic in your planning.

## Hestia *7.5ml ifer 5331*

The Goddess of the hearth. She has an inner presence and is not attached to people, power or outcomes. She lives in a centered state of grace creating beauty and welcome in her home. Use this when you are wanting stillness, patience and to live calmly within your truth.

## Demeter *7.5ml ifer 5333*

The Goddess of grain and mothering. She is the maternal one to whom we pray for nourishment and nurturing, or for when we wish to strengthen our ability to be the nurturing, compassionate, unconditionally loving mother.

## Aphrodite *7.5ml ifer 5334*

The Goddess of love embodies the alchemical power of love. Aphrodite is about sensuality and sexuality, and the ability to be both creative and procreative. Focused receptivity.

## Meditational Trilogy Kit *7.5ml ifer 5390*

Three meditational journey essences. Kit consists of 3 essences: Blue Star, Malva Zebrina, and Monkshood; and a leaflet with suggestions for use.

## Rose Collection Kit (12 essences) *7.5ml ifer 5395*

## Rose "Belle Story" *7.5ml ifer 5264*

I am for the assimilation of spiritual experience. I am the essences that one takes to synthesize these experiences into deep rooted change.

## Rose "Sarah van Fleet" *7.5ml ifer 5265*

I am for when change brings disharmony between the soul/heart reality and the physical reality.

## Rose-Red Climbing *7.5ml ifer 5266*

I am for having the strength and courage to open for higher purpose.

## Rose "Mdme. Legras de St. Germain" *7.5ml ifer 5267*

I am for regenerating Universal love when it has been burnt out by pain and fear in this lifetime and others.

## Rose "English Elegance" *7.5ml ifer 5268*

I am for linking with the cosmos and inhaling the cosmos' serenity.

## Rose "Cerise Bouquet" *7.5ml ifer 5269*

I am for opening to love.

## Rose "Konigin von Danemark" *7.5ml ifer 5270*

I am for conserving the soul's life forces while opening ever more to the vast spiritual planes/realities.

## Rose-yellow heirloom *7.5ml ifer 5271*

I am for having the confidence of knowing that you are at home in the Universe.

## Rose-pink heirloom *7.5ml ifer 5275*

I am for having the inner serenity that comes from confidence in divine goodness.

## Rose "Gertrude Jekyll" *7.5ml ifer 5272*

I am for integrating waves of expansion.

## Rose "Fruhlingsmorgen" *7.5ml ifer 5273*

I am for expanding the heart and solar plexus into another dimension.

## Rose "Bonica" *7.5ml ifer 5274*

I am about opening the crown chakra to hear one's higher self.

# **Dosage** Combinations

## **Alert and Alive** *30ml ifer 5550*

Take 2-4 drops when drowsy at inconvenient times or 4 times a day when one feels one is drowsing through life.

## **Creative Flow** *30ml ifer 5551*

Take anytime you want to support your creativity. Dissolves blocks and fosters connection to your soul's inspirations. Great for all creative endeavors, even creative problem solving.

## **Emergency Relief** *30ml ifer 5552*

Take as often as needed for acute crisis. To ease trauma on all levels. Supports emotional balance, courage, and protection during times of crisis. Maintains body/soul fusion during traumatic events.

## **Exaltation and Joy** *30ml ifer 5553*

Take to experience balance and joy. Brings a sense of calmness and self-love. Useful for times of unease.

## **Grieving** *30ml ifer 5554*

Use when you are facing grief. Helps release a lifetime reservoir of grief, painlessly through the heart. May bring the cleansing release of tears.

## **Life's Transitions** *30ml ifer 5555*

This essence is for when all that is safe and familiar is dissolving. Promotes balance during times of change.

## **Motivation** *30ml ifer 5556*

Use when you need focus and the will to move forward and accomplish. Treats the roots of procrastination.

## **Relaxation** *30ml ifer 5557*

Take this essence for general stress, jangling nerves or anxiety. Promotes a centered calmness and ease.

## **Restful Sleep** *30ml ifer 5558*

Take at bedtime to help relax your body, mind and soul into a soothing and healing sleep. Useful for times of tension that keep sleep away or to prevent tiring, over-active dream states.

## **Safe Boundaries** *30ml ifer 5559*

Same formula as Master Yarrow. Use for protection from energies and emotions that inappropriately invade your personal boundaries. Healer of the auric shield. Use when around difficult people or in difficult situations.

## **Vital Balance** *30ml ifer 5560*

Take a preventative or treatment to disharmony and dis-ease. This formula nurtures your balance bringing clarity and sharpness to the soul's vibration, fostering the connection between the vital earth energy and one's self. Use when you are feeling tired and vulnerable to colds and flu.

## **Worthiness** *30ml ifer 5561*

Take to promote healthy self-esteem and sense of self. Great for all ages.

# Healing Herbs
# **Bach Remedies**

Region : Hereford, England

Founded: 1988

DEVELOPER: Julian Barnard

Born in1947, Julian trained in Art and Design with an early career writing on architecture. He first met the Bach flower remedies in the mid seventies and learned from Nickie Murray at the Bach centre. He has written several books about the remedies including Guide to the Bach Flower Remedies (1979) and Healing Herbs of Edward Bach (1988), an illustrated book describing their healing indications and how the remedies are made.

ESSENCES: The Healing Herbs' Bach Flower Remedies are dedicated to maintaining the purity and quality of the 38 flower remedies discovered by Dr Bach. They are made according to the original and traditional methods of Dr Bach from the flowers and trees found in remote places in the English countryside. These flower remedies, preserved in organic brandy, work on the emotional and psychological states of mind and have gained a reputation of being effective and user friendly for everyday problems that manifest in today's ever increasing stressful world. They are safe to use for children, babies and animals.

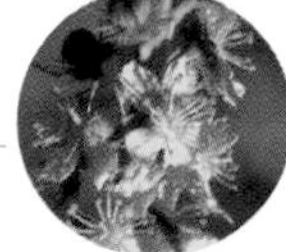

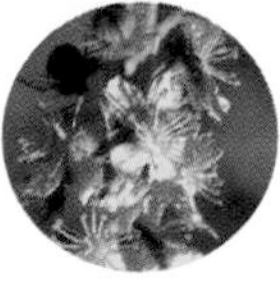

**Agrimony** *10ml ifer 1496 / 30ml ifer 1497*

Worry hidden by a carefree mask, apparently jovial but suffering; steadfast peace

**Aspen** *10ml ifer 1498 / 30ml ifer 1499*

Vague, unknown, haunting apprehension and premonitions; trusting the unknown

**Beech** *10ml ifer 1500 / 30ml ifer 1501*

Intolerant, critical, fussy; seeing more good in the world

**Centaury** *10ml ifer 1502 / 30ml ifer 1503*

Kind, quiet, gentle, anxious to serve, weak, dominated; an active and positive worker

**Cerato** *10ml ifer 1504 / 30ml ifer 1505*

Distrust of self and intuition, easily led and misguided; confidently seek individuality

**Cherry Plum** *10ml ifer 1506 / 30ml ifer 1507*

For the thought of losing control, of doing dreaded things; calmness and sanity

**Chestnut Bud** *10ml ifer 1508 / 30ml ifer 1509*

Failing to learn from life, repeating mistakes, lack of observation; learning from experience

**Chicory** *10ml ifer 1510 / 30ml ifer 1511*

Demanding, self-pity, self-love, possessive, hurt and tearful; love and care that gives freely to others

**Clematis** *10ml ifer 1512 / 30ml ifer 1513*

Dreamers, drowsy, absent-minded; brings down to earth

**Crab Apple** *10ml ifer 1516 / 30ml ifer 1517*

Feeling unclean, self-disgust, small things out of proportion; the cleansing remedy

**Elm** *10ml ifer 1518 / 30ml ifer 1519*

Capable people, with responsibility, who falter, temporarily overwhelmed; the strength to perform duty

**Gentian** *10ml ifer 1522 / 30ml ifer 1523*

Discouragement, doubt, despondency; take heart and have faith

**Gorse** *10ml ifer 1524 / 30ml ifer 1525*

No hope, accepting the difficulty, pointless to try; the sunshine of renewed hope

### Heather *10ml ifer 1526 / 30ml ifer 1527*

Longing for company, talkative, overconcern with self; tranquillity and kinship with all life

### Holly *10ml ifer 1528 / 30ml ifer 1529*

Jealousy, envy, revenge, anger, suspicion; the conquest of all will be through love

### Honeysuckle *10ml ifer 1530 / 30ml ifer 1531*

Living in memories; involved in present

### Hornbeam *10ml ifer 1532 / 30ml ifer 1533*

Feels weary and thinks can't cope; strengthens and supports

### Impatiens *10ml ifer 1534 / 30ml ifer 1535*

Irritated by constraints, quick, tense, impatient; gentle and forgiving

### Larch *10ml ifer 1536 / 30ml ifer 1537*

Expect failure, lack confidence and will to succeed; self-confident, try anything

### Mimulus *10ml ifer 1538 / 30ml ifer 1539*

Fright of specific, known things - animals, heights, pain etc., nervous, shy people; bravery

### Mustard *10ml ifer 1540 / 30ml ifer 1541*

Gloom suddenly clouds us, for no apparent reason; clarity

### Oak *10ml ifer 1542 / 30ml ifer 1543*

Persevering, despite difficulties, strong, patient, never giving in; admitting to limitation

### Olive *10ml ifer 1544 / 30ml ifer 1545*

Exhausted, no more strength, need physical and mental renewal; rested and supported

### Pine *10ml ifer 1546 / 30ml ifer 1547*

Self critical, self reproach, assuming blame, apologetic; relieves a sense of guilt

### Red Chestnut *10ml ifer 1548 / 30ml ifer 1549*

Worry for others, anticipating misfortune, projecting worry; trusting to life

### Rock Rose *10ml ifer 1550 / 30ml ifer 1551*

Feeling alarmed, intensely scared, horror, dread; the courage to face an emergency

### Rockwater *10ml ifer 1552 / 30ml ifer 1553*

Self-denial, stricture, rigidity, purist; broad outlook, understanding

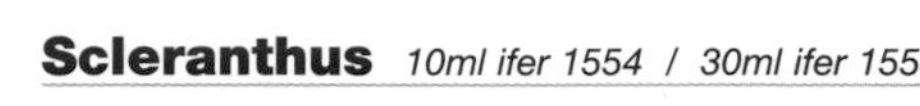

### Scleranthus *10ml ifer 1554 / 30ml ifer 1555*

Cannot resolve between two choices, indecision, alternating; balance and determination

### Star of Bethlehem *10ml ifer 1556 / 30ml ifer 1557*

For consolation and comfort in grief, after a fright or sudden alarm

### Sweet Chestnut *10ml ifer 1558 / 30ml ifer 1559*

Unendurable desolation; a light shining in the darkness

### Vervain *10ml ifer 1560 / 30ml ifer 1561*

Insistent, willlful, fervent, enthusiastic, stressed; quiet and tranquillity

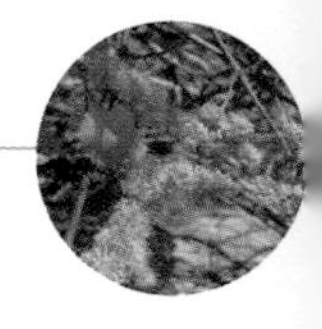

### Vine *10ml ifer 1562 / 30ml ifer 1563*

Dominating, tyrant, bully, demands obedience; loving leader and teacher, setting all at liberty

### Walnut *10ml ifer 1564 / 30ml ifer 1565*

Protection from outside influences, for change and the stages of development; the link breaker

### Water Violet *10ml ifer 1566 / 30ml ifer 1567*

Withdrawn, aloof, proud, self-reliant, quiet grief; peaceful and calm, wise in service

### White Chestnut *10ml ifer 1568 / 30ml ifer 1569*

Unresolved, circling thoughts; a calm, clear mind

### Wild Oat *10ml ifer 1570 / 30ml ifer 1571*

Lack of direction, unfulfilled, drifting; becoming definite and purposeful

### Wild Rose *10ml ifer 1572 / 30ml ifer 1573*

Lack of interest, resignation, no love or point in life; spirit of joy and adventure

### Willow 10ml ifer 1574 / 30ml ifer 1575

Dissatisfied, bitter, resentful, life is unfair, unjust; uncomplaining, acceptance

### Five Flower Remedy *10ml ifer 1520 / 30ml ifer 1521*

The rescue remedy combination of Dr Bach: Cherry Plum, Clematis, Impatiens, Star of Bethlehem and Rock Rose. For use in any sudden difficulty

### Five Flower Cream

*28gm ifer 2239 / 112gm ifer 2359 / 450gm ifer 4779 / 3x7gm ifer 5628*

# Himalayan **Flower** Enhancers

Region: Himalayas

Founded: 1991

DEVELOPER: A former landscape gardener, Tanmaya left his native Australia and spent 20 years as a spiritual seeker and nomad in India. He found the Himalayas a constant source of inspiration and revelation, seeking out the tranquillity and stillness embodied in the sacred mountains. The Parati Valley in the Khulamen area of the Himalayas produces an annual display of lush, vibrant flowers that is so legendary for its beauty that it is simply known as 'the valley of the flowers'.

ESSENCES: Tanmaya's essences are known as flower enhancers because they enhance what is right, rather than focusing on problems. They act as subtle catalysts for change, aligning us with our inner truth, gently releasing blockages and old thought patterns that no longer serve our growth. The names of the enhancers derive not from the plant names themselves, but rather from their therapeutic qualites, such as 'Ecstasy' and 'Let Go'.

By uncovering our inherent wholeness, healing and re-balancing can naturally take place. Not only do they aid meditation, but the Chakra Set is especially designed to empower the body's major energy centres (chakras) by gently dissolving any stored or blocked energy. Equally unique is the method by which they are made. He places the blossoms directly into pure locally-produced alcohol made from wild white roses, mountain spring water, wheat and sugar.

**Chakra Set** *(set of 8) 15ml ifer 2471*

**The Chakra Set**

This is the backbone of this line, containing 8 Himalayan Flower Enhancers, one for each of the 7 major chakras, facilitating gentle access, deepening and 'gratefulness' for celebration and sharing. Within the seven chakras lies the full spectrum of human experience, from sex and survival in the root chakra to union and transendence in the crown chakra. Enjoy the journey.

**Down to Earth** *(Root Chakra-base of spine) 15ml ifer 2436*

Enhances life force energy, connection with the earth. Helps with ungroundedness, sluggishness, anxiety around material existence.

**Well Being** *(Hara-centre of abdomen) 15ml ifer 2437*

Enhances connection with one's power, centering, stimulating creativity and integrating emotions,

**Strength** *(Solar plexus chakra) 15ml ifer 2438*

Enhances one's individuality, personal creativity, honesty, self worth, self-identity, power of manifestation in the material world.

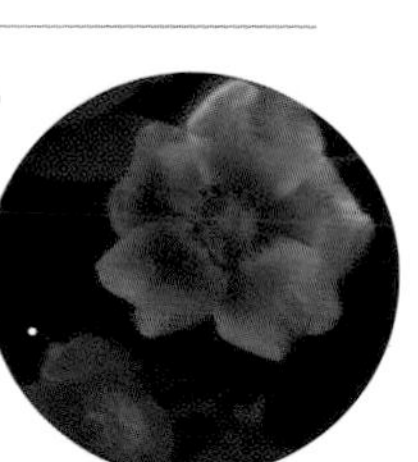

**Ecstasy** *(Heart chakra) 15ml ifer 2439*

Enhances love, compassion, sincerity, depth of feeling, empathy with all living things, transpersonal love. Helps with bitterness, jealousy, feelings of contraction.

**Authenticity** *(Throat chakra) 15ml ifer 2440*

Enhances expression, appreciation of aesthetics, pleasure and beauty, creativity, self authority. Helps in cases of shyness, fear of speaking one's truth, difficulties in communication.

**Clarity** *(Third eye chakra) 15ml ifer 2441*

Enhances clarity, awareness, intuition, wisdom, clairvoyance, ability to see into the heart of things, sense of universal self, meditation.

**Flight** *(Crown chakra - top of head) 15ml ifer 2442*

Enhances oneness, meditation, prayer, higher self, union of mind, body and spirit; sense of the formless. Helps with feelings of separateness, isolation.

**Gratefulness** *15ml ifer 2443*

Enhances sharing, universal brotherhood, wonder, awe. Helps with egocentric, judgemental, and selfish attitudes

# **Other** Essences

## Aura Cleaning *15ml ifer 2445*

Cleans and refreshes the aura adding lightness and sparkle. Excellent for use in bath or spraying over the body. Excellent room freshener.

## Blue Dragon *15ml ifer 2452*

Enhances focus, concentration, single-pointedness. Excellent for meditation. Pierces straight into the heart of matter revealing only one sky.

## Champagne *15ml ifer 2468*

Joyful, light, for celebration: particularly good at night.

## Children's Flower *15ml ifer 2446*

Protective essence for children. Helps the child maintain their original connection with the natural world. Invokes delight, playfulness, innocence, resilience, a sense of wonder and awe in the mysteries of life. Connects adults with their inner child.

## Chiron *15ml ifer 2449*

Gives insight into the wound which has disconnected us from our essence. For healers evokes shamanistic energies, channelling. Eases Chiron transits.

## Endurance *(formerly called Longevity - Himalayas/Sinai Desert)* *15ml ifer 2463*

Gives vitality, stamina, endurance.

## Expansion *15ml ifer 2455*

Specifically for the area of the chest, gives a feeling of expansion, openness, gentle relaxation.

## Gateway *15ml ifer 2459*

Assists in periods of transition, rights of passage, times of deep soul searching. Gives strength and resilience in times of inner turmoil.

## Goddess *(India/China) 15ml ifer 2461*

Enhances the goddess, the wisewoman; provokes beauty, grace, receptivity, feminine strength. (Moon/Venus energy)

## Golden Dawn *15ml ifer 2453*

For women, releases old wounds around sexuality. Centers one in a place of stillness where no wounds exist, and so allowing disidentification and gentle healing to happen by itself.

## Happiness *15ml ifer 2451*

Gives a radiance from within that sends a smile, a smoothing glow throughout the body. Relaxing.

## Healing *15ml ifer 2447*

For healers - gives the effect of a walk through a pine forest, clearing the channels for the healer, centering and bringing them back to their natural relationship with existence.

## Heart of Tantra *15ml ifer 2458*

Creates a circle of light between the root chakra and the heart. For men particularly it bridges the solar plexus with the heart, thus moving sex from power to love.

## Hidden Splendor *15ml ifer 2444*

Brings forth ones inner beauty. For reclaiming your birthright, your inner glory. Helps with feelings of worthlessness, insignificance, contraction.

## Isan (Neem-India) *15ml ifer 2465*

Helps integrate mind, body and spirit. Good to take after sessions or meditation. Strengthens one's ability to live one's truth.

## Let Go *15ml ifer 2454*

For relaxation, letting go into the flow.
A Pisces flower.

## Lotus (India) *15ml ifer 2464*

The philosopher's stone of flowers-symbol of enlightenment. Enhances all forms of spiritual healing. Acts as a booster for other essences. Opens crown chakra. Excellent to use with meditation.

## Morning Glory (India) *15ml ifer 2466*

Helps one get up and greet the morning with enthusiasm. Enhances vitality and reduces nervous behaviour.

## Nirjara *15ml ifer 2456*

A deconditioning essence, excellent for all work of deprogramming. Where there is conscious intent to change conditioned attitudes and patterns, this essence helps erase outmoded imprints from the cells. Supports transformation. A powerful healing essence.

## **Pluto** *15ml ifer 2450*

Brings consciousness to the shadow. Diffuses anger, frustration, old patterns of behaviour. Helps one surrender to change, seeing the big picture.

## **Renaissance** (Brazil) *15ml ifer 2467*

For rebirth. Assists in letting go of all that is not real and dissolving into that which has always been. A support for seekers during difficult times. (Made under a full Pisces moon together with Sandra Epstein, co-creator of Brazilian Rain Forest Essences.)

## **Sober Up** *15ml ifer 2469*

Grounding, stabilizing. Balances excess energy in the head. Good for alcohol excess and related problems.

## **Trust** *15ml ifer 2448*

Gives a sense of protection, trust. Heals wounds between lovers, creating the space for union to take place.

## **Veil of Dreams** (India) *15ml ifer 2462*

Step through the veil of dreams and into the mysteries. Excellent to take before sleeping, helps with remembering one's dreams. Use in conjunction with Clarity and Blue Dragon for psychic work.

## **Vital Spark** *15ml ifer 2457*

Helps regain ones center. Enhances vitality and life force, especially in situations of shock, fear, and extreme emotions. Helps one relax, let go, and surrender to the moment, thereby providing the space for healing to take place. Can be used for plants shocked due to replanting etc.

## **Warrior** *15ml ifer 2460*

Enhances masculine strength, groundedness, courage, male sexuality, strength of purpose. Best taken in conjunction with the heart chakra essence Ecstasy. (Sun/Mars energy)

# **Research** Essences

## **Rapa-Nui** *15ml ifer 4091*

Evoking ancient earth energy, healing past life wounds, merging into the ancient wisdom of Gaia. (Made with sea water at the oldest sacred site on Easter Island, under the dark of the moon, with obsidian from the island's largest volcano, and the flower of Mira-Tahiti - the last native shrub remaining on the island.)

## **Nirjara 2** *15ml ifer 4092*

Deconditioning, particularly in the mental body. Helps dissolve old thought forms and patterns that are no longer appropriate, allowing one to be in the emptiness of the moment. Supporting a fresh response to life's experiences – unencumbered by expectations and fears based on the past.

## **Pink Primula** *15ml ifer 4093*

Opening the heart to the pure delight and joy of simply being alive. Like many of these research essences was made at an elevation of approximately 3,000 metres, higher than any others I had made before.

## **Rock Primula** *15ml ifer 4094*

Quiet acceptance/connection with one's inner beauty/peace - regardless of what may be going on around you.

## **White Orchid** *15ml ifer 4095*

For accessing the angelic realms of the heart. Opens the higher octaves of the heart chakra, accessing love and acceptance. A very powerful and beautiful essence.

## **Purple Orchid** *15ml ifer 4096*

A doorway in. Accessing great depths within.

## **Astral Orchid** *15ml ifer 4097*

Connection with the Greater Mind. Non-personal understanding, channelling.

## **Opium Poppy** *15ml ifer 4098*

Helping to break free of addictive emotional patterns that keep us in the past.

## Gulaga Transformation Set *(consisting of 8 essences)*

*15ml ifer 5855*

This box set of 8 Himalayan Flower Enhancers is a group of essences to be used as an aid to rapid transformation and restructuring, both on a personal and organizational level.
Gulaga triggers an awareness of what no longer serves in ones life, and awakens the strength to change. The other seven essences support the process – helping create a smoother unfolding and integration – with courage, love and acceptance

## Cedar *15ml ifer 5853*

Made from the flower of the Deodar Cedar in the Himalayas in 1994. It came rushing in when I was putting together the Gulaga set as a support and to soften the edges of the Gulaga essence. Gives grounding and courage, stability, strength and vitality. Encourages deep roots into the earth so one's branches can reach high into the sky.

## Gateway *15ml ifer 2459*

(see description above)

## Gulaga *15ml ifer 4920*

Made during a solar eclipse from a red mushroom at the sacred site on Gulaga Mountain, on the far South Coast of Australia's eastern seaboard. A powerful essence for transformation. Ruthlessly exposing and clearing away all that is no longer appropriate or serving us on our journey. Realigning us with our life's purpose.

## Gulaga Crystal *15ml ifer 5852*

Made from a small piece of crystal from a vein running between Gulaga (the Mother) and Natchanuku (one of her sons), hills in New South Wales. Aligns the mind, crystallises intention, grounds new vision, strengthens resolve. Brings lightness, clarity and joy to complete the transition process initiated by the Gulaga essence.

## Let go *15ml ifer 2454*

(see description above)

## Nirjara *15ml ifer 2456*

(see description above)

## Nirjara 2 *15ml ifer 4092*

(see description above)

## White Orchid *15ml ifer 4095*

(see description above)

# Light Heart **Single Stock** Essences

Region: Suffolk, England

Founded: 1993

DEVELOPER. Rose Titchiner first began working with flower essences over 30 years ago. Since early childhood Rose sought answers to the fundamental questions of "Who are we? Why are we here? What is this?" In the last nine years, in her own search for healing and in response to her work as a spiritual healer and therapist, she joined with those in spirit who work with her, to co-create essences, with the intention of providing inspiration for the profound healing and awakening of consciousness at this time.

ESSENCES. These essences address the dynamics of spiritual, emotional, mental and physical healing in our lives and the conscious choice between love and fear in all areas of our experience. Most of the essences are made from plants growing organically in the two acres surrounding Rose's home or in nearby wildflower meadows, heathland or water meadows. Rose also makes environmental essences, in addition to essences co-created solely with intention. Included in the range are 42 single essences, 12 Combination essences and 9 Inspirational essences (including Space Clearing essences).

**Blue Delphinium** – *Delphinium sp*
*15ml ifer 5692*

Speaking out; speaking one's truth with honesty and integrity; for clear, strong, unambiguous speech; expression of spiritual truth; for developing the ability to listen - both to others, and within.
Indications: fear of speaking out and speaking one's truth; for releasing fears relating to speaking out, throat restrictions and inhibitions, speech difficulties.

**Blue Hibiscus** – *Hibiscus syriacus 'Blue Bird'*
*15ml ifer 5693*

Coming into one's full expression; 'Coming out'; for expressing our true nature – physically, vocally, creatively, and through how we live our life; feeling alive and fully present, within our body, on the earth.
Indications: for inhibition and judgement about expressing ourselves on any level; for when we are not comfortable with our body or our physical expression.

**Celandine** – *Ranunculus ficarius*
*15ml ifer 5694*

Joy; lightness; experiencing the joy and light of divine expression in all; for celebrating and expressing joy and appreciation; joyful musical inspiration (particularly singing).
Indications: for depression, pessimism, gloominess, S.A.D.; for whenever we need the inspiration of light and joy.

**Cherry Plum Fruit** – *Prunus serasifera* *15ml ifer 5695*

Centering; for embracing strong feelings without fearful or violent reaction, or suppression of feeling; for staying peacefully in the heart of feeling and uncovering greater love, self-knowledge and compassion.
Indications: fear of breakdown or collapse during times of strong emotional release of anger, grief, fear etc; for when we become reactive or disconnected from feeling.

**Comfrey** – *Symphytum aspermum*
*15ml ifer 5696*

Dynamic patience and stillness – recognising and embracing the opportunity and gift within our present experience; grounding; for meditation.
Indications: Fighting or resisting being where we are; feeling limited or restricted by circumstance; living for the future; impatience.

**Cowslip** – *Primula veris.* *15ml ifer 5697*

Soothing; comforting; nurturing 'mother' energy; feeling supported; awareness that we are not alone; being kind to ourselves; feeling able to ask for help; soothes and comforts young children and the elderly.
Indications: for when we feel stretched to the limit of our physical and emotional endurance and feel alone in our struggle; for worry; exhaustion; and those deprived of mothering.

**Crab Apple Fruit** – *Malus pumila* *15ml ifer 5802*

For allowing our body to return to its innate state of innocent health and vitality, by withdrawing the belief that we are guilty of creating disease and damage through some failing on our part.
Indications: Guilt, hopelessness, and feelings of failure in relation to health and one's ability to heal; belief that we only heal if we become perfect and pure.

**Crimean Snowdrop**
– *Galanthus plicatus* *15ml ifer 5803*

Return to pure essence; healing the memory of trauma and suffering wherever it is held, in our being, in an environment or in material objects.
Indications: Post-traumatic shock and memories of suffering that haunt; for healing objects and environments which retain a memory of suffering.

**Cyclamen** – *Cyclamen hybrida* *15ml ifer 5698*

Self Nurture; making time and space for oneself; nourishing one's body, mind, heart and soul; nurturing one's core energy and dreams; making time to centre and choose from the heart.
Indications: loss of sense of self and integrity; exhaustion; burn out; allowing one's life to be dictated to by external influences.

**Dandelion** – *Taraxacum officinale*
*15ml ifer 5699*

Letting go of held tension, defence and fear, for deep relaxation and peace – recognition of the God/Good in All.
Indications: for emotion held as physical tension; inability to relax; fearful defence; held in fear and trauma, post traumatic shock.

**Divine Embodiment** – *Stellaria holostea* *15ml ifer 5856*

with imprinted inspirational essence
For healing the cellular memory of suffering in the human body; for relaxing and expanding our cells and experiencing each cell, and the space between each cell, filled with the light of the absolute peace of divine embodiment - ending mortality and disease, and the separation between body and soul.

**Fleabane** – *Pulicaria dysenterica*
*15ml ifer 5700*

For keeping a positive view of what's happening to those around one and to the world in general; comforts and reassures the sensitive.
Indications: for anxiety, worry, insecurity, over-sensitivity, over-empathising with fearful perceptions of events in the lives of people around one or in the world in general.

**Golden Daffodil** – *Narcissus sp*
*15ml ifer 5701*

Divine Perception; for recognising that we are Divine, all knowing, infinitely powerful and creative; recognising the divine nature of all.
Indications: for whenever we feel powerless or ignorant (mere mortals); for when we need to connect with our Higher Self to get a greater overview of life.

**Goldenrod** – *Solidago virgaurea*
*15ml ifer 5702*

Inner Authority; integrity and self respect; following our inner knowing; peaceful assertiveness; becoming our own unconditionally loving and authoritative inner father.
Indications: loss of integrity, giving away our power, feeling diminished or crushed by another's judgement; submission to authority figures, bullying or social pressure.

**Gorse** – *Ulex europaeus* *15ml ifer 5703*

Self forgiveness; for letting go the judgement we hold against ourselves; for knowing that we are wholly worthy of love every moment of our lives regardless of what acts we have committed.
Indications: Guilt, self-judgement; for when we have been judged by others to have committed an act that is unforgivable.

**Honesty** – *Lunaria annua* *15ml ifer 5704*

Honesty without judgement; for acknowledging the full depth and range of our feelings; for recognising that the greatest gift we can give to ourselves and others is the unadorned expression of our human-ness.
Indications: hiding our true feelings for fear of judgement; self- judgement; sensitivity to judgement and criticism from others.

**Horse Chestnut** (Leaf Bud) - *Aesculus hippocastanum* .
*15ml ifer 5705*

For healing the experience of male physicality and sexuality; expression of unconditional love, integrity and embodiment of spirit through male physicality and sexuality.
Indications: for men who lack confidence in their physicality, sexual expression or virility; for women who are uncomfortable with male physicality and sexuality.

## **Lilac** – *Syringa vulgaris* *15ml ifer 5706*

Recognising that the apparent random chaos of life is in reality, a constant evolving creation of complex, interacting multi-dimensional order and form; for understanding complex ideas and systems; for evolving fluid, responsive management systems; steering a path through complexity by responding to the reality of the moment; for complex business and study projects.
Indicatons: Low self worth; fear of empowerment, success and abundance; for when it feels safer to be a victim of circumstance than to stand in one's own power.

## **Manuka** – *Kunzea scoparium* *15ml ifer 5707*

Forgiveness; for understanding that true forgiveness is the letting go of judgement of ourselves and others; for deep understanding & compassion for ourselves and others.
Indications: for personal or community relationships where there is much conflict, anger, and retribution, which it seems impossible to clear and forgive.

## **Orange Wallflower** – *Cheiranthus cheirii*
*15ml ifer 5708*

For knowing that we are the source of infinite love and abundance – that there is no lack, except in our perception.
Indications: fear of lack; fear of love being withheld or denied; loneliness, neediness in relationships, co-dependency; for when we block the flow of giving and receiving in our lives because of fear.

## **Peaceful Detachment** – *Achillea millefolium*
*15ml ifer 5806*

Peaceful detachment; divine union; for safe connection to others and ourselves at the level of 'higher truth' and higher love – beyond ego reaction, fear, identity and duality.
Indications: over empathy; over-sensitivity to, and over-involvement with the level of ego/emotional reactive drama in our own and other people's lives.

## **Physostegia** – *Physostegia virginiana* *15ml ifer 5709*

Integrity in interaction, centred interaction with others; able to respond appropriately, without being affected by strong influences or ego dynamics.
Indications: for when we deny our integrity in our interactions with others; overwhelm in work, study and crisis situations; conflict resolution. (Can be sprayed in offices, classrooms and conference rooms.)

## **Pink Cherry** – *Prunus sp* *15ml ifer 5710*

For a sense of deep, unconditional, tender love; heart softening and opening; nurtures and soothes; for unconditional love; inspires tender and sensitive communication.
Indications: for anyone needing love; for the inner child, and for children who need embracing and comforting; for those who didn't have sufficient mothering and love as children.

## **Pussy Willow** – *Salix daphnoides*
*15ml ifer 5711*

Flexibility born out of responding to the real flow in life – to what is truly comfortable and appropriate, to our inner rhythms and real sense of timing; knowing that life supports us if we support and honour ourselves on a daily basis.
Indications: Anger; resentment; rigidity; self-denial; denying our integrity – too much doing and never being.

## **Red Clover** – *Trifolium pratense* *15ml ifer 5863*

For knowing the reality of peace; recognising that by our fear we separate ourselves from knowing our ever-present good/God; knowing that we are always partnered in spirit.
Indications: mass panic, terror, fear, anxiety, panic attacks; for when we hook into fearful thought forms related to world events, or events around us.

## **Red Gladiolus** – *Gladiolus sp*
*15ml ifer 5712*

Healing women's experience of sexuality; expression of unconditional love, integrity and embodiment of spirit through female sexuality.
Indications; for women who have experienced a split between the spiritual expression of love and sexuality, and their actual physical and emotional experience (in reaction to abuse or sexual acts devoid of love and sensitivity).

## **Red Poppy** – *Papaver rhoeas.* *15ml ifer 5713*

For a fiery sense of self-esteem and self-worth; for constructive use of anger for positive change; setting boundaries without guilt.
Indications: swings between angry outbursts and suppressing anger; powerlessness, depression and frustration; when we get angry, then crumple into hopelessness and guilt; immune deficiency with patterns of powerlessness.

## **Rosebay Willowherb** - *Epilobium angustifolium*
*15ml ifer 5714*

For transforming our fear of expanded awareness and radical shifts in perception, for connection to the spirit in nature and the earth; grounds our awareness in our hearts, in the recognition of the divine in all.
Indications: fear of expanded awareness and fundamental shifts in perception; for when we feel disconnected from the natural world and the Earth.

## Sky Blue Comfrey

*– Symphytum aspermum*

*15ml ifer 5715*

Infinite peace - dynamic peace; knowing that we are infinite, that time and death are an illusion – that there is only now; inspires us to relax into the total peace of divine being and infinite safety and freedom from suffering.
Indications: fear of suffering and mortality, feelings of vulnerability and insecurity; fear of aging.

## Speedwell – *Veronica persica* *15ml ifer 5716*

Dynamic centred focus; being fully present and connected in the moment; seeing true; relaxed alert concentration; de-stresses; enhances intuition and meditation.
Indications: for stress, rushing, hyperactivity, poor attention span, lack of connection, concentration or focus; making careless mistakes, accident prone, clumsy; dreaming of the future, of ideas and schemes.

## Stitchwort – *Stellaria holostea*

*15ml ifer 5722*

Commitment to full embodiment as a divine being; grounding the light of divine perception and experience into all 'physical' matter and life experience.
Indications: Fear of fully incarnating and fully living, limiting fears of suffering and 'physical' mortality; feelings of acute vulnerability and sensitivity; cold feet.

## Sweet Pea – *Lathyrus odoratus*

*15ml ifer 5717*

Knowing that we are never alone; recognising the divine nature of all being, that we are not separate from Infinite Love, that we only separate ourselves; closeness to friends in spirit; communion with angels - our brothers and sisters in light.
Indications: for when we feel alone and cut off from love and spiritual support.

## The Rose – *Rosa ' Mme Isaac Pereire'* *15ml ifer 5804*

Full divine expression; divine 'Coming Out; for integrating and unfolding all aspects of our divine being and expressing that truth fully in the world, fulfilling our incarnation role at this time.
Indications: for those whose role challenges them to openly express the light of their truth and divinity in all areas of their life.

## True Power – *Crocus thomasinianus 'Royal'*

*15ml ifer 5864 / 30ml ifer 5865 / 50ml ifer 5866*

Realising that true power lies within us in the limitless love and truth of our being – that this is power and stature beyond measure, and can never be diminished, or taken by another.
Indications : Power struggles, jealousy, envy, hatred ,revenge, abuse of power, manipulation, distorted hunger for love and recognition, conflict resolution, peace meditation.

## Violet – *Viola odorata* *15ml ifer 5854*

For those in the public eye – encourages them to express truth and to maintain individual integrity, boundaries and privacy; balances the ego, dis-empowering the glamour of 'image' creation.
Indications: those who avoid public exposure fearing loss of boundaries and integrity, and fearing their own insecure ego being drawn into glamour.

## White Clover – *Trifolium repens* *15ml ifer 5718*

Infinite light; for transcending fear and allowing miracles to happen; knowing that we are eternally safe - beings of Light; changing our perception to one of unlimited possibility and joy.
Indications: Panic, shock, deeply held fear, terror, trauma; for whenever we identify with fear-based thought forms, perceptions and beliefs.

## White Yarrow – *Achillea millefolium*

*15ml ifer 5719*

Sovereignty; authority over our health – understanding that our 'physical bodies' are in fact fluid energy forms which reflect our beliefs about vulnerability, aging, illness, environmental toxicity etc.; knowing that in reality we are Divine, invulnerable and infinite.
Indications: fear of being vulnerable to 'external' agents - environmental pollution, radiation, viruses, cancer etc.

## Wild Cyclamen – *Cyclamen coum* *15ml ifer 5805*

Inner resourcefulness; self-sufficiency; self- guidance; for finding our own inner support, nurture, strength and counsel.
Indications: for times when we don't have outside support or help from others (except from spirit); for children who do not have sufficient support and nurture in their lives.

## Winter Jasmine – *Jasminum nudiflorum.* *15ml ifer 5720*

Light in the dark; inspiration and joy in our darkest times; uplift; inspiration from the natural world; feeling at home in winter.
Indications: for when it is hard to find the light; testing times; Seasonal Affective Disorder.

***These essences come in 15ml stock bottles ready for dilution***

# **Combination** Essences

### **Forgiveness** *30ml ifer 5095*

Forgiveness and Self Forgiveness; inspires one to release one's judgement, and view oneself and others with compassion and understanding.
Indications: for healing relationships where there is much conflict, old hurt, anger and grievance, which it seems impossible to clear and forgive; for guilt and self judgement.

### **Healing Grief** essence/spray

30ml ifer 5664 / 50ml ifer 5821

Embracing the full range of our grief, peacefully, without judgement; uncovering the healing that lies at the heart of grief; forgiveness; healing the memory of suffering; connection to spirit; new beginnings.
Indications: Grief and brokenheartedness of bereavement or relationship break-up; shock and trauma of loss; unresolved anger, bitterness and guilt; unfinished grieving.

### **Heart of Peace** essence/spray

30ml ifer 5647 / 50ml ifer 5648

Recognising that by choosing peace in place of fear we create safety and contribute to world peace; peaceful detachment from the level of emotional drama and trauma; divine perception that all is well - that we are innately invulnerable.
Indications: mass panic, terror, fear, anxiety; fearful perception of world events, or events around us.

### **Integrity in Interaction** essence/spray

30ml ifer 5090 / 50ml ifer 5413

Centred interaction with others: appropriate response and peaceful assertion, undisturbed by strong influences or ego dynamics; being open and willing to hear and understand other people's points of view.
Indications: for whenever we deny our integrity in our interactions with others; overwhelm and stress in work/study situations; conflict resolution.

### **Peace in a Storm**
(Crisis Combination)essence/cream/spray

30ml ifer 5086 / 50ml ifer 5106 / 50ml ifer 5412

Centred, peaceful, appropriate response in a crisis, peaceful connection to the moment; understanding and embracing strong feelings without overwhelm or fear; gentle release of anxiety, shock, anger and grief.
Indications: crisis, panic, shock, anxiety, extreme emotion, uncentred reaction or frozen response, - fear of breakdown or collapse.

### **Relationships** *30ml ifer 5655*

For integrity, independence, understanding, honest communication and unconditional love in relationships; encourages individual self-respect, appreciation and compassion in relationships.
Indications: Neediness, co-dependency, conflict, resentment, poor communication and unresolved issues in relationships; for loss of integrity and self-respect in relationships.

### **Self Esteem** *30ml Ifer 5087*

Confidence, integrity, self worth: honouring oneself, valuing one's understanding and knowing; self-assertion; for the courage to show one's true face and speak one's truth.
Indications: loss of integrity and confidence, feeling diminished and crushed by another's judgement or by authority figures; bowing to external influences, bullying or social pressure.

### **Self Expression** *30ml ifer 5092*

For releasing inhibition about expressing one's true nature, physically, vocally, creatively and through how one lives one's life; for letting go the fear of being judged, encourages expressiveness in art, dance, singing, acting, writing etc.
Indications: for whenever there is inhibition about expressing oneself on any level; for stage fright.

### **Self Healing** essence/cream

30ml ifer 5093 / 50ml ifer 5107

For confidence in one's ability to heal; authorising one's own healing; trusting one's intuition; fresh belief in healing after long term illness.
Indications: lack of confidence in one's ability to heal; feelings of powerlessness, fear, guilt, hopelessness and failure related to illness or injury. (Supports both conventional and complementary treatment).

### **Self Nurture** *30ml ifer 5088*

Self Nurture; making time and space to relax; nourishing and restoring one's body, mind and spirit; responding to comfortable, appropriate, real timing; knowing life supports us if we support and honour ourselves.
Indications: stress, exhaustion, burn-out; denying one's needs; too much 'doing' and never 'being'; allowing one's life to be dictated by external demands.

### **Sexual Healing** *30ml ifer 5091*

Healing one's experience of sexuality; expressing unconditional love, integrity and embodiment of spirit through sexuality; celebration and love of sexuality.
Indications: for those who have experienced a split between the spiritual expression of love and sexuality and their actual physical and emotional experience (resulting from abuse or sexual acts devoid of love and sensitivity).

**Sleep Well** essence/spray
*30ml ifer 5089 / 50ml ifer 5105*

Promotes deep, peaceful sleep: encourages one to let go of physical and emotional tension and stress; soothes and calms an anxious or overactive mind - helping one to feel relaxed and secure enough to sleep.
Indications: Sleeplessness.

**Women's Balance essence/cream**
*30ml ifer 5094 / 50ml ifer 5404*

To support women's balance on all levels, throughout their life cycles - from early puberty to menopause; for understanding and growing with the changing female cycles, life phases and roles.
Indications: for loss of emotional and physical balance related to changing female cycles, life phases and roles.

# **Inspirational** Essences

**Heart Mother** essence / spray
*30ml efer 5858 / 50ml efer 5859*

Balance; embodying the Mother within; maintaining through adequate nurture, the equilibrium point between self-denial and excessive need (emotional and physical); for healing our relationship with the earth and managing resources wisely.
Indications: emotional patterns (from inadequate or excessive mothering) related to blood sugar imbalance; depression; eating disorders; addiction..

**Infinite Abundance** - *30ml ifer 5099*

Relates to our beliefs about the source of love, money and other abundance in our lives. It helps us to know that we are the source of infinite love and abundance and that we are limited only by our own perceptions of who and what we are. For knowing that life supports us. For self nurture, creativity and the energy and self worth to bring about positive change.
Indications: Fear of lack; fear of expanded awareness.

**Infinite Light** – Environmental Space Clearing essence /spray
30ml ifer 5098 / 50ml ifer 5102 / 100ml ifer 5104

For healing and clearing the memory of trauma and suffering in an environment or in material objects; brings radiant light and love to buildings and landscape; lightens and clears the energy of the home, workplace and therapy rooms, as well as furniture, clothes and crystals.

**Infinite Peace** – Infinite Love / essence / spray
*30ml ifer 5097 / 50ml ifer 5101*

Divine perception; knowing that we are and always have been infinite, that time and death are an illusion; knowing we are the source of love and abundance – that there is no lack; recognising the innocent perfection of our true being; choosing love in place of fear; recognising the divine nature of all being.

**Light Anchor** – Imprinted Light essence/spray
*15ml ifer 5721 / 30ml ifer 5080 / 50ml ifer 5081 / 100ml ifer 5082*

Choosing Love in place of fear; anchoring our consciousness in the certainty of love, and the light of divine expression; for courage.
Indications: for whenever we lack courage and waver between choosing fear, mortality and powerlessness - or the certainty of love and divine reality; for clearing crystals and essences.

**Light Heart Anchor** essence/spray
*30ml ifer 5083 / 50ml ifer 5084 /100ml ifer 5085*

For joyful and peaceful expansion of multi-dimensional awareness, secure in the reality of the divine in all; knowing we are lovingly supported and partnered by the devas, angels and spiritual companions on this journey.
Indications: fear of expanded awareness and radical shifts in perception.

**Light Heart Space** - Personal Space Clearing essence/spray
*30ml ifer 5096 / 50ml ifer 5100 / 100ml ifer 5103*

For clearing and infusing one's personal energy field with light; responsibility for personal energy, integrity and boundaries; peaceful detachment from emotional drama; connection to divine perception; making time and space to relax and restore oneself.
Indications: oversensitivity, feeling over-empathic and drained; over-exposure to electromagnetic energy and radiation; for healers and therapists.

**Original Innocence** essence/spray
*30ml ifer 5665 / 50ml spray ifer 5751*

Ever-present essential innocence, wholeness and love; recognising that only judgement separates us from knowing the divine light and perfection of our true being; moving beyond duality and judgement.
Indications: deep feelings of guilt, failure and unworthiness; believing enlightenment is only achieved by reaching some unattainable goal of purity and perfection.

# Living **Essences** of Australia

## Region:
## Western Australia
## Founded:1977

DEVELOPERS: Vasudeva and Kadambii Barnao

Vasudeva and Kadambii live in Perth, Australia with their three children. They have been practicing spiritual meditation for many years which they credit with giving them the intuitive sensitivity and inner quiet to appreciate the subtleties of human nature and the many mysterious aspects of flowers. Vasudeva had a general interest in natural health practices and began researching and producing essences in 1977. In 1980 he and Kadambii formed the Australasian Flower Essence Academy (AFEA) which began a great expansion of research and development into the essences. In the late 1980's, through Kadambii's work with an aboriginal community, the AFEA research was ratified by the discovery of the ancient practices of the Nyoongah people. The AFEA pioneered the research and use of essences through acu-points and meridians, putting them into creams and lotions leading to their work being taught and used in hospitals

THE ESSENCES: Based in the South Western region of Australia, called "the Wildflower state", renowned for its unique and prolific flora, healing flower essences have been found in the field, in forest, deserts, on the kwongon sandplains, in the gorges, on the beaches and mountains. This corner of Australia is home to over 600 species of orchids. The Nyoongah people believed that flowers carried the colours of the Creator Spirit. There are over 200 remedies made and researched as well as Microvita creams for the relief of pain and arthritis, hypertension, stress and lethargy – they have also pioneered new diagnostic techniques for use with these flower essences.

### **Antiseptic Bush** *15ml ifer 1629*

⊕ Key Words: integrity sanctity cleansing alert focus

⊖ Key Words: compromising influenced distracted helpless

For cleansing oneself of negative influences in one's environment or a build up over time of such influences within oneself This essence helps a person to be amongst the different aspects of life and maintain inner sanctity by continual cleansing. In the case of negative or harmful aspects, or people, one is then able to live without a build up of negative energy.

### **Balga** (Blackboy) *15ml ifer 1631*

⊕ Key Words: maturity assertiveness balancing creativity

⊖ Key Words: destructive aggressive insensitive immaturity

For the maturing of the male principle or the man within. For both men and women the promoting of positive creativity that also nurtures an awareness of the needs of the environment while achieving goals, Helpful in balancing achievement with life sustaining qualities such as caring and community / family spirit.

### **Black Kangaroo Paw**
*15ml ifer 1632*

⊕ Key Words: forgiveness sensitivity Love positivity

⊖ Key Words: anger hatred negativity obsession hurt

The essence of forgiveness and love. To bring back the light and re-sensitise after resentment and heavy emotional traumas one can't seem to forget. Helpful in relationship break ups and grief/anger, obsessive cycles. Also for issues of control as in the cases of parents or other authority figures, which then get re-enacted in later life.

### **Blue China Orchid** *15ml ifer 1633*

⊕ Key Words: strengthen self control will renewal change

⊖ Key Words: addicted weak overwhelmed obsessive

To strengthen the Will and take back control of the Self. To realise the beauty of inner focus and consistency in establishing a fulfilling life. For those who feel too easily swayed and distracted because of lacking direction and purpose. Helpful in bringing new beginnings by breaking the hold of old patterns of behaviour that are deteriorating the quality of life. For breaking the spell of habitual patterns of behaviour. Used also for breaking the hold of substance addiction.

## Blue Leschenaultia *15ml ifer 1634*

⊕ Key Words: giving sharing open free generous

⊖ Key Words: voracity selfishness covetous hoarding petty.

The essence that inspires generosity and the openness to share what you have with others on all levels. The opening of a window in the soul that reveals the basic needs of fellow human beings and then rekindles the desire to give with grace and benevolence. Also helps to de-energise an unhealthy need to have and keep hold of material possessions.

## Brachycombe *15ml ifer 1636*

⊕ Key Words: tolerance impartial kindness humility appreciation

⊖ Key Words: voracity selfishness covetous hoarding petty.

To encourage respect and appreciation for people and their intrinsic value. For when criticism needs to be transformed into acceptance of others, their individual and differing expressions. Helpful for bridging communication and mutual respect problems in relationships.

## Brown Boronia *15ml ifer 1637*

⊕ Key Words: free release patience acceptance

⊖ Key Words: worry anxiety sleeplessness obsessive

To inspire the realisation that the journey of life will bring solutions, one needs patience and acceptance of the "here and now". For those who are worried and therefore miss out on joy. Helpful in relieving stress and sleeplessness caused by worry.

## Candle of Life *15ml ifer 3473*

⊕ Key Words: positivity optimism Light renewal

⊖ Key Words: hopelessness battling struggle past pain

This essence helps the person to switch on their light again, that is, to see they must reach out to the beauty around them and inside of them to feel that it is good to be alive. Whatever the past pain has been, or how long a person has been hurting and struggling to go on, positive life experiences wait for them on the horizon. The renewal of hope and optimism, when we are in touch with our inner Light, is always rewarded.

## Cape Bluebell *15ml ifer 1638*

⊕ Key Words: joy letting go freeing geniality friendly

⊖ Key Words: resentment jealousy bitterness envy blame

An essence enhancing inner renewal and freeing oneself from old baggage that has no part to play in a happy life. For dealing with issues of the past which leave a bitter taste. To re-experience the joy of making the most of possibilities in present and future relationships.

## Catspaw *15ml ifer 1639*

⊕ Key Words: speaking out courage clarity acknowledgement

⊖ Key Words: suppressed introverted disregarded hurt

To encourage expressing the hurt one feels, so that others may better realise your situation and respond. To release the pent up gut feelings and face what is really happening. This frees one from both expectation of fairness and the situation of being used by others. Helpful for equalising one-sided relationships and bringing reality to obligatory relationships

## Christmas Tree (Kanya) *15ml ifer 1640*

⊕ Key Words: responsible sharing caring maturity

⊖ Key Words: irresponsible selfish inconsistent immaturity

This essence helps settle the person, bringing inner contentment which enhances the enjoyment of the family or group. The person can then fulfill their responsibilities and reap the rewards of consistency and shared goals. For issues of responsibility in family and group life where duties and everyday pressure is causing an individual to become distant and avoid their share of the load. This affects the whole group as they must carry the extra burden, and problems of resentment soon arise.

## Correa *15ml ifer 1642*

⊕ Key Words: confidence Self esteem learning acceptance potential

⊖ Key Words: underconfidence regret Self recrimination inferiority complex

To inspire feelings of positivity and self esteem. Being able to learn from mistakes with acceptance and without blame or regret. From inner acceptance - to focus - to success. Helpful for overcoming negative self concepts with ensuing phases of stagnation or depression.

## Cowkicks *15ml ifer 1643*

⊕ Key Words: re-energize rebuild vigour

⊖ Key Words: shattered tired exhaustion trauma

The essence of recovery from trauma. To help rebuild and re-thread the subtle and physical bodies after a shattering experience, mentally and/or physically, thereby energizing them. To integrate such experiences into one's understanding and perspective on Life in a wise way and move forward with renewed vigour.

## Cowslip Orchid *15ml ifer 1644*

➕ Key Words: humility confidence Self assured inner satisfaction

⊖ Key Words: demanding selfish attention seeking competitive

This essence helps resolve problems of over-competitiveness and brings a person into a space where they are free to interact with others as an equal. The Self then comes from a deeper aspect where it can feel joy for another's successes without feeling inferior or unattended. For issues of craving recognition and acceptance from others.

## Dampiera *15ml ifer 1645*

➕ Key Words: flexibility open co-operative letting go

⊖ Key Words: rigidity suppressive serious up-tight

The essence of letting go and allowing Life to flow. For issues of holding on and rigidity of mind and body. For releasing the need that Life and people should conform to only one perspective. Helpful in times of change, grief and reconciliation for the person to allow the old day to go and the new day to be embraced with flexibility.

## Donkey Orchid *15ml ifer 1707*

➕ Key Words: detachment peace positivity release re-build trust

⊖ Key Words: blaming resentment revenge wronged suspicious

To inspire the release of people in your life who have wronged you. To detach from the feelings of revenge and start living for today. This essence invokes a life affirming positivity that dissolves any chips that may be on your shoulder.

## Fringed Lily Twiner *15ml ifer 1646*

➕ Key Words: gracious giving loving

⊖ Key Words: demanding self-centred resentful tantrums

This essence stimulates love and focus out towards others, and one becomes happy by giving. For loss of balanced perspective leading to introversion, being demanding and over concentrated on oneself and what one has or has not got.

## Fringed Mantis Orchid *15ml ifer 1647*

➕ Key Words: benevolence good intentions conscience straight forward

⊖ Key Words: interfering nosey gossiping deceptive control

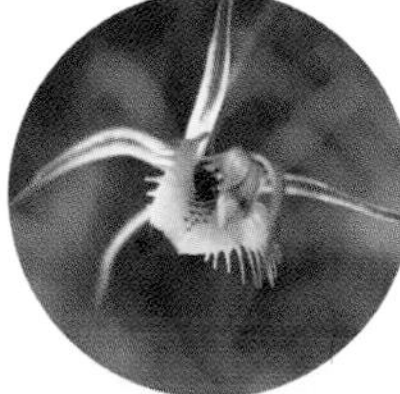

Frees the conscience which then naturally brings the mind back to balanced healthy pursuits.
For those who find themselves caught in an unhealthy curiosity about the affairs of others, who feel powerful with personal information and can't resist gossiping.

## Fuchsia Grevillea *15ml ifer 1648*

➕ Key Words: unifying truthful honesty integrity expression

⊖ Key Words: two-faced hypocrisy hidden negativity smug

To find the freedom of truthfully showing one's true thoughts and intentions. To be able to think, say, and be as one whole person without hiding any underlying negativity or to fall into hypocrisy.

## Fuchsia Gum *15ml ifer 1649*

➕ Key Words: comfortable at ease accepting contemplate

⊖ Key Words: fearful claustrophobia trapped irrational panic

For claustrophobia, both physical and emotional. To enable a person not to feel panic in a confined space or when feeling under threat. To allow the rush of energy and fear to be earthed so that rational thought can prevail.

## Geraldton Wax *15ml ifer 1651*

➕ Key Words: inner strength independent self assured

⊖ Key Words: compromised influenced pressured dominated obligatory

To strengthen oneself so as not to be pressured against one's will, or be routinely influenced by the desires of others who focus on you. Helpful for dominant/submissive relationships and for adolescents succumbing to peer group pressure.

## Giving Hands *15ml ifer 3474*

➕ Key Words: regeneration optimism inspiration joyous

⊖ Key Words: sadness abused heaviness hopelessness

To find the powers of regeneration and metamorphosis within. The essence to care for and heal oneself so one can bounce back after personal trauma and unload the feelings of heaviness. When this is achieved the renewed inspiration for Life and zest for living carries one through to positive experiences and gives scope for great fulfilment.

## Goddess Grasstree *15ml ifer 1652*

➕ Key Words: mature nurturing patient supportive unconditional love

⊖ Key Words: overbearing hard judgmental severe manipulative emotional clinging dependent

For the maturing of the female principle or woman within. For both men and women a metamorphosis to inner strength, nurturing sensitivity and loving wisdom that is not emotionally dependent. Helpful in releasing the feminine aspect into society.

## Golden Glory Grevillea *15ml ifer 1653*

+ Key Words: open sociable confident expressive detached

− Key Words: withdrawing aversion shy wary cut off

An essence of confidence for those who feel more comfortable withdrawing from people than dealing with criticism. Enables one to detach from the judgmental attitudes of others and feel free to join in social situations.

## Golden Waitsia *15ml ifer 1654*

+ Key Words: broadening carefree expansive adaptable

− Key Words: perfectionism worry petty small perspective

To re-ignite spontaneity and carefree feelings, to heal all aspects of anxiety linked to perfectionism. Helpful for those who worry about details, and also those needing to accept their present imperfect state of health and well being while convalescing from illness or trauma

## Green Rose *15ml ifer 1655*

+ Key Words: break-through change progress focus vigour

− Key Words: indolent stagnation resentment defeated

This essence helps fight stagnation and repetition of mistakes. For frustration. To enhance forward movement through a problem without sudden leaps back to square one. Helpful for maintaining disciplines and healthy habits for body, mind and spirit.

## Hairy Yellow Pea *15ml ifer 3361*

+ Key Words: decision patience direction wisdom calm

− Key Words: anxious scattered overwhelmed inexperienced

The essence of patience in finding direction in life which leads to peaceful settling of the mind. This patience allows time for the consolidation of experiences so one can make decisions with greater wisdom and determination , and not be influenced into erratic action driven by one's own anxiety.

## Happy Wanderer *15ml ifer 1656*

+ Key Words: Self assured independent determination capable

− Key Words: trepidation insecure under-confidence emotionally dependent

To inspire standing on one's own feet, to be able to achieve with one's own strength. For issues of dependency. Whether it is trepidation about striking out on a new path less travelled by others, being able to let go of the need for a backup person or simply fear of doing things alone. This essence inspires a realisation of self reliance and determination.

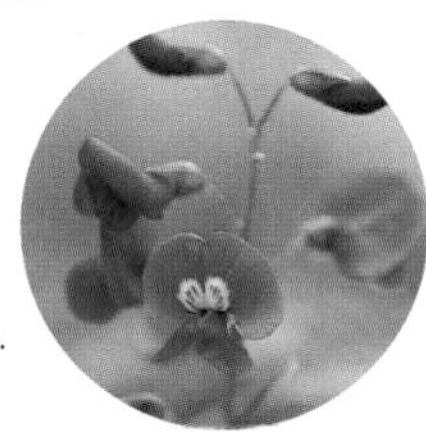

## Hops Bush *15ml ifer 1657*

+ Key Words: relaxation release rest peace

− Key Words: frenetic hyper over-active scattered energy stress

This essence earths excessive, scattered energy and re-establishes a natural and healthy flow which feeds the needs of activity without over stimulating. With this inner mental and physical peace the person feels back in control of their life and can have balanced states of rest and activity. For those who can't sleep or relax due to frenetic energy unbalancing them.

## Hybrid Pink Fairy/Cowslip Orchid *15ml ifer 1658*

+ Key Words: inner strength discriminating resilient stability

− Key Words: over-sensitive influenced reactionary emotional

This essence is as a filter and inner strengthener so that a person is not going up and down with the praise and condemnation of others. For those psychically sensitive, it helps to relieve the burden of that sensitivity by engendering a contentment generated by their own inner centre. Helpful also with pre-menstrual syndrome and sensitivity of pregnancy, creating instead a rosy glow of inner tranquility. Also for those wishing to overcome nervousness when speaking in public.
For those who are extra- sensitive to the thoughts and judgments of others.

## Illyarrie *15ml ifer 1659*

+ Key Words: fearless joy bright exuberant fun realization

− Key Words: downcast hurt avoiding suppressed memory fear

The essence of joy and courage to face and deal with past shadows and pain. To inspire the knowledge that there is no pain that can't be dealt with, it is never as bad as you fear, it will not overwhelm you, you are stronger than it. Helpful also in psychotherapy, rebirthing & past life therapy to uncover forgotten or hidden experiences affecting the present state of being.

## Leafless Orchid *15ml ifer 1661*

+ Key Words: centering energizing balance sustain wholeness

− Key Words: depleted tired worn out drained overwhelmed

This essence stimulates the inner core of one's being to take control of life situations. It helps one to come from a central energy where depth and breadth of vision ensures no energy is needlessly wasted on peripheral issues. The effect is to deepen understanding of what caring for and helping a person can really mean. To know also when to stand back for that person's deeper welfare. Helpful for feelings of depletion in those whose work or life is in the service of others.

## Macrozamia *15ml ifer 1662*

➕ Key Words: balance equilibrium release sexual wholeness love union

➖ Key Words: blocked stereotyped sexual problems negative images

For healing and restoring balance to all aspects of male/female, Yin/Yang energy flows. To release blockages to these primal and vital flows brought about by sexual trauma, underdevelopment, fear or loathing of the opposite sex and hormonal fluctuations. Also helpful in physical manifestations of these blockages such as for restoring balance to the water element in the body as this essence basically re-harmonizes the sex / water chakra.

## Many Headed Dryandra

*15ml ifer 1663*

➕ Key Words: dedication commitment inspired fulfillment consistent

➖ Key Words: irresponsible run away overwhelmed freaked out

This essence calms, strengthens and inspires the person to face and deal with their life and relationships so that stability and fulfillment come together for them at last. With new found consistency there is a deepening and maturing in all aspects of Life. For those with difficulties, such as panic and a need to run away when facing responsibility in work or family life.

## Mauve Melaleuca *15ml ifer 1666*

➕ Key Words: contentment idealism inner constant love

➖ Key Words: hurt anger disappointed needy frustrated

This essence inspires the realisation that idealism about love is important, that being loved is wonderful, it is eternally with us and sometimes also given to us from the external world. For healing those who are holding in sadness and great hurt, this is the essence of finding higher love. The depths of love these people long for are more surely found within the depths of themselves, where it can never leave them.

## Menzies Banksia *15ml ifer 1667*

➕ Key Words: freeing joyousness healing courage regeneration

➖ Key Words: fear trepidation hesitation pessimism pain

To move on through, and past, pain and into new experiences of life without fear. For those who have been hurt, expect to be hurt again and thus close doors of opportunity. Especially in the realms of human relations, this fear and hesitation blocks joyful new beginnings. This essence encourages regeneration, renewal and courage using painful experiences as an opportunity for greater depth.

## One-sided Bottlebrush

*15ml ifer 1668*

➕ Key Words: awareness in touch appreciation perspective

➖ Key Words: complaining burdened isolated

The essence of awareness and balance of focus. For those feeling they are unfairly carrying everyone's work-load on their own shoulders. For those feeling unsupported and overwhelmed, such as people in leadership positions or situations such as being a single parent or self employed. This essence helps one refocus on the contribution that others make, then sensitivity to their problems and burdens is born. This awareness and empathy can serve to improve everyone's situation.

## Orange Leschenaultia

*15ml ifer 1669*

➕ Key Words: softness tender sensitive compassion

➖ Key Words: hardened gruff intolerant selfish

This essence brings one in touch with the softness of life and empathy re-emerges. The hardened outer skin then becomes subtle and supple again, and is able to receive and give love. For those who have been gradually closing up and de-sensitising because of the harsh realities of life and human relations.

## Orange Spiked Pea *15ml ifer 1670*

➕ Key Words: expressive articulate calm communicate detached

➖ Key Words: angry hurt explosive uncontrolled provoked bottled up

To enhance full expression, response and articulation of feelings without being angered or provoked to violence. To inspire the detachment to let harsh words pass through you and not damage your equipoise. To stop and think and come from a higher aspect in yourself before reacting to hurt by producing more hurt.

## Pale Sundew *15ml ifer 1672*

➕ Key Words: kindness conscience perspective justice light

➖ Key Words: manipulative arrogant duplicity deception predatory

The essence of conscience. For those who get caught in rapacious, manipulative power playing for their own gain and lose sight of the reality of natural Karma where Life asserts justice. This essence raises the consciousness of the person to see the futility of what they are doing and its effects on others. As the light of conscience pierces the inner darkness a new person is born.

## Parakeelya *15ml ifer 1673*

+ Key Words: self esteem assertive dignity inner strength

− Key Words: withdraw unappreciated work horse compromising

The essence of self esteem and assertiveness. For hard working people feeling increasingly lonely and sad because they are unappreciated and treated like a work-horse. This essence restores the sense of self dignity, with an inner strength to not withdraw but be actively part of society and able to one's assert rights as an individual.

## Pincushion Hakea *15ml ifer 1674*

+ Key Words: open exploring accepting discriminating inquisitive

− Key Words: limited dogmatic closed defensive

The essence of opening up to new concepts and ideas. To take the fear out of the unknown and untried. To inspire full acceptance of the beliefs of others without feeling unduly persuaded against your better judgment. Helpful for those who feel intimidated by others, views and find themselves being automatically defensive and dogmatic.

## Pink Everlasting *15ml ifer 1675*

+ Key Words: sustaining responsive replenishing

− Key Words: empty dry unfulfilled burnt out

This essence is helpful in restoring the milk of human kindness to the hearts of those whose caring has run out. This happens because it is an emotionally based response. The kindness that will never run out comes from a much higher and richer source, beyond personal limitations of energy, and this is what this essence gets one in touch with. For those who feel dried out and have no more to give. For feelings of emptiness in dealing with people.

## Pink Fairy Orchid *15ml ifer 1676*

+ Key Words: serenity equipoise inner peace resilient composure

− Key Words: reacting disturbed stressed overwhelmed nervy

This essence calms the inner core enabling a person to carry their own peace with them and be discerning as to what elements of the external world they will allow to activate their attention. For those stressed by environmental chaos or pressure. Helpful for those easily influenced and changed by noises, clamour or emotionally charged environments.

## Pink Fountain Triggerplant *15ml ifer 1677*

+ Key Words: restoring vigour re-connecting vitality

− Key Words: exhausted unable to cope drained lifeless

This essence re-ignites the vital flame and restores its dynamism to the point where the person can take over this most essential responsibility. For those who are losing their inner vital force which keeps one alive, either by a slow draining on the physical level, or a cutting off in the subtle bodies.

## Pink Impatiens *15ml ifer 1678*

+ Key Words: courage prevail inner strength determination

− Key Words: compromised overwhelmed opposition struggle

To encourage maintaining the fight for one's morality amidst opposition. This essence promotes the inner strength of one's convictions to prevail without compromise even when the struggle seems long and potentially overwhelming. Helpful for those who feel they have to give in and accept defeat when they feel unsupported or unlucky in the ideals they strive for.

## Pink Trumpet Flower *15ml ifer 1679*

+ Key Words: focused purposeful achievement mental vigour

− Key Words: vague meandering unconnected unfocused

The essence of clarity and focus. To harness the inner strength of purpose and direct it towards important goals. Encourages achievement through new mental directness. Helpful for those who find difficulty in maintaining purpose, who feel they get lost half way through a thought process or activity. Also excellent for attaining healing objectives and for directing energy at childbirth.

## Pixie Mops *15ml ifer 1680*

+ Key Words: considerate compassion

− Key Words: resentful reactionary hurt hardening

This essence frees and strengthens the heart so that one does not become like the very people one resents.
In this way to become a helpful understanding person, such as is needed by yourself, and others in the world every day. For dependency / resentment cycles where a sensitive person becomes hard after being let down by other people.

## Purple & Red Kangaroo Paw
*15ml ifer 1685*

+ Key Words: openness sensitivity understanding

− Key Words: blaming arguing critisising reacting

This essence inspires partners to drop the blame game and concentrate on sensitivity to the other person, thus allowing constructive re-building of trust and other solutions. Helpful for objective self analysis and rebalancing of partnerships. For relationships with circular arguments of blame.

## Purple Enamel Orchid *15ml ifer 1681*

+ Key Words: openness sensitivity understanding vulnerability

− Key Words: blaming negative arguing criticizing reacting

This essence instills consistency in achievement and energy output. Helpful for those who do too little, then too much - and then collapse. The practical use of energy encourages better self esteem and confidence, proving oneself is then no longer an issue. Helpful also for those who feel defeated, useless and are feeling unable to prove to others that they can reach a goal.

## Purple Eremophila *15ml ifer 1682*

➕ Key Words: calm diplomatic balanced settled

⊖ Key Words: emotional messes confusion hopeless

To gain and maintain serene objectivity amidst very personal issues of the heart that threaten to unbalance you. This essence encourages the objectivity without compromising richness of feeling and sensitivity towards loved ones, and is very helpful in times of relationship upsets.

## Purple Flag Flower *15ml ifer 1683*

➕ Key Words: release relief unwind relax

⊖ Key Words: tense pressure stress anxious

To release build up of pressure and tension and allow healing relaxation of body and mind. To enhance the unwinding process and to release the sense of having to automatically react tensely to situations. Very helpful for those who feel rising stress and those who find themselves on the edge of a breakdown.

## Purple Nymph Waterlily (Liani) *15ml ifer 1684*

➕ Key Words: Selfless Love heart depth impartial freeing

⊖ Key Words: emotional frustration hurt unfulfilled

The essence of selfless service. To drink deep from the deeper side of one's Love nature. To not be caught in emotional traps in your dealings with fellow humans or your own Life path. To sensitise to a point beyond personalisation, freeing the heart with service. Helpful for those who are desiring to merge with the Uniyersal purpose and on all levels, practical and internal, share their treasures with others.

## Queensland Bottlebrush
*15ml ifer 1686*

➕ Key Words: at ease social interaction balanced energy

⊖ Key Words: discomfort drained hermit unsettled avoiding

This essence helps transmute reservations about the demands of being social into a liberated social manner. The change in focus to one's general internal direction ensures a healthy flow of energy and ability to enjoy and deal with people without hesitation. For feelings of restlessness, discomfort and tiredness that are accentuated in the company of others.

## Rabbit Orchid *15ml ifer 1687*

➕ Key Words: true Self revealing open depth honest

⊖ Key Words: masking obligatory shallow image insecure

This essence helps one not to rely on external images and masks and to desire honest and meaningful connections to people. For those who want to find their true and deeper Self Frustration with shallow, empty and obligatory relationships is brought to an end by seeking the greater depth in the Self and other people. Very revealing and freeing for inner growth, helpful also with all types of psychotherapy and counselling to get past protective facades to the inner riches.

## Red & Green Kangaroo Paw *15ml ifer 1690*

➕ Key Words: in touch patient sensitive closeness attentive

⊖ Key Words: absent distracted distant restless ambitious

To bring one back in touch with loved ones, promoting sensitivity. To be in the here and now, patiently, allowing time and space for closeness and the little joys of life together. Helpful for busy mums, dads and spouses who find their distracted behaviour is creating distance in relationships.

## Red Beak Orchid *15ml ifer 1688*

➕ Key Words: enthusiasm resolve holistic

⊖ Key Words: uninspired lethargic frustrated

This essence renews energy and inspiration to attend to all facets of life creatively and with equal enthusiasm. For those caught in a conflict between desire and duties, personal expression and responsibilities. Helpful for lethargy and listlessness, also adolescence and mid-life dilemmas of rebellion or frustration about duties and family ties.

## Red Feather Flower *15ml ifer 1689*

➕ Key Words: helpful sharing supportive enthusiasm energy

⊖ Key Words: lazy burdening isolated rebellious resentful

This essence helps a person rely on their own energy and be aware of sharing burdens in family and community life. The return of this energy flow then sees a general boost to overall energy output and creativity- in all areas of the person's endeavour. For problems with energy and, attitudes leading to laziness.

## Red Leschenaultia *15ml ifer 1691*

➕ Key Words: sensitize melting bliss Love closeness gentility

⊖ Key Words: cold harsh uncaring closed contempt for weakness

The essence of gentleness and sensitivity. To re-open the heart, engendering empathy with the problems of others which then becomes an opportunity for openness and the merging of souls. Especially helpful for couples and family relations where harshness and brittle attitudes are stopping the love, joy and closeness of life together.

## Reed Triggerplant *15ml ifer 3476*

➕ Key Words: rejuvenate restore withstand revitalize recover

⊖ Key Words: struggle exhausted worn down depleted not coping

This wildflower essence helps bring back the feeling of wholeness of being where one's integral self is restored. It works to heal and then integrate and revitalise the parts of the mind that are full of trauma, and therefore being kept isolated in the mind to prevent further trauma. Once the person feels their inner strength restored, the mind is unified and has the inherent ability to withstand the thrusts and parries of life.

## Ribbon Pea *15ml ifer 1692*

+ Key Words: fearless calm accepting positive

− Key Words: foreboding dread anxiety fear

To rise above fear and foreboding that stops us from taking positive attitudes and directions that are desired for a fulfilling life. Helpful for those who feel a sense of nameless dread and don't understand why they feel that way. Healing the panic of fear of annihilation.

## Rose Cone Flower *15ml ifer 1693*

+ Key Words: peace tranquility inner quiet at ease

− Key Words: tense stressed edgy disturbed hassled

The essence of holding peace and inner tranquility. For those who find environmental distractions and the company of people make them increasingly tense. This essence promotes an inner strengthening which enables the inner peace to hold despite external happenings. A person is then able to maintain themselves in all situations with equanimity and sweetness of mind. Helpful for parents and those in the "people" professions.

## Shy Blue Orchid *15ml ifer 1696*

+ Key Words: break through dynamism inspired free to express

− Key Words: oppressed powerless unresolved obstructed

Focuses spiritual energies that will consistently break up negative oppressive forces in the environment. This essence gives a sense of protection and dynamism where powerlessness has previously prevailed. This is a deep, internally inspiring and extremely subtle flower essence which is of great benefit to those dedicated to the Path of Light.

## Silver Princess Gum, Gungurra *15ml ifer 1697*

+ Key Words: challenge overcoming mastering persistence

− Key Words: giving up stagnancy rebellious frustrated

For inspiring inner strength of perseverance when things aren't working out. To keep caring for others and not give up or rebel. Encourages one to achieve goals despite the obstacles. Particularly effective for adolescent growing pains, getting students past learning dead-ends, establishing healthy disciplines (caring about ending an unhealthy addiction) and for those who feel in a stagnant malaise.

## Snakebush *15ml ifer 1699*

+ Key Words: fulfilled inner contentment independent Self Love

− Key Words: needy hurt bitterness submissive demanding

The essence of deep fulfilling Self Love. For those disillusioned by the lack of love from others who they have loved. This essence encourages a self contained yet caring attitude to others which brings about an inner emotional contentment. The "needy" feelings towards loved ones are then transformed into a sensitivity from a centre of Self Love.

## Snakevine *15ml ifer 1700*

+ Key Words: optimism confidence positivity encouragement

− Key Words: undermined attacked sad uneasy struggling

This essence brings back confidence and appreciation of our achievements even when all around is malice and doubt. For those who are the target for negativity and find they are losing vitality. With renewed vitality in our goals and objectives it is possible to move out of the sphere of influence of these negative projections into the free space of positivity and success.

## Southern Cross *15ml ifer 1701*

+ Key Words: understanding aware accepting empathy wisdom

− Key Words: judgmental inexperienced condemning short sighted

The essence of empathy, to help one get in touch with how l ife is experienced by others and to integrate this into one's understanding. To look at life from a perspective that encompasses all the possibilities a person can face and thus lose any judgmental attitudes. To inspire the realisation that " one day it could be me in that situation" and so also to prepare oneself for the twists and turns that life may present you with. Also helpful for those finding themselves in trauma and unable to cope due to lack of experience of such things.

## Spirit Faces (Banjine)

*15ml ifer 3362*

+ Key Words: perspective decentralizing Selfless appreciating

− Key Words: focus on self self engrossed fixated

This essence inspires an outlook where one's own concerns don't have to always be prominent. The world turns with or without you. The decentralising of one's focus brings one in touch with the beauty and joy that surrounds all life and one can appreciate it anew.

## Star of Bethlehem *15ml ifer 1708*

+ Key Words: resolutions creativity open mind hope opportunities

− Key Words: blocked hopelessness blank no options tunnel vision

The essence of creative solutions and breaking through. For those who feel there is no way out of their dilemmas, that they are facing locked doors on all sides. This essence brings about the realisation and mental force to break into the realms of infinite options and choice which have always been there. With new creativity and hope, life situations are completely turned around. Also helpful for releasing and manifesting the artistic and other creative talents in people.

## Start's Spider Orchid

*15ml ifer 3477*

⊕ Key Words: directness straightforward decisive resolving

⊖ Key Words: compromised avoiding messy unclear frustrating

The essence of directness and straightforwardness. Learning to deal with difficult people and situations in a benevolent but successful manner. To stimulate the mind to focus on what is real and important, bringing out the courage within to cut through emotional smoke screens in communications with people.

## Swan River Myrtle *15ml ifer 3475*

⊕ Key Words: fairness inner strength positivity insight

⊖ Key Words: suffering injustice or perpetrator of injustice victim of unfairness or unfair person

Healing with this flower manifests within oneself a non-compromising attitude towards fairness both from ourselves and from others. Secondly, it stops one getting emotionally caught when someone is unfair. By not accommodating another's unfairness, being taken for granted ends, this puts the responsibility on to the other person to examine their behaviour.

## Urchin Dryandra *15ml ifer 1703*

⊕ Key Words: happy Self appreciation Self worth

⊖ Key Words: inferiority victim sad down trodden

This essence boosts the sense of self worth and a person's understanding of how they got in their "victim" situation. For those with feelings of inferiority due to suffering unkindness from people they cared for. Helpful for those feeling down-trodden after relationship break ups and the underdog in an ongoing relationship.

## Ursinia *15ml ifer 1704*

⊕ Key Words: wisdom co-ordination integrating taking responsibility

⊖ Key Words: disillusioned disheartened criticizing unrealistic

The essence of integration and wisdom in working with groups of people or in the family. To accept the reality of group dynamics and retain idealism. To inspire one to work constructively with the group to keep the flow and growth in a healthy direction despite problems with egos, dishonest communication and other common destructive elements. One then works with and engenders positivity and deals effectively with negativity.

## Veronica *15ml ifer 1705*

⊕ Key Words: fellowship bridging open re-orientate expression

⊖ Key Words: isolated retiring lonely sad misunderstood

This essence re-orientates sensitivity towards others and the bridges one must make in order to bring about understanding. With this realisation comes the desire to meet people half way, or more if necessary, to engender friendship and fellowship. For those who feel misunderstood and therefore isolated and lonely.

## Violet Butterfly *15ml ifer 1706*

⊕ Key Words: restoring capacity regain Love recovery whole

⊖ Key Words: emotionally shattered trauma overwhelmed

This essence calms the flaring sensitivities and emotional pain that so stress a person. For healing those who are feeling emotionally shattered during and after relationship traumas, such as break-ups. During these experiences they despair of any possibility of having love in their life. This essence speeds their emotional recovery, healing the damage and allowing them to pass on through to the rest of their life.

## W. A. Smokebush *15ml ifer 1709*

⊕ Key Words: connected whole re-integrated clear headed

⊖ Key Words: vague disconnected directionless faint stress fear

This essence helps to re-integrate the subtle and more physical aspects of your being into a functioning whole again. Helpful also in cases of difficulty in concentration, fainting and after anaesthesia to promote quick recovery of mind/body connections so important for the healing processes. For anxiety, vagueness and feeling muddled caused by the mind and body separating in times of extreme stress.

## Wattle *15ml ifer 3479*

⊕ Key Words: alert wise mature aware responsible

⊖ Key Words: naive scattered vulnerable avoid facing reality

The essence to steady the mind-focus and inspire facing up to the realities and consequences of choices. To be alert to all aspects of a situation and be prepared to take them into account. To have a mature and wise view of Life. To avoid unnecessary dangers.

## White Eremophila *15ml ifer 1710*

⊕ Key Words: clarity perspective observing objectivity

⊖ Key Words: tangled up preconceived ideas reacting unclear

The essence of clarity for those engulfed in complexities and difficulties. To help one develop a broad perspective when messy situations are threatening to drag you down. Helpful in maintaining equipoise, consistency and direction in your life.

## White Nymph Waterlily (Liani) *15ml ifer 1711*

⊕ Key Words: Spiritual perspective emotional purification inner calm meditation

⊖ Key Words: desires denied frustrated caught lack of vision

For the uncovering of the deepest spiritual core. This is an essence of tranquility that encourages pulling back the layers to reach the soul level. It also inspires using the higher self to integrate and respond to Life from the most Universal perspective possible for one's evolution at the time, rather than one's personal perspective. Helpful for spiritual practices such as meditation.

## White Spider Orchid
*15ml ifer 1641*

⊕ Key Words: sustaining maintaining love rise above purpose

⊖ Key Words: overwhelmed sadness anguish introversion aversion

To bring love and caring to the darkest corners of the universe without being devastated by the insensitivity and overwhelming suffering around you. For those who seek to help make this planet a better place for all. Helpful and inspiring for those in the caring professions and in volunteer service, by engendering a higher perspective on the purpose of pain in the journey of the soul.

## Wild Violet *15ml ifer 1712*

⊕ Key Words: explore open courage happiness

⊖ Key Words: over cautious pessimistic apprehensive worry

The essence of balance between caution and courageous decision making. For those who feet unable to trust new opportunities in their life because of unknown outcomes, and find that this view stops them from experiencing life. It can also lead to a sense of fatalism and negativity about the flow of life in general. Helpfuil for worrying and pessimistic tendencies.

## Woolly Banksia *15ml ifer 1713*

⊕ Key Words: belief in success optimism renewed idealism

⊖ Key Words: fatalistic disheartened unsure sad defeatist

To be able to face new goals without fear of inevitable failure. For those who are losing heart this essence rekindles the desire to go ahead with ideals and goals when the struggle seems too much.
Helpful during long, tiring and seemingly pointless phases in the journey to reach one's higher aspirations.

## Woolly Smokebush *15ml ifer 1714*

⊕ Key Words: Self perspective humility objectivity

⊖ Key Words: dramatic exaggerating self orientated

The essence of perspective and humility. Helps one avoid the traps of glamour and self importance so that life is seen with objectivity. Without this objectivity situations and one's part in them can be dramatised beyond their importance and central vital issues can be neglected. Helpful for maintaining forward progress without distracting oneself.

## Yellow & Green Kangaroo Paw *15ml ifer 1718*

⊕ Key Words: tolerance encouraging understanding teaching

⊖ Key Words: hard perfectionist impatient chastising

The essence of tolerance and understanding for those frustrated by the mistakes of others. The realisation comes that there is value in making mistakes when a person is guided by the sincerity and benevolence of another. With this sensitivity, judgmental attitudes drop away and relationships prosper.

## Yellow Boronia *15ml ifer 1715*

⊕ Key Words: concentration study calm focus

⊖ Key Words: over active scattered restless shallow distracted

This essence is calming and centering for the mind. Inspires deeper contemplation. For those who can't focus or concentrate and follow a thought through. Helpful for students of all ages and those who have 4ifficulty with distraction.

## Yellow Cone Flower *15ml ifer 1716*

⊕ Key Words: self recognition positivity self esteem

⊖ Key Words: under valued inferiority complex unaccepted

This essence turns the perspective around to encourage a realisation that the first and most important opinion is the one you have about yourself. From this then comes personal objectives for growth and expansion built on positivity and self assessment rather than outside recognition. For those who have low self esteem because they feel they are not valued by others.

## Yellow Flag Flower *15ml ifer 1717*

⊕ Key Words: carefree light hearted jovial balanced strength

⊖ Key Words: stressed sombre glum up-tight unprepared

To have lightheartedness and calmness despite rising pressure and tension so that Inner peace and relationships with others do not suffer. To find fortitude and wisdom to handle stressful phases without making life one long hard chore. Helpful in keeping the mind in a positive frame where it can enjoy the garden of Life.

## Yellow Leschenaultia *15ml ifer 1719*

+ Key Words: open listening understanding wisdom learning

– Key Words: dismissive intolerant insensitive impatient arrogant

For stimulating open-mindedness which then receives knowledge and the concepts of others. This essence calms the mind and dispels the illusion that we hear even when we don't listen. The message people are trying to convey is then fully understood and relationships with others improve dramatically. Helpful with learning difficulties in children and adults including autism and attention deficit disorder. In learning not to assume that one does know, full expansion of consciousness is possible.

### Using the Flower Essence Creams and Lotions

These creams and lotions are made with the gentle properties of Australian wildflower essences mixed into a vegetable cream base. They are the result of more than fifteen years of research and development by Living Essences Laboratories in Perth, Western Australia. These preparations can be used in all bodywork therapies like massage, chiropractic, physiotherapy and reflexology plus as an everyday use for the person at home or at work.

## Body Bliss *250ml ifer 1664 / 500ml ifer 3419*

The flower essences Body Bliss works to reduce stress and promote a feeling of well-being and relaxation. If muscles are tight because of stress, a gentle massage with Body Bliss helps to ease tension and allows both body and mind to relax. Try using Body Bliss for conditions where a calming effect would be beneficial, for example, the temporary relief of the symptoms of tension headaches, tension pain and insomnia, and to ease anxiety which causes the tightening of the lungs, apply the lotion to the chest, back and neck. The lotion is an excellent massage medium; full results can be achieved with only one simple application

## Comfort Cream *125ml ifer 2331 / 240ml ifer 1671*

Microvita Pain Cream is like a first-aid kit in a bottle for muscular aches and pains and many other conditions where pain and discomfort are a problem. The flower essences in Pain Cream can be helpful for the temporary relief of the symptoms of muscles in spasm, pulled muscles torn ligaments, minor sprains and bruising, back and neck pain, sciatic pain, headaches, sinus pain, sunburn and insect bites and itches. Microvita Pain Cream will also provide temporary relief of menstrual

## Body Sports *240ml ifer 1665 / 500ml ifer 3458*

A body lotion which is useful for the temporary relief of general aches and pains. Body Sports provides an excellent massage medium, full results can be achieved with one simple application. Sports people in particular can try using Body Sports before sport or exercise to help prevent injuries. Rub the lotion into the legs, arms and back or any part of the body which may be prone to strain or injury. It is easily absorbed by the skin and can be used quite liberally if desired. The lotion also has an invigorating effect. Body Sports and the Pain Cream are based on a similar combination of flower essences, but Body Sports is formulated as a lotion for all-over application, whereas the Pain Cream is recommended for specific trouble spots.

## De-stress Moisturiser *125ml ifer 2333 / 240ml ifer 3315*

A Moisturising cream with stress relieving qualities. Using De-Stress Moisturiser daily can help to ease tension and allow both body and mind to relax, as well as improving skin lustre and appearance. To help reduce stress and promote a feeling of well-being and relaxation apply De-Stress Moisturiser as a moisturiser or after shave to the nerve rich facial area. De-Stress Moisturiser Cream and Body Bliss are based on a similar combination of flower essences, but the De-Stress Moisturiser has been specially formulated for use on the face.

## Easy Joint Cream *125ml ifer 2332 / 240ml ifer 1630*

This cream has been specially formulated for sufferers of Osteo arthritis. The therapeutic effects of the Arthritis Cream is derived from the specific flower essences which are recommended by Living Essences Laboratories for the symptomatic relief of the rigidity and the particular and different pain resulting from arthritic conditions. Regular daily application according to directions is essential for best results. The treatment takes four to six weeks to take effect, although many feel the benefits immediately, and some who have had their complaint for many years will need a longer time before the effects are fully felt. If the arthritis is spreading to the rest of the body or is in many places, it is best to apply the cream all over the body four times a day.

# **Combination** Essences

## Crisis Relief Drops

For times of shock and trauma. This essence combination is designed for times of crisis, when one finds it hard to cope with sudden events which impact negatively on one's vital force and nervous system.
COMBINATION OF ESSENCES: Cowkicks, Red Beak Orchid, Donkey Orchid, White Spider Orchid, Southern Cross.
ORAL DOSE: taken, one drop under the tongue, every twenty minutes or so, as needed, over a time of crisis and depletion.

## Essence of Emotions In Balance

Relieves Emotional Churning, Re-Affirms One'S Quiet Centre. This essence combination reflects internal causes for highly emotional states: Needing more clarity and an objective, balanced perspective, need for greater resiliency and dealing with relationship upsets calmly and realistically.
COMBINATION OF ESSENCES: White Nymph Waterlily, Goddess Grasstree, Purple Eremophila
ORAL DOSAGE: 6 drops in a glass of water in the evening.

## Essence of Positivity

Brightens Outlook, Rebuilds Capacity For Joy This essence combination reflects internal causes for lack of positivity: Being caught up in minute details, tending to be pessimistic, becoming glum and negative when becoming stressed, feelings of inevitable failure because of past experiences.
COMBINATION OF ESSENCES: Golden Waitsia, Wild Violet, Yellow Flag Flower, Woolly Banksia.
ORAL DOSAGE: 6 drops in a glass of water before bed.

### Essence of Clarity

Brings A Calm Focus, Centering Of Mental Energy This essence combination reflects internal causes for difficulties in concentration and meditation: Lack of Yang energy which encourages setting and achieving goals, scattered mental energy, inability to centralize energy, difficulty in focusing and carrying through an activity to its completion.
COMBINATION OF ESSENCES: Balga,Yellow Boronia, Leafless Orchid, Pink Trumpet.
ORAL DOSAGE: 6 drops in a glass of water before bedtime.

### Essence of Creativity

Opening Up To Expanded Thought. This essence combination reflects internal causes for blocked creativity: Being resigned to a lack of options and creative solutions, needing more flexibility, needing openness to learning, difficulty in focusing and carrying through an activity to its completion, being caught up in minute details.
COMBINATION OF ESSENCES: Star of Bethlehem, Dampiera, Yellow Leschenaultia, Pink Trumpet, Golden Waitsia.
ORAL DOSAGE: 6 drops in a glass of water around sunset.

### Essence of Energy

Revitalizing Energizing, Rebuilds Vigour This essence combination reflects internal causes for lack of energy: inner conflict between desires and responsibilities, the aftermath of shattering experiences, and loss of energy due to expectation of further painful experiences.
COMBINATION OF ESSENCES: Red Beak Orchid, Cowkicks, Menzies Banksia.
ORAL DOSAGE : 6 drops in a glass of water around sunset

### Essence of Inner Strength

Brings Back Vital Force. This essence combination reflects internal causes for lack of inner strength: Depletion of vital force, being easily unbalanced by outside influences, needing resilience, swinging between high and low energy levels.
COMBINATION OF ESSENCES: Pink Fountain Triggerplant, Hybrid Pink Fairy/Cowslip Orchid, Goddess Grasstree, Purple Enamel Orchid.
ORAL DOSAGE: 6 drops in a glass of water before 9pm.

### Essence of Relaxation

Releases Feelings Of Rising Pressure , Calms Scattered Frenetic Energy This essence combination reflects internal causes for the inability to relax: Needing more clarity and an objective balanced perspective, e,optional stress, irritability due to little quiet or private space, worry, feelings of rising pressure and states of frenetic, scattered energy.
COMBINATION OF ESSENCES: White Nymph and Purple Nymph Waterlily, Rosecone Flower, Brown Boronia, Purple Flag Flower, Hops Bush.
ORAL DOSAGE: 6 drops in a glass of water in the evening.

### Sneezease

Allergic reactions effecting the sinuses are very debilitating. An allergic reaction is the body's response to a perceived threat. It is the over reaction to environmental factors which causes the majority of allergic reactions. This essence is designed to ameliorate this overreaction, by breaking down overly sensitive defensive programming. Take one drop on top of the tongue and apply to centre of forehead, fontanel and acupuncture points, Du20 and Du18 every hour.

## Essence Mists

### Love Life Plus for Men Chakra Mist

Balances the sex chakra in men. Yogic science teaches that the psychic centre called the Svadisthan Chakra, conditions sex life and the hormonal secretions of the reproductive glands. Imbalance in these glands affects Libido, Courage, Aggressive Tendencies and Vulnerability. Spray around Pubic area, sacral vertebrae, and along the centre or the head starting at the hairline on the front of the head to the top of the back of the neck. The healing effect of this essence combination builds, so it needs to be used on a daily basis and not only when symptoms are present.

### Love Life Plus for Women Chakra Mist

Balances the sex chakra in woman. Yogic science teaches that the psychic centre called the Svadisthan Chakra conditions sex life and the hormonal secretions of the reproductive glands. Imbalance in these glands affects Libido, PMT, Period pain, and symptoms of Menopause. Spray around Pubic area, sacral vertebrae, and navel area six times per day. The healing affect of this essence combination builds so it needs to be used on a daily basis and not only when symptoms are present.

### Relaxation and Harmony Mist

Often we enter a house or building and although the surroundings are aesthetically pleasant we feel unsettled or uncomfortable. In such situations we register negative subtle vibrations that permeate the atmosphere of the building. These vibrations lie beyond the frequency that our physical senses can register, however our subconscious does register these vibrations and that is why we feel uncomfortable or unsettled. In our home, habitual stress and disharmonious reactions impregnate our environment with stress and discordant vibrations. Such atmospheres support or feed the stress and disharmony within us, compounding the undesirable discord between others and ourselves. Within our own atmosphere or aura we may need to overcome the stress and disharmony that builds up over the day. The Relaxation and Harmony Spray is designed to be sprayed into our surroundings and or around oneself to help overcome stress and disharmony. The flowers used in the relaxation and harmony spray are designed to clear ones environment of stress, disharmony, lethargy and intimidating vibrations.

### Travelease Mist

Many find travel de-vitalising, stressful and disorientating for the body clock. Traveleaze is designed to minimize the negative affects of travel and bring a speedy recovery from the above symptoms. Spray the back of neck hourly for the duration of travel. After reaching the destination use as needed.

# Living Tree **Orchid** Essences

## Region: West Sussex, England

## Founded: 1998

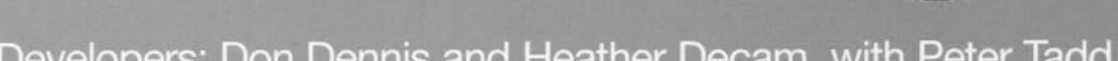

Developers: Don Dennis and Heather Decam, with Peter Tadd

Don Dennis first encountered the Bach Remedies in his students days when he came over to England from the USA. His interest in orchids stems from meeting SSK of the Dancing Light Orchid Essences, who inspired him to grow a few. That few is now several hundred! Heather Decam has always felt a quiet yet deep connection with nature, and together they have been exploring the spiritual and healing qualities of the orchids though the essence making. Their mutual friend Peter Tadd has been involved from the outset in providing a detailed analysis of the qualities and actions of each essence, and in helping to establish a deeper and detailed understanding of the energetic aspects of the process of essence making. The method of making the essences is designed to have a minimum of energetic footprint from the makers.

The Essences: Almost 10% of flowering plants are orchids, and they are grown by an estimated 4 million people worldwide, yet very little research has been done into their healing qualities as essences. Andreas Korte of Germany pointed out that they are able to reach into the chakras above the body – a key point, confirmed by Peter Tadd independently – and Shabd-sangeet Khalsa took the pioneering step of making essences with tropical orchids grown within a greenhouse environment. The orchids of the Living Tree line are quite varied, with a focus on the Phragmipediums and Paphiopedilums, but including some tropical orchids which are not commonly encountered. Being lovingly looked after enables a rich process of interaction for Don and Heather in the process of working with the orchids.

### **Unveiling Affection** *Phragmipedium Hanne Popow*

*15ml ifer 4116*

For loving and nurturing oneself, as well as opening one's heart with affection to those around one. Good for anyone who has ever felt emotionally bereft, or who has difficulty valuing and caring for themselves. To hold affection in your heart, for both self and others.

### **White Beauty Aura Spray**

*Phalenopsis aphrodite & Rose Quartz, with rose otto oil*

*120ml ifer 5538*

Nurturing and de-stressing. Envelopes one with unconditional love, akin to that of a mother for a newborn child. Refreshing, and mildly relaxing, can be used as a post-trauma spray for both people and animals.

### **Messenger of the Heart** *Phragmipedium Grouville*

*15ml ifer 4660*

To give voice to the heart. To communicate what one is feeling, without fear of the consequences for speaking one's truth. To help one to be more aware of what is deeply valued within one's heart. Picture a messenger on a white horse, galloping along in one's heart: within this image one can find all the qualities of this essence.

### **Clear Mind** *Aeranthes grandiflora & aquamarine gemstone*

*15ml ifer 5196*

Clearing and calming the mind. Clarity of perception & reflection. Eases mental stress. Clarity of a pale gemstone; calm of a cool, cloudless, full moon night with no breeze. Reflection by the quiet lake of the mind.

*also: Clear Mind Aura Spray with grapefruit, sandalwood & rose otto oils*
*120ml ifer 5199*

### **Golden Radiance**

*Phragmipedium St. Ouen*

*15ml ifer 5415*

To bring one into awareness of the radiance of one's inner light. Opens the throat chakra; clears negative thought forms from the brow chakra; opens the ajana centre between the eyebrows. Brings out a golden light within the inner chamber of the heart, inviting this light to connect with the throat chakra. Expands the auric field laterally. Helpful in times of stress or anxiety, bringing a light in the darkness. Fundamentally not a remedy, but rather an essence for one's being.

*also: Golden Radiance Aura Spray with bergamot and rose otto oils*
*120ml ifer 5467.*

## Renewing Life *Phragmipedium Carol Kanzer*

*15ml ifer 5477*

Clears ancient negative energetic patterns from the 10th, 12th, and root chakras, renewing one's inherent health. A very gentle, quiet essence, yet profound in its reach. The root chakra governs cellular patterning, so renewal at this level, combined with the higher chakra action, makes this essence a subject for on-going research at the IFER.

## Clearing The Way / Self Belief

*Phragmipedium Don Wimbur*

*15ml ifer 5522*

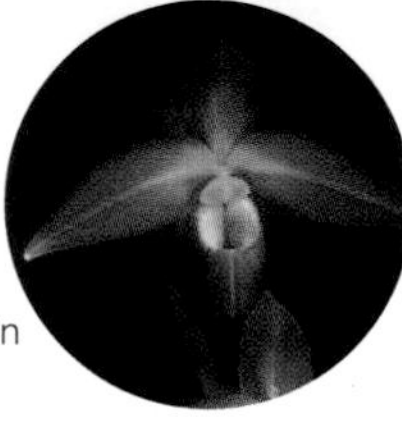

This essence helps to relax tension in the 8th chakra, and strengthens the definition of the petals of the crown chakra, which serves to strengthen one's belief in one's own inner resources, and one's ability to move forward with projects and goals.

## Time Zone / Being in Time

*Phragmipedium Ainsworthii*

*15ml ifer 5504*

Harmonizes the body's cycles with the cycles of nature around one. This is a gentle process of calibration, which also helps one to manage one's time better, especially when there is the sense of having too much to do and too little time to do it in. This essence helps one have a greater sense of 'pace' to the daily demands on one's time.

**Time Zone** is the name given in part to this essence, as it provides very effective help in adjusting to a new time zone when travelling. The body can immediately harmonize with the time-cycles of the local area.

**Being in Time** describes another aspect of this essence: how in general terms it helps us to cope more gracefully with existing in time, with being creatures that are subject to the rhythms of time. It also helps those who are reluctantly incarnate to enter more fully into the here and now.

## Angelic Canopy *Laeliocattleya Angel Love*

*15ml ifer 5621*

An essence that brings balm to one's wounds, Angelic Canopy brings nurture to those who are in grief or despair, or who have lost hope. Helps one to go beyond the immediate response to things and events. Releases the tension from the flight vs. fight response, helping to increase one's sense of security. Helps one to re-align to the values of life. Works especially on the relationship between the 10th and 11th chakras, to help the alignment to one's higher purpose. "All things can be done in Grace." (See photo on back cover.)

## Serendipity *Paphiopedilum Predatious*

*15ml ifer 5851*

Very helpful when one is bogged down with too many responsibilities, or just feeling stuck. Works to align one's preparedness to move into action with deeper dimensions of of one's being. Helps bring new insights in one's meditation. An antidote to being in a rut.

## Happy Relief *a four orchid essence combination*

*15ml ifer 5861*

Our first combination, this essence had the surprising effect of making one feel quietly happy, and at the same time clearing stress and shock. Clears tension from the limbic centre and the baihui point on the top of the head (the "place of a hundred gatherings" in the Chinese tradition, which governs the major meridians.). Brings a sense of happiness and gentle yet strong vitality.

## Happy Relief Aura Spray

*120ml ifer 5731*

As above, but working from the outside in.

## Active Serenity *a five orchid essence combination*

*15ml ifer 5862*

The same combination as Happy Relief, but with the addition of Devata. Working primarily on the mental body centres, this combination is excellent for stress and fatigue. Stress held in the brain stem and alta major chakra (back of the head) is dissolved, and also supports the frontal lobes and crown chakra. For clarity and mental energy which is calm yet energized.

## Active Serenity Aura Spray

*120ml ifer 5732*

As above, but working from the outside in.

## Walking to the Earth's Rhythm

*Paphiopedilum St. Swithin*

*15ml ifer 5602*

For helping us to reconnect with walking in harmony with the rhythm of the Earth herself. This is a calm and soothing essence, good for helping one to gently come back to earth after deep meditations. Works to repair very old ruptures within the etheric matrix of the throat chakra. For 'listening with the feet'. About knowing how to walk, and where to walk.

## Devata *Comparetia speciosa*

*15ml ifer 5816*

If one thinks of the higher and positive qualities of Queen Elizabeth I, one will gain insight at one level into the qualities essence. Its note is of the essence of the mature feminine: wondrous, warm, beautiful, quietly regal, insistent but not aggressive, and with a charismatic integrity. Knows that Beauty is the handmaiden to Truth. This essence is also concerned with the integrity of the mind, and with protecting the depth of the feminine. The archetype of Athena also resonates with this essence, whose name embodies a goal: the spiritual potential of the human heart of the soul. (See photo on front cover.)

## Core of Being *Nanodes medusae*

*15ml ifer 5609*

Gentle yet profound, this essence enters into one's "causal body", which underlies the etheric, astral, and emotional bodies. Core of Being serves to align, strengthen, and calm the causal body.

# Pacific **Essences**

Region: Canada,

North West Pacific

Founded: 1983

DEVELOPER: Sabina Pettitt

Sabina is a lover of Life, People and Nature. She brings this passion to all aspects of her healing work - as an acupuncturist, counsellor, a flower essence practitioner and developer. She has studied Ayurveda with Deepak Chopra as well as being certified by him in Primordial Sound Meditation. Her spiritual Training in Arhatic Yoga and Pranic Healing is an ongoing commitment to healing herself and the Planet.

ESSENCES: The Pacific Essences are subtle energy remedies from the plant, sea and mineral kingdoms. They are delicate energy imprints of their source and can impact on the human energy system in a life supporting way. Made from plants and sea life which grow or live on the Canadian Coast, they are made at the location where they are found and no life is destroyed during the process. The sea essences carry a very different energy from the flower remedies - The 48 flowers carry an etheric, gentle, dancing soft energy which produce subtle shifts, whereas the 24 sea essences are clearly about transformations in consciousness.

There are also three powerful combinations in the Range - Abundance, Heart Spirit and Balancer - which assist one to promote 'abundance consciousness' in the mind body and spirit, to heal old heart wounds and embrace the presence of love - and to balance and harmonise in times of stress or trauma.

## **Flower** essences

### Alum Root *7.5ml ifer 2386 / 25ml ifer 2397*

Key Words: Grace, Trust, Light-hearted, Beauty
Challenges: Power struggles, Conflict
Affirmation: I can respond to all conflict with grace and ease.

### Arbutus *7.5ml ifer 1766 / 25ml ifer 1767*

Key Words: Spirit, Integrity
Challenges: Homesickness, Longing, Abandonment
Affirmation: I joyfully express Spirit. I appreciate the wisdom of life.

### Bluebell *7.5ml ifer 1776 / 25ml ifer 1777*

Key Words: Openness, Communication, Self-expression
Challenges: Limitation, Shyness, Tongue-tied, Uncomfortable, Fatigue
Affirmation: I am willing and able to express myself.

### Blue Camas *7.5ml ifer 1772 / 25ml ifer 1773*

Key Words: Conscious, Balance, Perspective, Integration
Challenges: Learning disabilities, Inability to learn from experience
Affirmation: I am creative and practical.

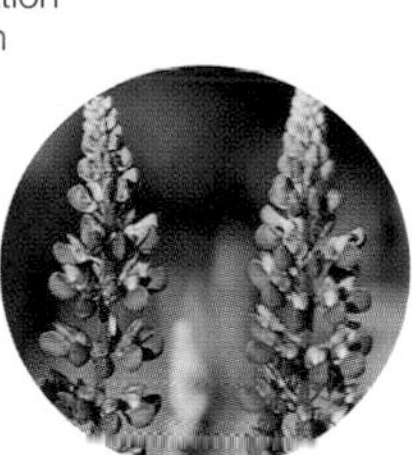

### Blue Lupin
*7.5ml ifer 1774 / 25ml ifer 1775*

Key Words: Clarity, Focus
Challenges: Confusion, Frustration, Despair
Affirmation: I can see clearly. I can think clearly.

### Camellia *7.5ml ifer 1780 / 25ml ifer 1781*

Key Words: Vision, Openness, Self-expression, Opening
Challenges: Guilt, Shame, Closed to new experience
Affirmation: I am true to myself. I am open to life experience.

### Candystick
*7.5ml ifer 1782 / 25ml ifer 1783*

Key Words: Survival, Purpose
Challenge: Free Will
Affirmation: I am willing to take responsibility for my choices. I accept the free will of other beings.

## Chickweed
*7.5ml ifer 1784 / 25ml ifer 1785*

Key Words: Present, Available, Response-ability
Challenges: Bitterness, Resentment, Unavailable
Affirmation: I am able to respond to life as it unfolds before me. I am available and present.

## Death Camas *7.5ml ifer 1786 / 25ml ifer 1787*

Key Words: Rebirth-ing, Beginnings, Ecstasy, Transformation
Challenges: New beginnings, Change
Affirmation: I am in tune with the Infinite. I go with the flow.

## Douglas Aster
*7.5ml ifer 2387 / 25ml ifer 2398*

Key Words: Expansion, Generosity, Adaptability, Radiance
Challenges: Attachment, Ego, Clinging
Affirmation: From the centre of my being I radiate generosity and love.

## Easter Lily *7.5ml ifer 1789 / 25ml ifer 1790*

Key Words: Truth, Purity, Integrity, Honesty, Authenticity
Challenges: Duplicity, Dishonesty, Illusion
Affirmation: I am who I am. I am that I am.

## Fairy Bell *7.5ml ifer 2388 / 25ml ifer 2399*

Key Words: Lightness of being
Challenges: Ambiguity, Resistance, Depression, Vulnerability
Affirmation: I am at ease. This too shall pass.

## Fireweed *7.5ml ifer 1791 / 25ml ifer 1792*

Key Words: Love, Loving, Lovable, Compassion/Service
Challenges: Coldness, Uncaring, Inability to feel, Emotional wounds
Affirmation: I am loving and lovable.

## Forsythia *7.5ml ifer 1793 / 25ml ifer 1794*

Key Words: Transformation, Motivation
Challenge: Self-destruction
Affirmation: I am willing to change. I have the inner resources and energy required to change.

## Fuchsia *7.5ml ifer 2389 / 25ml ifer 2407*

Key Words: Balance, Self-actualization, Re-creation
Challenges: Procrastination, Sloth and Torpor
Affirmation: I am the change I wish to see in the world.

## Goatsbeard *7.5ml ifer 1795 / 25ml ifer 1796*

Key Words: Fantasy, Meditation, Creative Visualization, Rejuvenation
Challenges: Tension, Tightness, Holding
Affirmation: I feel tension and stress dissolving.

## Grape Hyacinth
*7.5ml ifer 1797 / 25ml ifer 1798*

Key Words: Balance, Perspective
Challenges: Shock, Trauma, Despair
Affirmation: I am balanced and whole.

## Grass Widow *7.5ml ifer 1799 / 25ml ifer 1800*

Key Word: Freedom
Challenge: Fear of being judged by others
Affirmation: I release limitation. I am unlimited.

## Harvest lily
*7.5ml ifer 1801 / 25ml ifer 1802*

Key Words: Community, Relationship, Resolution
Challenges: Social interaction
Affirmation: I radiate my beauty and vitality. I recognize the beauty and vitality in others.

## Hooker's Onion *7.5ml ifer 1804 / 25ml ifer 1805*

Key Words: Light, Freedom, Inspiration, Creativity, Spontaneity
Challenges: Overwhelmed, Frustrated, Stuck, Dense, Heavy
Affirmation: I am Light. I am a clear channel for Light and Creativity.

## Indian Pipe
*7.5ml ifer 2390 / 25ml ifer 2406*

Key Words: Reconciliation, Reverence
Challenges: Illusion, Separation
Affirmation: We are all one.

## Lily of the Valley *7.5ml ifer 1811 / 25ml ifer 1812*

Key Words: Simplicity, Innocence
Challenges: Sophistication, Over-Control, Rigidity
Affirmation: I embrace life with an open heart. I embrace my own uniqueness.

## Narcissus *7.5ml ifer 1818 / 25ml ifer 1819*

Key Words: Safety, Nurturing
Challenges: Worry, Anxiety
Affirmation: I am safe.

## Nootka Rose

*7.5ml ifer 1826 / 25ml ifer 1827*

Key Words: Enthusiasm (en theos - in God), Love
Challenges: Weariness, Abuse, Abandonment
Affirmation: I am an aspect of the Divine. I am a spark of the Infinite.

## Orange Honeysuckle *7.5ml ifer 1828 / 25ml ifer 1829*

Key Words: Creative Expression, Inner direction, Creativity
Challenges: Identity, Lost, Anger
Affirmation: I am creative. I find rest and calm in the full expression of my creativity.

## Ox-Eye Daisy

*7.5ml ifer 1830 / 25ml ifer 1831*

Key Word: Perspective
Challenges: Over-focused, Not being able to see the forest for the trees
Affirmation: I am able to see things differently.

## Pearly Everlasting *7.5ml ifer 2391 / 25ml ifer 2405*

Key Words: Commitment, Devotion, Service
Challenges: Perspective, Anger
Affirmation: I am committed to this process of growing together in love and harmony.

## Periwinkle

*7.5ml ifer 1832 / 25ml ifer 1833*

Key Words: Remembering, Centred
Challenges: Confusion, Forgetfulness, Despair, Depression
Affirmation: I am uplifted. I remember who I am.

## Pipsissewa *7.5ml ifer 1837 / 25ml ifer 1838*

Key Words: Decisive, Choices
Challenge: Indecisiveness
Affirmation: I am able to choose. I can trust my energy and follow my heart.

## Plantain *7.5ml ifer 1839 / 25ml ifer 1840*

Key Words: Purification, Cleansing
Challenges: Poisonous thought and attitudes, Resentment
Affirmation: I release all obstacles to growth and healing. I release thoughts which are not life supporting to myself or others.

## Poison Hemlock *7.5ml ifer 1841 / 25ml ifer 1842*

Key Words: Releasing, Faith
Challenge: Holding on to old structures and beliefs
Affirmation: I let go.

## Polyanthus

*7.5ml ifer 1843 / 25ml ifer 1844*

Key Word: Abundance, Self-worth
Challenges: Unworthiness
Affirmation: I am willing to receive. I deserve to receive.

## Poplar *7.5ml ifer 2392 / 25ml ifer 2404*

Key Words: Healing, Innocence, Yielding
Challenges: Separation
Affirmation: I allow myself to be moved by Spirit.

## Purple Crocus

*7.5ml ifer 1845 / 25ml ifer 1846*

Key Word: Feeling embraced
Challenges: Grief, Deep sadness
Affirmation: I allow myself to be exactly where I am.

## Purple Magnolia *7.5ml ifer 1847 / 25ml ifer 1848*

Key Words: Opening, Intimacy, Sensuality
Challenges: Coldness, Frigidity, Withdrawal from life
Affirmation: I celebrate life.

## Red Huckleberry

*7.5ml ifer 2393 / 25ml ifer 2403*

Key Words: Introspection, Digestion, Nourishment
Challenges: Being not Doing
Affirmation: It is safe to retreat and go within.

## Salal *7.5ml ifer 1850 / 25ml ifer 1851*

Key Word: Forgiveness, Forgiving
Challenges: Grudges, Resentment
Affirmation: I am forgiving. I forgive myself and release the past.

## Salmonberry

*7.5ml ifer 1852 / 25ml ifer 1853*

Key Words: Physical alignment, Physical expression
Challenges: Physical, mental, emotional, and spiritual alignment
Affirmation: I celebrate my physical embodiment.

## Silver Birch
*7.5ml ifer 2394 / 25ml ifer 2402*

Key Words: Conception, Manifestation
Challenges: Control
Affirmation: I am flexible and strong. I am able to conceive.

## Snowberry *7.5ml ifer 1868 / 25ml ifer 1869*

Key Words: Acceptance, Enthusiasm
Challenge: Resistance
Affirmation: I embrace my life experience.

## Snowdrop *7.5ml ifer 1870 / 25ml ifer 1871*

Key Words: Hope, Delight, Release
Challenges: Fear, Restriction
Affirmation: I can let go and experience joy.

## Twin Flower *7.5ml ifer 1879 / 25ml ifer 1880*

Key Words: Peace of mind, Acceptance, Compassion
Challenges: Judgment, Criticism
Affirmation: I do not understand what anything is for, and so I accept what is without criticism.

## Vanilla Leaf
*7.5ml ifer 1881 / 25ml ifer 1882*

Key Word: Self-esteem
Challenge: Self-loathing
Affirmation: I love myself. I celebrate who I am.

## Viburnum *7.5ml ifer 1883 / 25ml ifer 1884*

Key Words: Intuition, Channel, Relaxed, Insight
Challenges: Self-doubt, Insecurity
Affirmation: I am a channel for creative intelligence.

## Wallflower *7.5ml ifer 2395 / 25ml ifer 2401*

Key Words: Expression, Sharing, Communication
Challenges: Sensory deficits, Autism
Affirmation: My senses are alive and I can share my perceptions with you.

## Weigela *7.5ml ifer 1885 / 25ml ifer 1886*

Key Words: Integration, Alignment, Teaching
Challenges: Disassociation, Speechless
Affirmation: I am an embodiment of wisdom.

## Windflower *7.5ml ifer 1887 / 25ml ifer 1888*

Key Words: Grounding, Spirit
Challenges: Scattered, Spaced out
Affirmation: I know who I am.

## Yellow Pond-Lily
*7.5ml ifer 2396 / 25ml ifer 2400*

Key Words: Strength, Security, Letting Go/Centering
Challenges: Attachment, Doubt
Affirmation: I am not my feelings.

# Sea essences

## Anemone *7.5ml ifer 1764 / 25ml ifer 1765*

Key Words: Allowing, Empowerment, Response-ability
Challenges: Victim, Powerlessness, Blame, Controlling
Affirmation: I am able to respond with trust and openness.

## Barnacle *7.5ml ifer 1770 / 25ml ifer 1771*

Key Words: Intuitive, Yielding, Nurturing
Challenges: Tough, Resistant, Stubborn
Affirmation: I embrace the softness within.

## Brown Kelp *7.5ml ifer 1778 / 25ml ifer 1779*

Key Words: Clarity, Freedom
Challenges: Confusion, Fixation
Affirmation: I can let go of this position.

## Chiton *7.5ml ifer 2334 / 25ml ifer 2346*

Key Words: Flexibility, Gentleness
Challenges: Rigidity
Affirmation: I maintain flexibility within my physical structure.

## Coral *7.5ml ifer 2335 / 25ml ifer 2356*

Key Words: Harmony, Cooperation
Challenges: Conflict, Fear
Affirmation: I can live harmoniously in community. Only fear prevents me from living in paradise.

## Diatoms *7.5ml ifer 2336 / 25ml ifer 2358*

Key Words: Source, Love, Consciousness, Grace, Dharma/Purpose
Challenges: Darkness, Stuckness
Affirmation: Heart is my centre.

## Dolphin *7.5ml ifer 2337 / 25ml ifer 2355*

Key Words: Playful, Lighthearted, Higher communication, Lightheartedness
Challenges: Seriousness, Melancholy
Affirmation: I dance my life light heartedly.

## Hermit Crab *7.5ml ifer 2338 / 25ml ifer 2354*

Key Words: Contentment, Ease, Comfortable with self
Challenges: Loneliness, Avoidance
Affirmation: I am content and at peace with my solitude.

## Jellyfish *7.5ml ifer 1807 / 25ml ifer 1808*

Key Words: Fluid, Flexible, Present, Embracing
Challenges: Stuck, Rigid
Affirmation: Be Here Now.

## Moon Snail *7.5ml ifer 1814 / 25ml ifer 1815*

Key Words: Curiosity, Innocence, Illumination
Challenges: Rigid Beliefs and Attitudes
Affirmation: I am free. My mind is filled with Light.

## Mussel *7.5ml ifer 1816 / 25ml ifer 1817*

Key Words: Creativity, Transformation
Challenges: Irritability, Frustration
Affirmation: I am creative and powerful.

## Pink Seaweed *7.5ml ifer 1835 / 25ml ifer 1836*

Key Words: Grounded, Secure, Patient, Grounding
Challenges: Change, Inflexibility
Affirmation: I am grounded and secure. I move in the flow of life.

## Rainbow Kelp *7.5ml ifer 2339 / 25ml ifer 2353*

Key Words: Alchemy, Potentiality
Challenges: Reactivity
Affirmation: I am able to respond with my full potential.

## Sand Dollar *7.5ml ifer 1854 / 25ml ifer 1855*

Key Words: Reality, Truth
Challenges: Illusion, Limitation
Affirmation: I am willing to expand my awareness.

## Sea Horse *7.5ml ifer 2340 / 25ml ifer 2352*

Key Words: Life Force, Expression
Challenges: Paralysis, Lazy
Affirmation: I feel the life force in my physical body. There is no loss of power in gentleness.

## Sea Lettuce *7.5ml ifer 2341 / 25ml ifer 2351*

Key Words: Purifying, Healing, Purification
Challenges: Facing the dark side
Affirmation: I shine the light of healing on my dark side. My dark side is dissolved in the green light of healing.

## Sea Palm *7.5ml ifer 1862 / 25ml ifer 1863*

Key Words: Flowing, Allowing, Be-ing
Challenges: Busy, Preoccupied, Controlling
Affirmation: I am fully present.

## Sea Turtle *7.5ml ifer 2342 / 25ml ifer 2350*

Key Words: At home, Present, Available, Grace
Challenges: Busy-ness, Awkwardness
Affirmation: I 'lumber' through my life with grace and charm.

## Sponge *7.5ml ifer 2343 / 25ml ifer 2349*

Key Words: Inner Peace, Wonder
Challenges: Victim consciousness, Opinionated
Affirmation: As I am able/willing to release judgment, hope and wonder blossom.

## 'Staghorn' Algae *7.5ml ifer 2344 / 25ml ifer 2348*

Key Words: Steadiness, Inner Security
Challenges: Self-knowledge
Affirmation: I remember who I am in the midst of conflict and turmoil.

## Starfish *7.5ml ifer 1875 / 25ml ifer 1876*

Key Words: Willingness, Releasing
Challenges: Attachment, Clinging
Affirmation: I accept the unfoldment of life.

## Surfgrass *7.5ml ifer 1877 / 25ml ifer 1878*

Key Words: Courage, Flexibility
Challenges: Pride, Ego
Affirmation: I am powerful and flexible.

## Urchin *7.5ml ifer 1864 / 25ml ifer 1865*

Key Words: Exploration, Safety, Focus
Challenges: Fear of the unknown
Affirmation: It is safe to explore my hidden potential. I am protected when I bring more awareness to light.

## Whale *7.5ml ifer 2345 / 25ml ifer 2347*

Key Words: Telepathy, Clairsentience, Human Potential, Expansion
Challenges: Ethnocentricity, Arrogance
Affirmation: I am able to access my full mental potential.

# **Combination** essences

## Abundance

*25ml ifer 1762 / 25ml oil ifer 1763 / 50ml spray ifer 5152*

Helps us to realize our full potential at all levels of our being and in any area of our life we chose to focus on. Empowers us and, as our self-imposed limitations fall away, we are able to discover and nurture our unlimited potential. It has helped individuals to manifest physical health, to nurture relationships, to discover their power to manifest, and to be willing to accept the energy of financial prosperity.

## Abundance Program *ifer 3009*

This 22 day program incorporates the use of the Abundance essence, the Abundance Oil, written exercises and meditations to help us to discover and to focus on our goals. Assists one to manifest their dreams and discover their personal power in terms of creating their own reality.

## Balancer

*25ml ifer 1768 / 25ml oil ifer 1769 / 50ml spray ifer 5421*

For use in times of stress, overwhelm and emergency situations. Brings life energy to all the chakras and gently promotes an even flow of energy through the meridians so that in moments of shock or trauma we are given the necessary energetic resources with which to cope with our immediate challenge. May also be used when we are physically depleted and/or ill. Not just for acute situations, Balancer can be taken at times of inner turmoil as it has a grounding and settling effect that helps us to stay present.

## Heart Spirit

*25ml ifer 1803 / 25ml oil ifer 5192 / 50ml spray ifer 5422*

A synergistic formula of 21 essences connected to all levels of heart energy that has transformed lives by assisting in the release old heart pain. Enables us to move to a place of seeing ourselves, others and our life circumstances "through the eyes of the heart". Sets up a magnetic resonance of loving energy in the auric field which attracts more loving and life supporting energy to us.

## NEW****Available June 2002.

## Abundance of the Heart kit *ifer 5876*

*33 steps to contacting and activating your Higher Self.*

Utilizing both Abundance and Heart Spirit energies as well as Dolphin, Diatoms, Fuchsia and Indian Pipe, this program of daily exercises gently leads you to the discovery of who you really are and enables you to respond to people and life situations from an enlightened and light hearted place. It is the next octave of transformation and Self-acceptance after creating the foundation and structure for new possibilities in the original Abundance Program.

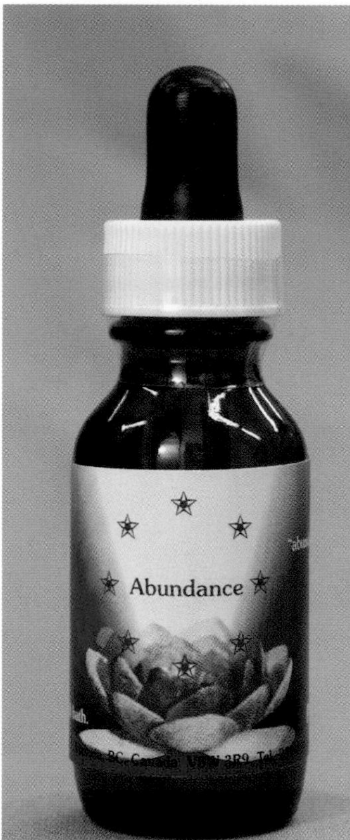


Sabina Pettitt is a true pioneer in the essence world in a number of respects: extending the making of essences into the area of working with plants and creatures of the sea; bridging the worlds of acupuncture and essences (Vasu & Kadambii of the Living Essences also have done this); and in bringing essences into supporting our need for abundance in our lives.

The Abundance Essence, oil, and spray, are all helpful in allowing one to manifest positive changes in one's life, to assist one in experiencing abundance in whichever area of life one is intending to fulfil.

# Petite Fleur **Essences**

Region: Texas, USA

Founded: 1981

DEVELOPER: Judy Griffin is a fourth generation flower essences maker,her Italian mother, grandmother, and great grandmother all having made flower essences before her. Not only did Judy continue on this tradition but expanded her knowledge bytraining in Chinese, Indian, Native American herbalist disciplines. A master herbalist with a PhD in nutrition, she has five books to her name. The Petites were created in response to the health challenges of her children, which led her to discover an holistic approach that incorporated the mind, body and spirit. The Petite Fleur are used internationally by allopathic and complimentary healthcare practitioners.

THE ESSENCES: The Petites are organically grown in Texas by Judy and are specifically designed to enhance the neurological and physiological systems of the body, as well as the spirit. Judy recognised that each flower has its own unique resonance or signature manifested by their particular fragrance, colour, shape, texture and personality. The Native Texans strengthen character and focus on enhancing the immunesystem by balancing inappropriate flight and flight stress responses while the Antique Roses enhance the nervous system.

## **Petite Fleur** Essences

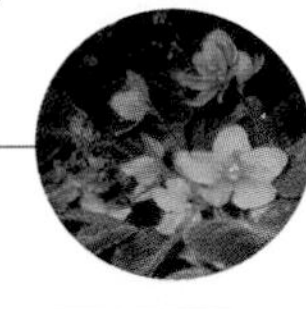

**African Violet** *3.8ml ifer 1930*

Nurturing from the soul; fulfilling love

**Alfredo de Damas** *3.8ml ifer 1931*

Constructive habits, enhances memory

**Amaryllis** *3.8ml ifer 1933*

Aids parasitic relations

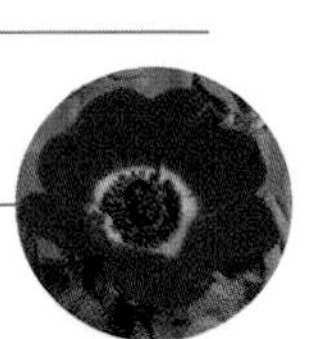

**Anemone** *3.8ml ifer 1934*

Overcomes 'life is a struggle'

**Aquilegia Columbine** *3.8ml ifer 1937*

Mother issues

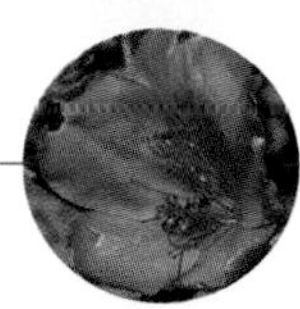

**Azalea** *3.8ml ifer 1940*

Promotes creativity; new ideas

**Babies Breath** *3.8ml ifer 1941*

Overcomes resistance to new ideas

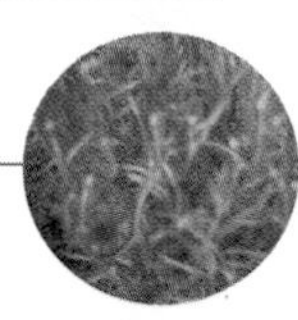

**Bachelor Button** *3.8ml ifer 1942*

Releases past painful experiences

**Bamboo** *3.8ml ifer 1943*

Promotes inner guidance.

**Basil** *3.8ml ifer 1944*

Reduces inferiority complex

**Begonia** *3.8ml ifer 1945*

Releases feeling threatened

**Blue Danube Aster** *3.8ml ifer 1946*

Enhances the power of concentration

**Bluebonnet** *3.8ml ifer 1947*

Promotes destiny and character

**Bougainvillea** *3.8ml ifer 1949*

Reduces chronic pain

**Bouquet of Harmony** *3.8ml ifer 3001*

Self-harmony; less stress

**Carrot** *3.8ml ifer 1952*

Promotes organizational skills

**Chamomile** *3.8ml ifer 1955*

Releases disappointment; swallowing hurt

**Christmas Cactus** *3.8ml ifer 1958*

Reinforces character strengths

**Crepe Myrtle** *3.8ml ifer 1962*

Promotes speaking your mind

**Crossandra** *3.8ml ifer 1963*

Encourages life changes

**Daffodil** *3.8ml ifer 1965*

Reduces shyness

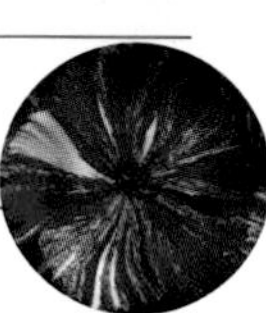

**Dianthus** *3.8ml ifer 1970*

Increases inner joy

**Dill** *3.8ml ifer 1971*

Reduces the fear of being alone

**Echinacea** *3.8ml ifer 1972*

Purifies thoughts, opinions

**Fortuniana** *3.8ml ifer 1978*

Integrates the personality with the Universal Soul

**Gaillardia** *3.8ml ifer 1981*

Encourages doing the 'impossible'

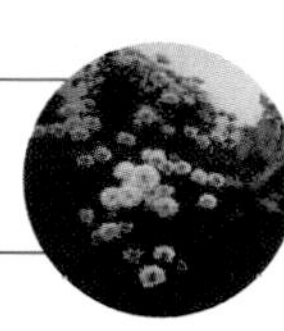

**Garden Mum** *3.8ml ifer 1982*

Releases critical thoughts

**Gardenia** *3.8ml ifer1983*

Attract mate; long-range goals

**Indian Hawthorne** *3.8ml ifer 1986*

Encourages unconditional love

**Indian Paintbrush** *3.8ml ifer 1987*

Enhances success consciousness

**Iris** *3.8ml ifer 1988*

Reduces mental stress

**Japanese Magnolia** *3.8ml ifer 1989*

Releases victim consciousness

**Jasmine** *3.8ml ifer 1990*

Reduces rebelliousness

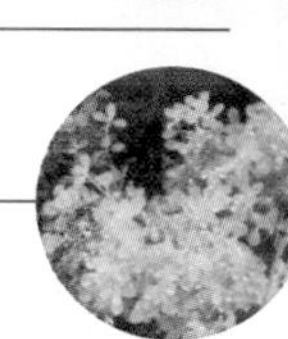

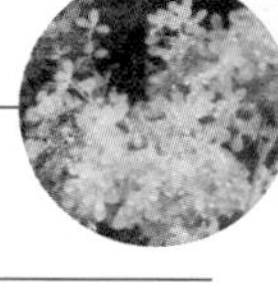

**Knotted Marjoram** *3.8ml ifer 1991*

Enhances attention to details

**Kolanchoe** *3.8ml ifer 1992*

Overcomes the illusion of opposites

**Lady Eubanksia** *3.8ml ifer 1993*

Wisdom and understanding to teach others

**Lantana** *3.8ml ifer 1994*

Aids oversensitive and allergic reactions

**Lemon Grass** *3.8ml ifer 1995*

Releases 'Love hurts'; parental conflicts

**Ligustrum** *3.8ml ifer 1996*

Increases self-assertion

**Lilac** *3.8ml ifer 1997*

Forgiveness; letting go

**Lily** *3.8ml ifer 1998*

Releases fear of failure

**Magnolia** *3.8ml ifer 2004*

Enhances self-appreciation

**Marigold** *3.8ml ifer 2007*

Balances male and female energy

**Meadow Sage** *3.8ml ifer 2009*

Aids in expressing strong emotions

**Mexican Oregano** *3.8ml ifer 2012*

Quick respond to new situations

**Morning Glory** *3.8ml ifer 2013*

Releases living in the past

**Moss Rose** *3.8ml ifer 2014*

Releases 'Never satisfied'

**Mushroom** *3.8ml ifer 2015*

Helps foresee and accept change

**Narcissus** *3.8ml ifer 2016*

Aids one who feels left out

**Old Blush** *3.8ml ifer 2018*

Stamina through decisiveness

**Onion** *3.8ml ifer 2019*

Releases preconceived opinions

**Orchid, Dancing Lady** *3.8ml ifer 2020*

Makes peace with my past

**Pansy** *3.8ml ifer 2021*

Transcends grief over past loves; loss of a loved one

**Penta** *3.8ml ifer 2023*

Enhances feeling safe to love

**Peppermint** *3.8ml ifer 2024*

Releases fear of loss

**Periwinkle** *3.8ml ifer 2025*

Clears past experiences

**Pine** *3.8ml ifer 2026*

Learn from past mistakes

**Pink Geranium** *3.8ml ifer 2027*

Releases suppressed anger

**Pink Rose** *3.8ml ifer 2028*

Reduces fat complex

**Poppy** *3.8ml ifer 2029*

Releases high expectations

**Primrose** *3.8ml ifer 2030*

Accept love from others

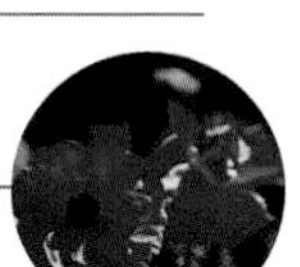

**Ranunculus** *3.8ml ifer 2033*

Abuse issues

**Red Carnation** *3.8ml ifer 2034*

Enhances self-worth

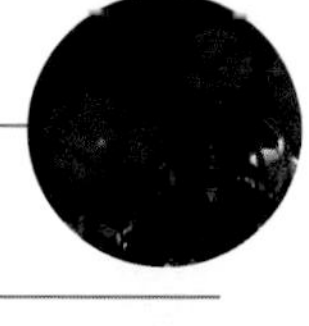

**Red Rose** *3.8ml ifer 2036*

Negative thoughts and feelings

**Rose Campion** *3.8ml ifer 2038*

Releases outdated beliefs

**Rose of Sharon** *3.8ml ifer 2039*

Feeling burdened by responsibility

**Salvia** *3.8ml ifer 2042*

Enhances self-esteem

**Shrimp** *3.8ml ifer 2044*

Reduces feeling overwhelmed; fear of aging

**Silver Lace** *3.8ml ifer 2045*

Insight from setbacks

**Snapdragon** *3.8ml ifer 2047*

Increases discernment

**Stock** *3.8ml ifer 2050*

Aids easily distracted individuals

**Sunflower** *3.8ml ifer 2052*

Releases feeling of separation, loneliness

**Tiger's Jaw Cactus** *3.8ml ifer 2057*

Overcomes procrastination

**Vanilla** *3.8ml ifer 2058*

Protection; children's remedy

**Verbena** *3.8ml ifer 3002*

Inner peace; better sleep

**Viridiflora** *3.8ml ifer 2060*

Personal power, balances chakras

**Wandering Jew** *3.8ml ifer 2061*

For individuals easily discouraged

**White Carnation** *3.8ml ifer 2063*

Reduces willfulness; increases willpower

**White Hyacinth** *3.8ml ifer 2064*

Reduces traumatic experiences

**White Petunia** *3.8ml ifer 2065*

Aids in better decisions

**White Rose** *3.8ml ifer 2066*

Enhances positive attitude

**Wisteria** *3.8ml ifer 2069*

Increases inner faith; opens heart

**Yellow Rose** *3.8ml ifer 2071*

Develops higher purpose

**Zinnea** *3.8ml ifer 2072*

Nurtures the inner child

# **Petite Fleur** combinations

Petite Fleur Essence combined with Essential Oils.
Fragrant perfume blends for the following conditions:

**Abate Anger** *3.8ml ifer 1929*

calms inner conflict, hypertension, and suppressed anger

**Allergy** *3.8ml ifer 1932*

reduces sneezing, wheezing, and sinus congestion

**Cold and Flu** *3.8ml ifer 1960*

reduces viral and upper respiratory symptoms

**Deep Sleep** *3.8ml ifer 1968*

alleviates anxiety and insomnia patterns

**Fatigue** *3.8ml ifer 4968*

use for muscular aches, chronic fatigue, and fibromyalgia

**Female Balance** *3.8ml ifer 1975*

hormone balance, reduces pms, mood swings, and hormonal changes

**Bouquet of Harmony** *3.8ml ifer 3001*

reduces anxiety, fear, beneficial during emergencies; apply as needed

**Inner Strength** *3.8ml ifer 4693*

builds character under adversity, enhances immunity during stress

**Male** *3.8ml ifer 2005*

enhances motivation, drive, and self worth

**Manage Pain** *3.8ml ifer 4858*

for chronic and acute pain like, migraines or minor injury

**Energy** *3.8ml ifer 1973*

increases stamina, endurance, and memory

**Passion** *3.8ml ifer 2022*

increases enthusiasm, spontaneity, creativity, and romance

**Reduce Stress** *3.8ml ifer 3883*

promotes inner calm; very effective for children and pets

**Regenerate** *3.8ml ifer 4969*

reduces tendency to scar, regenerating cell growth in tissue

**Self Image** *3.8ml ifer 2043*

enhances self esteem, supports chemically dependents during detox

**Stop Smoking** *3.8ml ifer 2051*

reduces compulsive urges, benefits hyperactivity and A.D.D.

**Weight** *3.8ml ifer 2062*

aids in reducing compulsive eating habits and food cravings

## The Native Texans

**Anise Hyssop** *3.8ml ifer 1935*

Apprehension before an audience or exam

**Borage** *3.8ml ifer 1948*

Learning to stand on my own

**Bronze Fennel** *3.8ml ifer 1951*

Enhances imagination, visualization techniques

**Catnip** *3.8ml ifer 1953*

Enhances social skills, making friends

**Cinnamon Basil** *3.8ml ifer 1959*

Strength during adversity

**Curry** *3.8ml ifer 1964*

Spontaneous action thinking on your feet

**Dandelion** *3.8ml ifer 1966*

Answers from dreams; overcomes fretful dreams

**Day Lily** *3.8ml ifer 1967*

Reduces stress in major lifestyle changes

**Delphinium** *3.8ml ifer 1969*

Attention deficit, forgetfulness

**Foxglove** *3.8ml ifer 1979*

Attracts fulfilling personal relationships

**French Lavender** *3.8ml ifer 1980*

Releases unexpressed desires

**Iberis Candytuft** *3.8ml ifer 1985*

Aids wounded healers

**Lobelia** *3.8ml ifer 1999*

Learning to say no

**Mexican Bush Sage** *3.8ml ifer 2010*

Enhances uniqueness without peer pressure

**Mexican Hat** *3.8ml ifer 2011*

Prosperity and fulfilment

**Purple Garden Sage** *3.8ml ifer 2031*

Focuses on what is valuable in love relationships

**Rain Lily** *3.8ml ifer 2032*

Aids in reconciliation between friends and lovers

**Red Malva** *3.8ml ifer 2035*

Guidance for spiritual development

**Rosemary** *3.8ml ifer 2040*

Releases painful memories

**Salad Burnet** *3.8ml ifer 2041*

Helps overcome unfulfilled desires in relationships

**Soapwort** *3.8ml ifer 2048*

Clairaudience; new ideas

**Spike Lavender** *3.8ml ifer 2049*

Encourages cooperation

**Sweet Annie** *3.8ml ifer 2053*

Enhances public image, bringing out the best in public

**Tansy** *3.8ml ifer 2054*

Protects from environmental pollution

**Thyme** *3.8ml ifer 2056*

Attracts beneficial spirits and friends

**Wild Oats** *3.8ml ifer 2067*

Develops sense of humour

**Wild Wood Violets** *3.8ml ifer 2068*

Look within for answers

**Yarrow** *3.8ml ifer 2070*

Anti inflammatory and increases the potency of the Petites

## Antique Rose collection

**Alfredo de Damas** *3.8ml ifer 1931*

Constructive habits, enhances memory

**Archduke Charles** *3.8ml ifer 1938*

Encourages intimacy and commitment

**Autumn Damask** *3.8ml ifer 1939*

Disappointment about past loves

**Cecil Brunner** *3.8ml ifer 1954*

Defines boundaries in relationships

**Champney's Pink Cluster** *3.8ml ifer 1956*

Learning to love through respect

**Cherokee Rose** *3.8ml ifer 1957*

Reduces mood swings

**Country Marilou** *3.8ml ifer 1961*

Encourages inner strength and security

**Fairy Rose** *3.8ml ifer 1974*

Helps overcome inhibitions

**Fimbriata** *3.8ml ifer 1976*

Encourages an ongoing passion for life

**Fortune's Double Yellow** *3.8ml ifer 1977*

Allows desires to gracefully unfold

**Fortuniana** *3.8ml ifer 1978*

Unites with the universal soul

**Gruss an Aachen** *3.8ml ifer 1984*

Releases settling for less in relationships

**Lady Eubanksia** *3.8ml ifer 1993*

Wisdom and understanding to teach others

**Louis Phillipe** *3.8ml ifer 2000*

Feeling love has passed you by

**Madame Alfred Carriere** *3.8ml ifer 2001*

Prophetic dreams

**Madame Louis Levique** *3.8ml ifer 2002*

Fear of losing control

**Maggie** *3.8ml ifer2003*

Perceiving hidden aspects in others

**Marie Pavie** *3.8ml ifer 2006*

Following your heart in relationships

**Marquise Bocella** *3.8ml ifer 2008*

Encourages trust in long term relationships

**Old Blush** *3.8ml ifer 2018*

Enhances energy and stamina

**Silver Moon** *3.8ml ifer 2046*

Reduces restless thoughts, head chatter

**Viridiflora** *3.8ml ifer 2060*

Enhances personal power

## Feng Shui Sprays

**Attraction** *120 ml ifer 5741*

**Clearing** *120 ml ifer 5740*

**Enhancement** *120 ml i fer 5743*

**Harmonize & Balance** *120 ml ifer 5742*

# Spiritual **Remedies** of Italy

## Region: North Eastern Italy
## Founded: 1995

DEVELOPERS: Paulo and Guilio
Growing up in a town in North Eastern Italy, Paulo always appreciated the beauty of flowers, but as with many of us got caught up in a hectic business career. He travelled to France to visit a friend in 1990, and stumbled across Flower Essences at a European Conference. He soon became engrossed, and began to combine business with his new love - by importing and distributing the essences in Italy. A while later he met Guilio, a therapist deeply involved with natural and vibrational healing, who guided Paulo to make his own essences. With his life long friend (also called Paulo) he went back to the places of his childhood - and through guidance made the 'Luce' (pronounced Lu-chay) essence which is used to great effect today.

ESSENCE: 'Luce' or 'Light' essence, is made from pure spring water that has been energised with a healing symbol. The Symbol itself was discovered when Guilio received a message - He was to go to a sacred place where he was to dig a hole of a certain depth and find a rock. Following the indications thus received, the rock was split in two and in it lay the symbol - an ancient drawing of the universe which had also been used by Native American Indians. This symbol was then charged onto the water, which received its healing qualities.

### Luce / Light essence

*15ml ifer 4796 / 50ml cream ifer 4797 / 100ml spray 4798*

Purely based on vibrational principles, this essence enhances the energy level of the whole cellular system. It stimulates the subtle levels of the being and reaches the innermost aspects of our spirit. It also stimulates energy points located on the body. The colour and gem vibrational constituents of the remedy stimulate and balance the chakras giving an ovorall and immediate physical benefit. The mineral and vegetal constituents come from highly charged locations, where both soil and vegetation have the ability to regenerate the body.

# Star Essences of California

Region: California, USA and Peru, South America
Founded: 1994

DEVELOPERS: Star Riparetti and Roger Valencia
Star Riparetti had a 14 year career in vibrational medicine as chief technician and director of the School of Nuclear Medicine at the Cancer Foundation of Santa Barbara, then moved to the other end of the spectrum – from isotopes to essences of flowers – both energetic medicine. Star has been working with flower essences for over 14 years and is accredited by the Bach Society and FES.
Roger Valencia is the Peruvian connection for the Andean orchid flower essence project. Born in Cuzco and educated in Lima, he has Degrees in business, chemistry and tourism. He is fluent in five languages including Quechua, one of the languages of the indigenous people of Peru. He is an avid botanist who loves wild orchids and has written a book about Andean orchids.

ESSENCES: These essences bring together the two continents of North and South America in the partnership of the two developers and the ingredients used in the essences. Angel Rejuvenation Spray was previously called Rejuvenation Spray and gained the word 'Angel' in its name after being used by an ex-nun who described seeing a huge angel and being very moved. Happy Pet has received good feedback for use on pets and wild animals

## Angel Rejuvenation Spray *60ml ifer 3481*

A miraculous blend of the Andean Orchid flower essence Epidendrum ibaguense, the Winay Winah Orchid (Winay Winah means Forever Young in Quechua). Winay Winah is a few hours hike from Machu Picchu on the Inca trail in the rain forest/cloud forest at around 10,000 feet . The essence was prepared at the sacred site of Machu Picchu, Peru and is a synergistic blend of the flower essence with pure essential oils of Frankincense, Lavender and Geranium which are known for their qualities of being rejuvenating, cleansing, antiseptic and uplifting. They are in a base of distilled activated sacred healing water. Reported to clear headaches, lift the spirit to a higher vibration, bring instant clarity and many a smile.

## Happy Pet *60ml drops ifer 4600 / 60ml aura spray ifer 5599*

Animals (wild and domestic) respond extremely well to vibrational essences. This combination has proven effective time and time again, for all kinds of pet upsets including moving, animal incidents and accidents, and transitions. Excellent for when pets travel. Use this essence to speed the recovery process. Add the essence to their water, directly on their paws, in their mouths, on their fur, or on your hands and pet them.

Epidendrum ibaguense

# Wild Earth Animal Essences

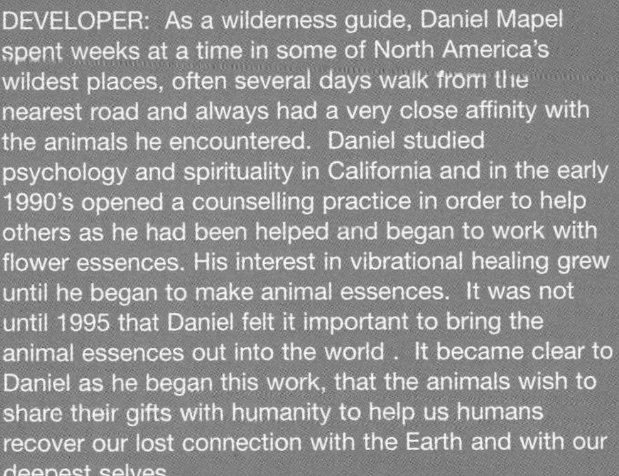

Region: Virginia, USA
Founded: 1995

DEVELOPER: As a wilderness guide, Daniel Mapel spent weeks at a time in some of North America's wildest places, often several days walk from the nearest road and always had a very close affinity with the animals he encountered. Daniel studied psychology and spirituality in California and in the early 1990's opened a counselling practice in order to help others as he had been helped and began to work with flower essences. His interest in vibrational healing grew until he began to make animal essences. It was not until 1995 that Daniel felt it important to bring the animal essences out into the world . It became clear to Daniel as he began this work, that the animals wish to share their gifts with humanity to help us humans recover our lost connection with the Earth and with our deepest selves.

THE ESSENCES: Wild Earth Animal Essences are natural, energetic formulas which nurture us with the wisdom and power of wild animals. Animal essences are "vibrational remedies" – each of the essences contains the vibrational imprint and energy of the animal but does not contain any animal parts. This is held in a solution of brandy and distilled water. There are 41 individual animal essences.

No animals were captured or harmed to develop these products. The essences are made during a ceremonial process of attunement in the wild. The spirit of the animal is invoked and there is meditation and prayerful attunement with each animal.

## North American Animals

### Bear *30ml ifer 3819*

Supports one in incubating ideas, plans, and dreams and bringing them to fruition. For tapping into the power of the unconscious mind. For cultivating strength, groundedness, and power.

### Beaver *30ml ifer 3834*

As the master architect and builder, provides support for creating the design of one's life. Facilitates planning, creating and problem solving. Especially supportive in the beginning of new projects.

### Buffalo *30ml ifer 3818*

For slowing down, grounding, and connecting with the rhythms of the Earth. Nurtures sacredness and stillness and encourages calm and contemplation. Enhances feelings of gratitude for the gift of all life.

### Butterfly *30ml ifer 3817*

As a catalyst for transformation, supports one in times of emotional and spiritual transition. For letting go and moving forward. Nurtures lightness, grace, and a balance of vulnerability and strength.

### Canada Goose *30ml ifer 3839*

For connecting with life as part of a sacred circle. Supports those who have lost their way. For becoming aware of the Great Cycle within and without of birth, death, and renewal.

### Crow *30ml ifer 3828*

Supports developing one's intuitive ability and shamanic power. For moving between the realms, for piercing through Illusion. "Open your eyes, open your ears, all is not as it appears."

### Deer *30ml ifer 3814*

For cultivating great awareness and calm. Encourages gentleness and peace. For seeing with great clarity what is going on around and within oneself. For cultivating humility and trust in gentle ways.

### Dolphin *30ml ifer 3816*

As the great teacher of play and unconditional love, enhances feelings of joy, laughter and delight, as well as compassion for oneself and others. Enhances dream recall and psychic development.

## Dove *30ml ifer 3829*

Nurtures feelings of peace, calm, and stillness at the heart of one's life. Quiets the thinking mind. Allows one to experience the glory of God in the present moment. For appreciating simplicity.

## Dragonfly *30ml ifer 3827*

As the master of illusion, supports one in traveling between the dimensions and opening to spiritual energies. For waking up from personal illusions. For relaxing and resting after busy periods.

## Eagle *30ml ifer 3812*

For soaring above earthly matters to gain perspective and clarity. Enhances spiritual and creative vision. Facilitates opening to the divine for creative inspiration. For connecting with divine guidance. For soaring with Great Spirit.

## Fox *30ml ifer 3835*

For developing independence of thought and confidence in one's decisions. Helps one find clever solutions when facing difficult situations. For breaking out of societal conditioning and finding one's own way.

## Frog *30ml ifer 3841*

Facilitates experiencing the everyday world as miraculous. Provides strength and certainty for those undergoing deep emotional and spiritual changes. For embracing change and transformation as the constant of life.

## Hummingbird *30ml ifer 3815*

Nurtures feelings of joy and delight at the gift of being alive. For "lightening up." Assists with gentle purification and cleansing. Helpful in times of physical transition (travel, moving house, etc).

## Mountain Lion *30ml ifer 3813*

Encourages purposeful action. Provides powerful support for manifesting one's dreams and visions. Supports one in staying true to oneself. Encourages the ability to walk one's talk.

## Otter *30ml ifer 3821*

Helps one access one's playful child-self. Encourages one to experience life as a joyful, fun game. For increasing humor, laughter, joy, and delight at being alive.

## Owl *30ml ifer 3820*

For accessing and acting upon one's highest wisdom. For seeing clearly through one's darkness. Encourages clarity of mind, intuition, and seeing and speaking the truth.

## Peacock *30ml ifer 3833*

Nurtures a sense of fullness, completion, and wholeness. For claiming one's authenticity and authority. Enhances confidence and supports self-esteem. For calling forth spiritual abundance.

## Rabbit *30ml ifer 3826*

For support in creating abundance at all levels of one's life.Nurtures creativity and manifestation in all aspects of one's life.Helps one to create the life of one's dreams.

## Raccoon *30ml ifer 3838*

Supports one in uncovering and accepting hidden aspects of the self. For unmasking the Truth. For moving with gentleness and ease between life's many roles — (ie: mother, wife, employee, sister, etc).

## Robin *30ml ifer 3837*

For nurturing and mothering oneself. Helps build a healthy adult ego. Supports one's ability to be a loving parent; for living in family harmony. A harbinger of spring, hope and happiness within the self.

## Salamander *30ml ifer 3831*

For connecting with the mysteries of the Earth. For grounding and finding Power through one's connection with the mysteries of transformation and regeneration. For deepening into the present.

## Salmon *30ml ifer 3836*

For cultivating awareness of life as a journey Home to the Divine. Helps one to find spiritual meaning and purpose. For moving forward with perseverance toward one's destiny, while surrendering to the divine.

## Seal *30ml ifer 3830*

As the great teacher of ease and effortlessness, supports one in learning to put forth effort and then allowing things to unfold naturally. For flowing through life with grace and ease, and for ease in one's body.

## Snake *30ml ifer 3823*

As a shamanic teacher, facilitates initiation into the deepest, transpersonal realms of the psyche. Provides powerful support for transformation at the deepest levels. For awakening to the deepest mysteries of Creation.

## Spider *30ml ifer 3825*

As the "Weaver of the Web," facilitates inner connection and integration. Nurtures a sense of belonging, connection and Wholeness, For tying together that which has felt separate within oneself.

## Squirrel *30ml ifer 3840*

Supports one in finding a dynamic integration of work and play. Raises awareness of one's spirited inner child. Helps turn any task into a delightful game. Enhances one's ability to gather and store resources.

## Swan *30ml ifer 3824*

For expanding one's capacity to acknowledge and accept one's own goodness and beauty. Nurtures a sense of Grace and facilitates seeing everything as a mirror of the Divine. Enhances self-esteem.

## Turtle *30ml ifer 3822*

For slowing down and experiencing deep grounding and Oneness with the Earth. Provides emotional and psychic protection for feeling safe when dealing with intense situations and environments.

## Whale *30ml ifer 3842*

For connecting with higher planes of consciousness beyond the earth-realm. For spiritual expansion at the deepest levels. Calms and clears the mind. For exploring the "big picture" of reality.

## Wild Horse *30ml ifer 3832*

Nurtures a sense of loving openness, belonging, and connection with others. Encourages strength, stamina and power. Gently opens the Heart chakra. Good for those who have "lost heart."

## Wolf *30ml ifer 3811*

Assists in defining relationships and setting healthy boundaries with others. Encourages sociability and community. For knowing the truth and acting upon it. Nurtures integrity and honoring lifetimes commitments.

# **African/Asian** Animals

## Cheetah *30ml ifer 5132*

For accomplishing tasks with great speed, efficiency, and focus. Provides a "jump-start" when feeling stuck or blocked. Helps one to get moving after a decision has been made. For efficient use of time and resources.

## Chimpanzee *30ml ifer 5133*

For connecting with the simplicity and joy of being alive. Provides support for those who feel socially inhibited or self-conscious. Nurtures playfulness, curiosity, and self-expression.

## Elephant *30ml ifer 5134*

For establishing deep grounding and spiritual expansion. Enhances telepathic communication over distances, and supports one in listening to others and to oneself. For remembering what is important.

## Gazelle *30ml ifer 5135*

Provides support for facing one's vulnerability and for learning the strength of healthy vulnerability. For being safe in the world. Helps one to develop a highly tuned sense of alertness and awareness.

## Giraffe *30ml ifer 5136*

For developing the ability to see the terrain of one's life from an expanded and clear perspective. For spiritual expansion and vision while at the same time remaining well grounded.

## Hippo *30ml ifer 5137*

Provides deep grounding and support for facing unresolved emotional issues. Supports those who need to learn to understand and be with their feelings. Encourages an integrated experience of the physical and emotional realms.

## Lion *30ml ifer 5138*

For claiming one's deepest personal authority and spiritual power. Encourages courage, fearlessness, leadership, achievement, and success. Nurtures a sense of well being and strength.

## Zebra *30ml ifer 5139*

Nurtures a profound integration of the opposites. For moving beyond black-and-white thinking, and for letting go of projections. For seeing the real truth behind what might at first seem masked or hidden.

## Tiger *30ml ifer 5140*

For quieting the mind and coming into the pure, raw awareness and power of the present moment. For becoming strong and focused. Nurtures a sense of spiritual strength and mastery. For cultivating an unwavering mind.

# General Guidelines on using Essences

The Individual essences are sold at 'stock' concentrate, while the 'combination' essences are normally sold at 'dosage' strength. The dosage instructions for each line of individual stock essences are given in the appendix. All the ready-to-use combination bottles of the line are bought with user-friendly instructions printed on the label.

Flower essences can be used internally and externally.

1. INTERNAL USE

Stock concentrate CAN be taken directly from the stock bottle but if you are taking it for more than a couple of days it is recommended and is more economical to make up your own dosage bottle. Another reason for making up a dosage bottle is when you want to take more than one essence at any one time. It is simply a lot easier to carry one dosage bottle with you than half a dozen Stock bottles!!

*How do I make up a dosage bottle from and individual stock bottle?*

Individual flower essence developers give guidance on how to make up a dosage bottle.
However the general guideline is:
a) Take a clean glass dropper bottle (eg. a 30ml). Fill with one quarter alcohol (choose from brandy/vodka/cognac) and three quarters spring water.

NB. Those with a sensitivity to alcohol may want to use an equal amount of apple cider vinegar or vegetable glycerine as a substitute for the brandy which is simply acting as a preservative for the water. Alternatively, a few drops can be placed in a cup of boiling water and the alcohol will quickly evaporate. Essences can also be mixed into pure water only, however they must be kept refrigerated and full potency will only last a few days.
b) Add 2 to 7 drops of your stock essence. This may depend on the ranges of essences you are working with, so consult the developer's recommendation if you wish in the appendix and JUST AS IMPORTANT is for you to use your own intuitive guidance.

*How can I combine individual essence choices into one dosage bottle?*

You may use more than one stock essence at any one time from a number of different producers so long as each essence addresses the SAME issue. It is generally suggested that a total number of stock essences combined into one dosage bottle is limited to 5 or 7.

*How do I use my dosage bottle?*

There are 4 simple things to be aware of:

*a. How many drops should I take?*

Individual developers have different recommendations for the amount of drops to be taken so you can consult the appendix for guidance. If you have made a blend from MORE THAN ONE essence range there is no hard and fast rule so as a guideline, take 2 to 7 drops.

*b. How often should I take the drops?*

Individual developers have different recommendations for the frequency of taking drops so you can consult the appendix for guidance. However as a guideline, take your drops first thing in the morning and last thing at night and more often if you feel you would like to. It is important to note that it is the frequency (the number of times the essences are taken) not the amount taken that increases the strength of their effect. Having the bottle by your bed ensures that you don't forget to take it!!

*c. How should I take the drops?*

Place drops UNDER the tongue or in a glass of water and sip at intervals. You could also put your essences in a bottle of water so that your body is receiving the healing message of the essence throughout the day. In the case of the Petite Fleur Essences, apply topically only, 2 drops on the wrist.

*d. For how many days should I take the drops?*

As a general guideline, take your dosage drops for two to four weeks. If addressing a psychological or emotional condition and benefit is not noticed within a week, consider the possibility that a different essence may be more appropriate for you at this time, as the right essence should be helping within that time-frame as a general rule.

2. EXTERNAL USE

It is equally effective to apply remedies either:

1) Directly on the skin, 2 or 3 drops of stock or dosage on the wrists or other area of the body.

2) In the bath (or foot bath or spa bath), 2 to 11 drops as a general rule. Baths are a great way to administer essences to young children!

3) Sprayed into the body's energy field, 12" over the head and generally around the body. You can buy the ready-to-use sprays and mists of the various essence ranges and you can also make you own by adding some stock drops to a clean, new spray bottle (preferably glass) filled with spring water. You can be guided by the developer and/or your own intuition as to the number of drops to use! A small amount of alcohol may be added as a preservative. You could also add some of your favourite essential oils.

4) Add essences to face creams, moisturisers,

5) Add drops to an aromatherapy burner, humidifier, air conditioner, or feng shui water feature.

**CARE FOR YOUR ESSENCES!!!!**

Please be sure to keep your bottle away from excessive heat and light over an extended period of time and any form of electromagnetic radiation.

# The Developer's Guide to Dosages

The use of essences is more of an art than a science, and it therefore arises that most of the developers have slightly different recommendations for the taking of their essences. *No harm will come from not following these guidelines.* It is simply that each developer has found certain levels of dosage preparation most effective with their products. Professional therapists will also utlilize their own method and approach to this question, as they deem it appropriate.

**Alaskan Flower, Gem and Environmental Essences:**

Use 2 drops from each
remedy added to a 30 ml dosage bottle. Take 4 drops of dosage 4 times daily. The average length of a dosage cycle is 30 to 40 days and for this you would need to make up 2 or 3 dosage bottles.

**Aloha (Hawaiin) Flower Essences:**

Use 7 drops from stock added to a 30ml dosage bottle. Take 3 to 7 drops of dosage, 3 times daily. Crisis situations:, take 3 to 7 drops of stock or dosage every 5 minutes until the crisis passes.

**Araretama Rainforest Essences of Brazil:**

See 'General Guidelines'.

**Australian Bush Flower Essences:**

Use 7 drops from each stock remedy added to a 30ml stock dosage bottle. Take 7 drops of dosage morning and night. Take dosage or Combination bottles daily for a 2 week period or for a month or more in cases of more physical or longstanding emotional problems.

**Bach Combination Remedies of France:**

Take 4 drops of the Combination 4 times daily in a glass of water.

**Bailey Flower Essences:**

From stock concentrate where the essence is to be taken over more than a day or so, we recommend a dosage bottle be prepared (ie. a 10ml bottle filled with spring water or filled with 50% water to 50% vodka). Use 3 drops from each stock essence to make the dosage bottle. Take 3 drops of dosage 3 times daily.

**Bloesem Remedies of the Netherlands:**

See 'General Guidelines'.

**Dancing Light Orchid Essences:**

Take 1 or 2 drops under the tongue straight from the stock bottle.

**Findhorn Essences:**

Use 7 drops of dosage under the tongue for 2 weeks. Traumatic situations, take every 15 minutes until the symptoms subside

**Flower Essences of Fox Mountain:**

Use 2 to 4 drops from each stock remedy added to a 30ml dosage bottle. Take 4 drops 4 times per day for 28 days.

**Healing Herbs Bach Remedies:**

Use 2 drops from each stock remedy added to a 30ml dosage bottle. If Five Flower remedy is chosen, then 4 drops of stock are used. Take 4 drops, 4 times a day. For short term or immediate issues, add 2 drops of each stock essence to a glass of water and sip at regular intervals until relief is obtained.

**Himalayan Flower Enhancers:**

See 'General Guidelines'.

**Light Heart Essences:**

Please refer to directions given on all bottles including stock bottles.

**Living Essences of Australia:**

See 'General Guidelines' for making up a dosage bottle from a stock remedy. From a stock or dosage bottle, take 1 drop under the tongue or in a glass of water 6 times daily. The dosage bottle will last between 6 to 8 weeks. At the end of this period, assess how deeply the healing has gone within and whether it would be helpful to continue for another 6 to 8 weeks to ensure completion.

**Living Tree Orchid Essences:**

Take 1 or 2 drops under the tongue straight from the stock bottle.

**Pacific Essences:**

Take 11 drops of stock or dosage concentrate in the morning and evening, under the tongue or in a glass of water. Essences can be added to a full bath, use 22-44 drops of stock or dosage concentrate.

**Petite Fleur Essences of Texas:**

Place 2 drops on the wrist or heart centre. For topical application only as a general rule.

**Spriitual Remedies of Italy:**

For oral use at times of acute distress, 2 to 8 drops every ten to fifteen minutes. During easier times, 4 drops are to be taken 3 times a day. When working with the spray or the cream, apply a small quantity several times a day or whenever required.

**Star Essences of California**:

Please refer to instructions on the essence labels.

**Wild Earth Animal Essences:**

Take 5 to 7 drops, 3 to 4 times per day, for 2 to 3 weeks, but not with food. However, Daniel encourages people to "experiment and do what feels right" with these essences! The benefits of taking the essences is enhanced by quietly reflecting upon the qualities of the animal. May also be added to a warm bath. With alcohol sensitivity, the drops can be placed in a cup of boiling water and the alcohol will quickly evaporate.

# Listing of Essences by Symptoms and other Categories

1. Abundance/Prosperity
2. Abuse Issues
3. Addictions
4. Anger/Frustration
5. Arrogance
6. Balance/Centering
7. Being in the Present
8. Catalyst/Enhancer
9. Cellular Renewal
10. Child and Parent
11. Cleansing/Detoxification
12. Commitment/Responsibility

13. Communication/Expression of Feelings
14. Confusion/Turmoil/Focus/Clarity
15. Connecting with Nature
16. Courage/Feeling Afraid
17. Courage/Fright/Terror
18. Creativity/Inspiration
19. Critical/Judgemental
20. Death/Dying
21. Decision Making
22. Despair/Loss of Hope
23. Digestive System
24. Dominance/Subservience

25. Energy Movement
26. Energy/Vitality/Fatigue/Exhaustion
27. Experiencing Wonder
28. Forgiveness/Letting Go
29. Grief/Sadness/the need to cry
30. Grounding
31. Guilt/Shame
32. Happiness/Joy
33. Healing & Nurturing the Heart
34. Inner Guidance/Intuition
35. Inner Strength/Will Power
36. Insecurity

37. Insensitivity
38. Jealousy/Envy
39. Life Purpose/Direction
40. Loneliness/Isolation/Alienation/Abandonment

41. Love/Self Love/Self Acceptance
42. Masculine/Feminine Harmony & Balance
43. Mental Focus/Learning/Memory
44. Motivation/Apathy
45. Muscular Tension
46. Negative Thoughts/Negative Feelings
47. Nurturing & Support
48. Obsession

49. Overly Sensitive
50. Panic/Emergencies/Trauma/Accidents/Shock
51. Patience/Tolerance
52. Protection/Boundaries
53. Recuperation/Convalescence
54. Releasing the Past/Release
55. Resistance to Change/Flexibility/Moving On
56. Self Confidence/Self Esteem/Independence
57. Selfishness/Care for Others/Compassion
58. Serenity/Inner Peace
59. Sexuality/Passion
60. Skin Matters

61. Sleep Patterns
62. Space Clearing
63. Spinal Alignment & Movement
64. Spiritual Awakening/Meditation
65. Stagnation/Blockages
66. Stress/Anxiety/Worry
67. Transitions/Change
68. Travel Aids
69. Trust
70. Understanding & Integration
71. Victim Mentality
72. Winter Lows

73. Womanhood
74. Workaholic Tendencies

## 1. Abundance/Prosperity

1040 Blueberry Pollen
1042 Bog Blueberry
2796 Papala Kepau
2430 Seiva
1294 Bistort
4903 Ground Elder
4205 Ground Ivy
4209 Love
2365 Moneyplant
3168 Abund Essence
1345 Bauhinia
1348 Bluebell
1349 Boab
5785 Christmas Bell
1357 Dog Rose
1359 Five Corners
1379 Philotheca
1394 Sunshine Wattle
2203 Harebell
2224 Laurel
5767 Prosperity
3517 Sea Rocket
5229 Malva Zebrina
5231 Money Plant
5232 Money Plant - White
2440 Authenticity (5th Chakra)
2436 Down To Earth
2443 Gratefulness
2448 Trust
5099 Infinite Abundance
5708 Orange Wallflower
5711 Pussy Willow
1762 Abundance Essence
1763 Abundance Oil
3009 Abundance Program Kit
5152 Abundance Spray
1771 Barnacle
1792 Fireweed
1844 Polyanthus
1930 African Violet
2012 Mexican Oregano
3818 Buffalo
3826 Rabbit
3840 Squirrel

## 2. Abuse Issues

1032 Balsam Poplar
1016 Portage Glacier
3216 Rhodochrosite
1210 Tundra Twayblade
4842 Aftershock Myst
2729 Avocado
2767 Panini-Awa'aw
5836 Intimacy Myst
2428 Assá
2373 Evening Primrose
4964 Giant Stropharia
2370 Impatiens
2377 Little Inky Cap
4209 Love
2367 Myoona
2366 Red Poppy
4207 Sneezewort
2382 Snowdrop
2372 Terra
1349 Boab
1346 Billy Goat Plum
2226 Confid
2230 Emergency Essence
1359 Five Corners
1361 Fringed Violet
1360 Flannel Flower
1374 Mlountain Devil
1380 Pink Mulla Mulla
1382 Red Helmet Orchid
2232 Sexuality Essence
3508 Balsam
2216 Holy Thorn
2414 Karma Clear
3515 Rose Alba
2225 Rowan
2217 Sea Pink
5330 Artemis
5215 Crested Iris
5303 Healer
5306 Master Yarrow
5242 Queen of the Meadow
5316 Release Trauma
5559 Safe Boundaries
5327 Trauma Relief
1517 Crab Apple
2436 Down To Earth
2453 Golden Dawn
2454 Let Go
2456 Nirjara
2448 Trust
2437 Well Being
5692 Blue Delphinium
5698 Cyclamen
5702 Goldenrod
5705 Horse Chestnut
5090 Integrity In Interaction
5413 Integrity In Interact. Spray
5709 Physostegia
5712 Red Gladiolus
5713 Red Poppy
5091 Sexual Healing
3474 Giving Hands
1794 Forsythia
1803 Heart Spirit Essence
1827 Nootka Rose
2349 Sponge
1865 Urchin
2033 Ranunculus
2058 Vanilla
3837 Robin
3832 Wild Horse

## 3. Addictions

1114 Labrador Tea
1016 Portage Glacier
4133 Purification
5120 Purification Spray
2734 Coffee
4213 Empowerment
2747 Kou
2756 Naio
2776 Pua - Kenikeni
2428 Assá
2422 Imbe
5160 Tassi
2378 Borage
4204 Greater Celandine
1349 Boab
1350 Boronia
1351 Bottlebrush
1361 Fringed Violet
4554 Monga Waratah
1389 Southern Cross
1392 Sturt Desert Rose
1393 Sundew
1398 Waratah
1399 Wedding Bush
2215 Apple
3509 Globe Thistle
3507 Hazel
5768 Transformation
5200 Agrimony
5212 Clematis "Ernest Markham"
1497 Agrimony
2436 Down To Earth
2454 Let Go
2466 Morning Glory
4098 Opium Poppy
2437 Well Being
5032 Freedom
5665 Original Innocence
5751 Original Innocence Spray
5713 Red Poppy
1633 Blue China Orchid
1634 Blue Leschenaultia
1655 Green Rose
1697 Silver Princess Gum
1794 Forsythia
1865 Urchin
1931 Alfredo De Damas
1980 French Lavender
2043 Self-Image
2051 Stop Smoking
2065 White Petunia
3812 Eagle

## 4. Anger/Frustration

1038 Blue Elf Viola
1134 Mountain Wormwood
3228 Tiger's Eye
2790 Akia
2743 Impatiens
2748 Kukui
2755 Mai'a (Banana)
2772 Pleomele Fragrans
5840 Stress Relief Myst
2783 'Uala
2429 Moara
4107 Thini-A
5493 Anger & Frustration
1299 Bracken (Aqu. Extract)
1301 Buttercup
3330 Childhood
2370 Impatiens
2377 Little Inky Cap
2368 Red Henbit
2379 Sensitive Weed
2382 Snowdrop
1356 Dagger Hakea
1369 Kangaroo Paw
1374 Mountain Devil
1382 Red Helmet Orchid
1385 Rough Bluebell
1388 Slender Rice Flower
1402 yellow Cowslip Orchid
2414 Karma Clear
3514 Monkeyflower
2225 Rowan
5324 Calm Time
5325 Child Glow
5331 Hestia
5221 Horseradish
5225 Ivory Hollyhock
5243 Red Hollyhock
1501 Beech
1507 Cherry Plum
1529 Holly
1535 Impatiens
1561 Vervain
1563 Vine
1575 Willow
2439 Ecstasy (4th Chakra)
2450 Pluto
2438 Strength
2437 Well Being

5030 Harmony
5692 Blue Delphinium
5704 Honesty
5707 Manuka
5711 Pussy Willow
5713 Red Poppy
1632 Black Kangaroo Paw
1654 Golden Waitsia
1666 Mauve Melaleuca
1670 Orange Spiked Pea Flower
1672 Pale Sundew
1691 Red Leschenaultia
1711 White Nymph Waterlily
5862 Active Serenity
5732 Active Serenity Spray
5538 White Beauty Aura Spray
1775 Blue Lupin
1783 Candystick
1817 Mussel
1829 Orange Honeysuckle
2405 Pearly Everlasting
1840 Plantain
1929 Abate Anger
3001 Bouquet Of Harmony
1982 Garden Mum
1996 Ligustrum
2009 Meadow Sage
2027 Pink Geranium
3829 Dove

## 5. Arrogance

2736 Cup of Gold
2779 Spider Lily
2423 Bromelia 1
2365 Moneyplant
1364 Gymea Lily
1365 Hibbertia
1385 Rough Bluebelll
1388 Slender Rice Flower
2222 Lime
2209 Willow Herb
5252 Sunflower
5261 Wild Ginger
1501 Beech
1567 Water Violet
2439 Ecstasy (4th Chakra)
2438 Strength (3rd Chakra)
4095 White Orchid
5710 Pink Cherry
1672 Pale Sundew
1719 Yellow Leschenaultia
2347 Whale
2016 Narcissus
2029 Poppy
3816 Dolphin
3815 Hummingbird
3821 Otter

## 6. Balance/Centering

3185 Aventurine
1032 Balsam Poplar
1098 Green Fairy Orchid
1100 Grove Sandwort
3204 Jadeite Jade
1114 Labrador Tea
1120 Lady's Slipper
1122 Lamb's Quarters
1144 Opium Poppy
1150 Pineapple Weed
1168 River Beauty
3219 Ruby
1020 Solstice Storm
1200 Sunflower
1202 Sweetgale
3230 Turquoise
1212 Twinflower
1218 White Spruce
1224 Wild Rhubarb
2738 Hau
5837 Office Harmony Myst
2768 Pa-Nini-O-Ka
5838 Protection Myst
2784 Ulei
2785 Water Poppy
2432 Ararybá
2428 Assá
4781 Kundalini
2435 Obaiti
5167 Red Gel & Oil
2434 Renascer
4107 Thini-A
5158 Yatê
3885 Arizona Fir
1305 Firethorn
5461 Shock & Trauma
1334 Thrift
1335 Tranquility
2380 Alternanthera
2365 Moneyplant
4208 Protection
2379 Sensitive Weed
2376 Tansy
3167 Adol Essence
1347 Black-eyed Susan
1352 Bush Fuchsia
4812 Calm and Clear Essence
4813 Calm and Clear Mist
4823 Calm and Clear Cream
1355 Crowea
1365 Hibbertia
1367 Isopogon
1368 Jacaranda
1378 Peach Flowered Tea-Tree
1383 Red Lily
1386 She Oak
1396 Talll Yellow Top
1402 Yellow Cowslip Orchid
2205 Daisy
2411 First Aid
4914 First Aid Gel
3509 Globe Thistle
2203 Harebell
2217 Sea Pink
2413 Spiritual Marriage
3519 Wild Pansy
5208 California Poppy
5210 Chive
5312 Pre Trauma
5265 Rose "Sarah Van Fleet"
5252 Sunflower
5311 Vital Balance
5560 Vital Balance
1543 Oak
1555 Scleranthus
1569 White Chestnut
2442 Flight (7th Chakra)
2453 Golden Dawn
2447 Healing
2458 Heart Of Tantra
2465 Isan
4091 Rapa-Nui
2469 Sober Up
2437 Well Being (2nd Chakra)
5035 Energy
5695 Cherry Plum Fruit
5647 Heart Of Peace
5648 Heart Of Peace Spray
5090 Integrity In Interaction
5413 Integrity In Interact. Spray
5086 Peace In A Storm
2080 Emotions In Balance
1661 Leafless Orchid
1681 Purple Enamel Orchid
5862 Active Serenity
5732 Active Serenity Aura Spray
5602 Walking to the Earth's Rhythm
5609 Core of Being
1768 Balancer Essence
1769 Balancer Oil
5421 Balancer Spray
1773 Blue Camas
1779 Brown Kelp
2407 Fuchsia
1798 Grape Hyacinth
1831 Ox Eye Daisy
2353 Rainbow Kelp
2349 Sponge
1884 Viburnum
1888 Windflower
2400 Yellow Pond Lily
2060 Viridiflora
2070 Yarrow
4796 Luce / Light Essence
4797 Luce / Light Essence Cream
4798 Luce / Light Essence Spray
3481 Angel Rejuvention Spray
3818 Buffalo
3817 Butterfly
3814 Deer
3829 Dove
5136 Giraffe
3813 Mountain Lion
3825 Spider

## 7. Being in the Present

2434 Renascer
2363 Clematis
4964 Giant Strophania
2368 Red Henbit
2230 Meditation
1383 Red Lily
1393 Sundew
5550 Alert & Alive
5212 Clematis "Ernest Markham"
1513 Clematis
1531 Honeysuckle
5033 Focus
5602 Walking To The Earth's Rhythm
5504 Time Zone / Being In Time
1785 Chickweed
1808 Jellyfish
1838 Pipsissewa
2350 Sea Turtle
1869 Snowberry
3818 Buffalo
3814 Deer
3829 Dove
3831 Salamander
3830 Seal
5139 Tiger
3822 Turtle

## 8. Catalyst/Enhancer

5131 Mana
2369 Rainbow
2368 Red Henbit
5221 Horseradish
5236 Pale Corydalis
4843 Empowerment Myst
5816 Devata
5131 Mana
1794 Forsythia
4796 Luce / Light Essence

## 9. Cellular Renewal

1216 White Fireweed
2428 Assá
2213 Ragged Robin
3518 Watercress
5213 Comfrey
5235 Mugwort
2456 Nirjara
5696 Comfrey
5802 Crab Apple Fruit
5706 Lilac
5711 Pussy Willow
5477 Renewing Life
5602 Walking To The Earth's Rhythm
2356 Coral
2358 Diatoms
1961 Country Marilou
1985 Iberis Candytuft
2041 Salad Burnet

## 10. Child & Parent

1100 Grove Sandwort
1138 Northern Lady's Slipper
1150 Pineapple Weed
1190 Sticky Geranium
1200 Sunflower
2733 Chinese Violet
5835 Family Harmony Myst
2763 Noni
2773 Plumbago
2783 'Uala
3352 Sea Campion
1339 Witch Hazel
2373 Evening Primrose
2375 Field Scabious
2370 Impatiens
4209 Love
2367 Mycena
4208 Protection
2379 Sensitive Weed
4206 Smooth Hawksbeard
2382 Snowdrop
3167 Adol Essence
1348 Bluebell
1350 Boronia
1351 Bottlebrush
1370 Kapok Bush
1371 Little Flannel Flower
1374 Mountain Devil
1382 Red Helmet Orchid
1400 Wild Potato Bush
3508 Balsam
2216 Holy Thorn
2414 Karma Clear
3515 Rose Alba
5203 Blackberry
5323 Boundaries
5207 Buttercup
5324 Calm Time
5209 Chamomile
5325 Child Glow
5215 Crested Iris
5333 Demeter
5326 Initiative
5228 Lovage
5327 Trauma Relief
5328 Worthiness
5561 Worthiness
5853 Cedar
2446 Children's Flower
2443 Gratefulness
5030 Harmony
5697 Cowslip
5700 Fleabane
5702 Goldenrod
5710 Pink Cherry
1652 Goddess Grasstree
4660 Messenger Of The Heart
4116 Unveiling Affection
5621 Loving Grace
1767 Arbutus
1771 Barnacle
1805 Hooker's Onion
1937 Aquilegia Columbine
1955 Chamomile
1962 Crepe Myrtle
1995 Lemon Grass
2052 Sunflower
3837 Robin

## 11.Cleansing / Detoxification

1032 Balsam Poplar
3187 Black Tourmaline
1092 Grass Of Parnassus
1010 Liard Hot Springs
3210 Moonstone
1012 Northern Lights
1140 Northern Twayblade
1016 Portage Glacier
4133 Purification
5120 Purification Spray
3219 Ruby
3224 Smoky Quartz
1020 Solstice Storm
3225 Spectrolite
1204 Sweetgrass
3230 Turquoise
2728 Amazon Swordplant
5834 Anti-Tox Myst
2729 Avocado
2734 Coffee
2745 Kamani
2765 Ohelo
2782 Ti (Or Ki)
2435 Obaiti
2431 Ybá
2375 Field Scabious
2383 Foxglove
4964 Giant Strophania
4204 Greater Celandine
4205 Ground Ivy
2367 Mycena (Mushroom)
2382 Snowdrop
1343 Angelsword
3337 Green Essence
4810 Purifying Essence
1400 Wild Potato Bush
2213 Ragged Robin
5768 Transformation
3518 Watercress
5204 Bloodroot
5216 Dandelion
5219 Garlic
5250 Spiderwort
1517 Crab Apple
2445 Aura Cleaning
2464 Lotus
2466 Morning Glory
2456 Nirjara
4098 Opium Poppy
5802 Crab Apple Fruit
5803 Crimean Snowdrop
5098 Infinite Light
5806 Peaceful Detachment
1629 Antiseptic Bush
1632 Black Kangaroo Paw
1638 Cape Bluebell
2356 Coral
1815 Moon Snail
1840 Plantain
2351 Sea Lettuce
1933 Amaryllis
1966 Dandelion
1969 Delphinium
1972 Echinacea
4796 Luce / Light Essence
4797 Luce / Light Essence Cream
4798 Luce / Light Essence Spray
3481 Angel Rejuventation Spray
3815 Hummingbird

## 12. Commitment / Responsibility

3221 Sapphire
1228 Willow
5787 Floral Orquidea
2378 Borage
2363 Clematis
2383 Foxglove
4962 Goldenrod
2365 Moneyplant
2368 Red Henbit
1351 Bottlebrush
1364 Gymea Lily
1366 Illawarra Flame Tree
1368 Jacaranda
1369 Kangaroo Paw
1370 Kapok Bush
1378 Peach-flowered Tea-tree
2231 Relationship Essence
1389 Southern Cross
1399 Wedding Bush
2215 Apple
3515 Rose Alba
5333 Demeter
5559 Safe Boundaries
5853 Cedar
2436 Down To Earth
2448 Trust
5698 Cyclamen
5702 Goldenrod
5713 Red Poppy
1640 Christmas Tree
1663 Many Headed Dryandra
1688 Red Beak Orchid
1704 Ursinia
3479 Wattle
2405 Pearly Everlasting
2350 Sea Turtle
1878 Surfgrass
1938 Archduke Charles
2039 Rose Of Sharon
2071 Yellow Rose
3813 Mountain Lion
3811 Wolf

## 13. Communication / Expression of Feelings

3186 Azurite
1038 Blue Elf Viola
1098 Green Fairy Orchid
1106 Horsetail
1212 Twinflower
2728 Amazon Swordplant
4210 Family Harmony
5835 Family Harmony Myst
2744 Jade Vine
5837 Office Harmony Myst

2797 Port St. John's Vine
2798 Pua Kala
2783 'Uala
2425 Celebração
2421 Jumping Child
4781 Kundalini
2433 Revelação
1299 Bracken (Aqu. Extract)
2373 Evening Primrose
2375 Field Scabious
4962 Goldenrod
2370 Impatiens
2377 Little Inky Cap
2381 Purple Flower
2366 Red Poppy
4207 Sneezewort
2382 Snowdrop
2374 Yellow Star Tulip
1348 Bluebell
1352 Bush Fuchsia
1353 Bush Gardenia
1356 Dagger Hakea
1357 Dog Rose
2226 Confid Essence
1360 Flannel Flower
2236 Heartsong Essence
1369 Kangaroo Paw
1381 Red Grevillea
2231 Relationship Essence
1395 Tall Mulla Mulla
2210 Broom
2361 Holy Grail
2216 Holy Thorn
3512 Lady's Mantle
3519 Wild Pansy
5214 Cosmos
5253 Sweet Pea
1497 Agrimony
1539 Mimulus
2440 Authenticity (5th Chakra)
2438 Strength (3rd Chakra)
2437 Well Being (2nd Chakra)
5692 Blue Delphinium
5693 Blue Hibiscus
5694 Celandine
5655 Relationships
5804 The Rose (Mme. Isaac Pereire)
1639 Catspaw
1670 Orange Spiked Pea Flower
1705 Veronica
4660 Messenger of the Heart
1777 Bluebell
1772 Blue Camas
2355 Dolphin
1790 Easter Lily
1815 Moon Snail
2352 Sea Horse
2401 Wallflower
2347 Whale
1935 Anise Hyssop
1955 Chamomile
1962 Crepe Myrtle
2008 Marquise Bocella
3816 Dolphin
5134 Elephant
3820 Owl

## 14. Confusion/Turmoil/ Focus/Clarity

1026 Alder
3184 Aquamarine
1036 Bladderwort
1000 Chalice Well
3194 Citrine
3196 Diamond
3199 Fluorite Combo
1148 Paper Birch
3220 Rutilated Quartz
3229 Topaz
2731 Bamboo Orchid
2747 Kou
2793 Mamaki
2753 Mamane
2757 Nana-Honua
2795 Pakalana
2769 Papaya
2780 Stenogyne Calaminthoides
5174 Magenta Gel & Oil
5159 Marupiara
2435 Obaiti
2434 Renascer
4107 Thini-A
5158 Yatê
5492 Confusion
1331 Solomon's Seal
1335 Tranquility
2364 Angelica
2378 Borage
2363 Clematis
2368 Red Henbit
2366 Red Poppy
2376 Tansy
2372 Terra
1350 Boronia
1352 Bush Fuchsia
4823 Calm & Clear Cream
4812 Calm & Clear Essence
4813 Calm & Clear Mist
2228 Cognis Essence
1368 Jacaranda
1373 Mint Bush
1377 Paw Paw
1393 Sundew
3421 Wise Action
2219 Birch
2210 Broom
2415 Clear Light
2205 Daisy
2218 Scots Pine
3519 Wild Pansy
5217 Dill
5230 Mauve Mullein
5234 Moonshine Yarrow
5239 Purple Bee Palm
5248 Shasta Daisy
1505 Cerato
1541 Mustard
1555 Scleranthus
1569 White Chestnut
1571 Wild Oat
2452 Blue Dragon
2441 Clarity (6th Chakra)
2459 Gateway
4920 Gulaga
2450 Pluto
2462 Veil Of Dreams
5702 Goldenrod
5090 Integrity In Interaction
5413 Integrity In Interaction Spray
5706 Lilac
5711 Pussy Willow
1637 Brown Boronia
2084 Concentration & Meditation
2080 Emotions In Balance
1654 Golden Waitsia
3361 Hairy Yellow Pea
1682 Purple Eremophila
3477 Start's Spider Orchid
1710 White Eremophila
1711 White Nymph Waterlily
5862 Active Serenity
5732 Active Serenity Aura Spray
5602 Walking To The Earth's Rhythm
5199 Clear Mind Aura Spray
5196 Clear Mind Essence
1775 Blue Lupin
1779 Brown Kelp
1812 Lily Of The Valley
1833 Periwinkle
1838 Pipsissewa
2353 Rainbow Kelp
2348 "Staghorn" Algae
1957 Cherokee Rose
2035 Red Malva
2065 White Petunia
3814 Deer
3812 Eagle
3835 Fox
3820 Owl
3825 Spider
5139 Tiger
3842 Whale
5140 Zebra

## 15. Connecting w/ Nature

1048 Cassandra
1060 Comandra
1094 Green Bells Of Ireland
1096 Green Bog Orchid
1132 Moschatel
1140 Northern Twayblade
2426 Embó Rudá
2380 Alternanthera
2381 Purple Flower
1362 Green Spider Orchid
3510 Grass Of Parnassus
2361 Holy Grail
3513 Mallow
2218 Scots Pine
5242 Queen Of The Meadow
5261 Wild Ginger
2446 Children's Flower
2447 Healing
4091 Rapa-Nui
5714 Rosebay Willowherb
5602 Walking To The Earth's Rhythm
2355 Dolphin
2404 Poplar
1884 Viburnum
2347 Whale
1978 Fortuniana
2056 Thyme
5134 Elephant

## 16. Courage/Feeling Afraid

3214 Peridot
1156 Prickly Wild Rose
1184 Soapberry
5838 Protection Myst
2786 Wiliwili
2423 Bromelia 1
5787 Floral Orquidea
4781 Kundalini
2434 Renascer
4107 Thini-A
2378 Borage
2377 Little Inky Cap
2371 Orchid
2366 Red Poppy
2379 Sensitive Weed
2382 Snowdrop
1357 Dog Rose

2230 Emergency Essence
4814 Emergency Mist
1363 Grey Spider Flower
1364 Gymea Lily
1392 Sturt Desert Rose
1395 Talll Mullla Mulla
1398 Waratah
5330 Artemis
1539 Mimulus
1549 Red Chestnut
2436 Down To Earth (1st Chakra)
2460 Warrior
1639 Catspaw
1659 Illyarrie
1678 Pink Impatiens
3477 Start's Spider Orchid
5522 Clearing The Way / Self Belief
4660 Messenger of the Heart
5816 Devata
2398 Douglas Aster
1800 Grace Widow
1878 Surfgrass
1933 Amaryllis
1948 Borage
1972 Echinacea
1981 Gaillardia
3815 Hummingbird
5138 Lion
3813 Mountain Lion

## 17. Courage/Fright/Terror

3344 Soul Support
2735 Cotton
2765 Ohelo
3493 Fears
4208 Protection
2372 Terra
1358 Dog Rose of the Wild Forces
2230 Emergency Essence
4814 Emergency Mist
1362 Green Spider Orchid
1363 Grey Spider Flower
1398 Waratah
2411 First Aid
4914 First Aid Gel
3511 Iona Pennywort
2212 Thistle
5206 Borage
5213 Comfrey
5552 Emergency Relief
5306 Master Yarrow
5559 Safe Boundaries
1499 Aspen
1507 Cherry Plum
1551 Rock Rose
5853 Cedar
2459 Gateway
2457 Vital Spark
2437 Well Being (2nd Chakra)
5036 Courage
5695 Cherry Plum Fruit
5803 Crimean Snowdrop
5699 Dandelion
5647 Heart of Peace
5648 Heart of Peace Spray
5080 Light Anchor
5086 Peace In A Storm
1692 Ribbon Pea
1709 W. A. Smokebush
1787 Death Camas
1871 Snowdrop
3001 Bouquet of Harmony
1959 Cinnamon Basil

## 18. Creativity/Inspiration

1222 Wild Iris
1224 Wild Rhubarb
5157 Indaiá
5174 Magenta Gel & Oil
3353 Oribá
2427 Pyatã
5167 Red Gel & Oil
5169 Yellow Gel & Oil
1338 Welsh Poppy
2380 Alternanthera
2383 Foxglove
4963 Ground Elder
2369 Rainbow
2368 Red Henbit
2372 Terra
2374 Yellow Star Tulip
2236 Creativity Essence
1397 Turkey Bush
2361 Holy Grail
2216 Holy Thorn
3515 Rose Alba
2207 Spotted Orchid
5334 Aphrodite
5203 Blackberry
5214 Cosmos
5551 Creative Flow
5224 Iris "Flight Of The Butterlies"
5248 Shasta Daisy
1513 Clematis
4097 Astral Orchid
2440 Authenticity (5th Chakra)
2441 Clarity (6th Chakra)
5694 Celandine
5698 Cyclamen
5706 Lilac
1631 Balga Blackboy
2082 Creativity
1685 Purple & Red Kangaroo Paw
1697 Silver Princess Gum
1708 Star Of Bethlehem
1713 Woolly Banksia
5851 Serendipity
2346 Chiton
1805 Hooker's Onion
1815 Moon Snail
1829 Orange Honeysuckle
1871 Snowdrop
1940 Azalea
1951 Bronze Fennel
1957 Cherokee Rose
1958 Christmas Cactus
3834 Beaver
3812 Eagle
3826 Rabbit

## 19. Critical/Judgemental

1058 Columbine
3213 Pearl
1186 Sphagnum Moss
2786 Wiliwili
4204 Greater Celandine
3147 Freshwater Mangrove
1402 Yellow Cowslip Orchid
3511 Iona Pennywort
2414 Karma Clear
2222 Lime
2225 Rowan
2207 Spotted Orchid
2209 Willow Herb
1501 Beech
2439 Ecstasy (4th Chakra)
2443 Gratefulness
2444 Hidden Splendor
2438 Strength (3rd Chakra)
5703 Gorse
5707 Manuka
1648 Fuchsia Grevillea
1701 Southern Cross
1704 Ursinia
1718 Yellow & Green Kangaroo Paw
4116 Unveiling Affection
1817 Mussel
1840 Plantain
1851 Salal
1880 Twin Flower
1929 Abate Anger
1982 Garden Mum
2019 Onion
2047 Snapdragon
3821 Otter

## 20. Death/Dying

2364 Angelica
4209 Love
2365 Moneyplant
3306 Autumn Leaves
1350 Boronia
1351 Bottlebrush
1354 Bush Iris
3305 Lichen
3511 Iona Pennywort
3516 Rose Water Lily
2202 Stonecrop
5554 Grieving
5223 Hyssop
5258 White Bleeding Heart
5259 White Foxglove
2454 Let Go
2448 Trust
2437 Well Being (2nd Chakra)
4095 White Orchid
5695 Cherry Plum Fruit
5080 Light Anchor
5806 Peaceful Detachment
1846 Purple Crocus
1876 Starfish
2400 Yellow Pond Lily
3001 Bouquet Of Harmony
1971 Dill
2021 Pansy
2024 Peppermint
3817 Butterfly
3829 Dove
3823 Snake

## 21. Decision Making

2371 Orchid
2376 Tansy
4812 Calm and Clear Essence
4813 Calm and Clear Mist
4823 Calm and Clear Cream
1355 Crowea
1368 Jacaranda
1377 Paw Paw
1387 Silver Princess
1393 Sundew
3794 Defining Edges
4938 Stepping Ahead Now
5332 Athena
5551 Creative Flow
5229 Malva Zebrina
5233 Monkshood
5522 Clearing The Way
5851 Serendipity
5199 Clear Mind Aura Spray
5196 Clear Mind Essence
5816 Devata

1838 Pipsissewa
3812 Eagle
3813 Mountain Lion
3820 Owl

## 22. Despair/Loss of Hope

1016 Portage Glacier
4133 Purification
5120 Purification Spray
3344 Soul Support
1208 Tundra Rose
2790 Akia
2732 Bougainvillea
2757 Nana-Honua
2765 Ohelo
2772 Pleomele Fragrans
2777 Pua-Pilo
2778 Pukiawe
5787 Floral Orquidea
2421 Jumping Child
2427 Pyatã
5162 Rudá
2431 Ybá
1294 Bistort
1299 Bracken (Aqu. Extract)
3330 Childhood
3902 Depression & Despair
3493 Fears
1311 Leopardsbane
3526 Transition
2364 Angelica
2378 Borage
4964 Giant Stropharia
2368 Red Henbit
2372 Terra
1354 Bush Iris
2230 Emergency Essence
1357 Dog Rose
1370 Kapok Bush
1373 Mint Bush
1386 She Oak
1394 Sunshine Wattle
1396 Talll Yellow Top
1398 Waratah
2206 Gorse
3511 Iona Pennywort
3515 Rose Alba
3516 Rose Water Lily
5325 Child Glow
5225 Ivory Hollyhock
5243 Red Hollyhock
1507 Cherry Plum
1517 Crab Apple
1519 Elm
1520 Five Flower Remedy
1523 Gentian
1525 Gorse
1531 Honeysuckle
1533 Hornbeam
1541 Mustard
1543 Oak
1559 Sweet Chestnut
2459 Gateway
4093 Pink Primula
4096 Purple Orchid
2438 Strength (3rd Chakra)
2448 Trust
5037 Joy
5080 Light Anchor
5086 Peace In A Storm
5713 Red Poppy
5621 Loving Grace
1775 Blue Lupin
2399 Fairy Bell
1798 Grape Hyacinth
1833 Periwinkle
2353 Rainbow Kelp
2401 Wallflower
1939 Autumn Damask
2000 Louis Phillipe
2006 Marie Pavié
2036 Red Rose
3812 Eagle
3821 Otter
3832 Wild Horse

## 23. Digestive System

2364 Angelica
1345 Bauhinia
1347 Black Eyed Susan
1350 Boronia
1355 Crowea
1357 Dog Rose
1377 Paw Paw
1378 Peach Flowerd Tea-tree
1381 Red Grevillea
2215 Apple
2213 Ragged Robin
5220 Ginseng
5240 Purple Loosestrife
2447 Healing
2438 Strength (3rd Chakra)
5697 Cowslip
5699 Dandelion
5700 Fleabane
1663 Many Headed Dryandra
1687 Rabbit Orchid
1688 Red Beak Orchid
1712 Wild Violet
1716 Yellow Cone Flower
1775 Blue Lupin
1800 Grass Widow
1840 Plantain
2349 Sponge
1888 Windflower
1943 Bamboo
1963 Crossandra
2014 Moss Rose
2024 Peppermint
2027 Pink Geranium
2030 Primrose (Evening)
2062 Weight

## 24. Dominance / Subserviance

1182 Sitka Spruce Pollen
1200 Sunflower
2740 Hinahina-Ku-Kahakai
2752 Macadamia
2774 Pua Melia (Plumeria)
2779 Spider Lily
2425 Celebração
5788 Floral Soberania
3330 Childhood
1313 Lilac
3339 Yang
3340 Yin
4204 Greater Celandine
2377 Little Inky Cap
2371 Orchid
1347 Black-Eyed Susan
1349 Boab
1364 Gymea Lily
1365 Hibbertia
1366 Illawarra Flame Tree
1367 Isopogon
1385 Rough Bluebelll
1402 Yellow Cowslip Orchid
2222 Lime
3514 Monkeyflower
2217 Sea Pink
5768 Transformation
2209 Willow Herb
5252 Sunflower
1501 Beech
1503 Centaury
1563 Vine
1565 Walnut
2438 Strength (3rd Chakra)
2460 Warrior
5702 Goldenrod
5090 Integrity In Interaction
5413 Integrity In Interaction Spray
5713 Red Poppy
5655 Relationships
1647 Fringed Mantis Orchid
1651 Geraldton Wax
1699 Snakebush
4116 Unveiling Affection
1765 Anemone
1785 Chickweed
1812 Lily of the Valley
1842 Poison Hemlock
1863 Sea Palm
2402 Silver Birch
1946 Blue Danube Aster
2002 Madame Louis Levique
2010 Mexican Bush Sage
2029 Poppy
2049 Spike Lavender

## 25. Energy Movement

3188 Bloodstone
3191 Carnelian
3198 Fluorite
3199 Fluorite Combo
1120 Lady's Slipper
3210 Moonstone
1150 Pineapple Weed
1202 Sweetgale
3229 Topaz
1224 Wild Rhubarb
5834 Anti-tox Myst
2730 Awapuhi-Melemele
2733 Chinese Violet
2738 Hau
2748 Kukui
2749 La'au'-Aila
5131 Mana
2775 Poha
1304 Early Purple Orchid
3493 Fears
4964 Giant Stropharia
2368 Red Henbit
4206 Smooth Hawksbeard
3429 Clearing Blockages
3428 Clearing Inner Pathways
3427 Dance of Creation
2217 Sea Pink
3519 Wild Pansy
5244 Rose Campion
5254 Tomato
2464 Lotus
2460 Warrior
5862 Active Serenity
5732 Active Serenity Spray
1777 Bluebell
2356 Coral
2355 Dolphin
1796 Goatsbeard
1817 Mussel
1829 Orange Honeysuckle
1855 Sand Dollar

2352 Sea Horse
1871 Snowdrop
2349 Sponge
1964 Curry
1973 Energy
2050 Stock
2054 Tansy
5132 Cheetah

## 26. Energy / Vitality / Fatigue / Exhaustion

3190 Brazilian Quartz
3191 Carnelian
1092 Grass of Parnassus
4134 Guardian
5121 Guardian Spray
3211 Opal
1144 Opium Poppy
3212 Orange Calcite
1016 Portage Glacier
4133 Purification
5120 Purification Spray
1190 Sticky Geranium
2730 Awapuhi-Melemele
2750 Lehua
2751 Lotus
5131 Mana
2778 Pukiawe
5786 Floral Caju
2421 Jumping Child
2427 Pyatã
5167 Red Gel & Oil
2430 Seiva
5160 Tassi
2431 Ybá
1338 Welsh Poppy
4964 Giant Stropharia
2370 Impatiens
4208 Protection
2368 Red Henbit
2379 Sensitive Weed
4206 Smooth Hawksbeard
2382 Snowdrop
1342 Alpine Mint Bush
1344 Banksia Robur
2227 Dynamis Essence
1361 Fringed Violet
1372 Macrocarpa
1373 Mint Bush
1376 Old Man Banksia
1377 Paw Paw
1400 Wild Potato Bush
2220 Elder
2206 Gorse
2096 Life Force
2217 Sea Pink
2221 Sycamore
2223 Valerian
3519 Wild Pansy
5550 Alert & Alive
5330 Artemis
5553 Exaltation & Joy
5301 Exaltation of Flowers
5237 Penstemon
5243 Red Hollyhock
5314 Trauma Ease
1519 Elm
1361 Fringed Violet
1533 Hornbeam
1373 Mint Bush
1543 Oak
1545 Olive
1377 Paw Paw
1557 Star Of Bethlehem
1573 Wild Rose
5853 Cedar
2436 Down To Earth (1st Chakra)
2463 Endurance
2447 Healing
2466 Morning Glory
2457 Vital Spark
5035 Energy
5698 Cyclamen
5711 Pussy Willow
5713 Red Poppy
1643 Cowkicks
2078 Energy
2081 Inner Strength
1661 Leafless Orchid
2331 Pain Cream
1675 Pink Everlasting
1677 Pink Fountain Triggerplant
1681 Purple Enamel Orchid
1688 Red Beak Orchid
3476 Reed Trigger Plant
1696 Shy Blue Orchid
2333 Skin Lustre Cream
1641 White Spider Orchid
1713 Woolly Banksia
5862 Active Serenity
5732 Active Serenity Spray
5861 Happy Relief
5731 Happy Relief Aura Spray
5602 Walking To The Earth's Rhythm
5609 Core Of Being
1777 Bluebell
2355 Dolphin
2398 Douglas Aster
1790 Easter Lily
2407 Fuchsia
1796 Goatsbeard
1827 Nootka Rose
2352 Sea Horse
1869 Snowberry
2349 Sponge
2347 Whale
1954 Cécil Brünner
1973 Energy
4968 Fatigue
2018 Old Blush
2044 Shrimp
2060 Viridiflora
3813 Mountain Lion

## 27. Experiencing Wonder

3230 Turquoise
2732 Bougainvillea
2367 Mycena (Mushroom)
3422 Wonderous Heart
3516 Rose Water Lily
5325 Child Glow
5243 Red Hollyhock
2452 Blue Dragon
2446 Children's Flower
2449 Chiron
2455 Expansion
2442 Flight (7th Chakra)
2443 Gratefulness
2444 Hidden Splendor
5694 Celandine
5538 White Beauty Aura Spray
2349 Sponge
1966 Dandelion
1974 Fairy Rose
1978 Fortuniana
1987 Indian Paintbrush
2001 Madame Alfred Carriere
2056 Thyme
2070 Yarrow
3841 Frog

## 28. Forgiveness/Letting Go

2428 Assá
2383 Foxglove
2377 Little Inky Cap
4209 Love
2365 Moneyplant
2367 Mycena
2381 Purple Flower
2369 Rainbow
2384 Rue
4206 Smooth Hawksbeard
2382 Snowdrop
1351 Bottlebrush
1356 Dagger Hakea
1374 Mountain Devil
1392 Sturt Desert Rose
3507 Hazel
2414 Karma Clear
2412 Revelation
2225 Rowan
2208 Scottish Primrose
2202 Stonecrop
5203 Blackberry
5216 Dandelion
5221 Horseradish
5223 Hyssop
5244 Rose Campion
5251 Star Chickweed
2439 Ecstasy (4th Chakra)
2454 Let Go
4095 White Orchid
5095 Forgiveness
5703 Gorse
5707 Manuka
5665 Original Innocence
5751 Original Innocence Spray
5710 Pink Cherry
1632 Black Kangaroo Paw
1645 Dampiera
1680 Pixie Mops
5621 Loving Grace
1803 Heart Spirit Essence
1842 Poison Hemlock
1851 Salal
2402 Silver Birch
1871 Snowdrop
1876 Starfish
2025 Periwinkle
2026 Pine
2067 Wild Oats
3817 Butterfly
3820 Dove

## 29. Grief / Sadness / The Need to Cry

1052 Chiming Bells
3192 Chrysocolla
3209 Montana Rhodochrosite
1168 River Beauty
1178 Single Delight
2421 Jumping Child
3353 Oribá
1299 Bracken (Aqu. Extract)
1308 Grief
5494 Sadness & Loneliness
2370 Impatiens
4209 Love
2367 Mycena (Mushroom)
2382 Snowdrop
1348 Bluebell

1350 Boronia
1351 Bottlebrush
1360 Flannel Flower
1371 Little Flannel Flower
1380 Pink Mulla Mulla
1384 Red Suva Frangipani
1391 Sturt Desert Pea
2411 First Aid
4914 First Aid Gel
3509 Globe Thistle
3510 Grass Of Parnassus
2412 Revelation
2214 Snowdrop
5209 Chamomile
5325 Child Glow
5554 Grieving
5243 Red Hollyhock
5258 White Bleeding Heart
1497 Agrimony
1523 Gentian
1525 Gorse
1531 Honeysuckle
1541 Mustard
1557 Star Of Bethlehem
1573 Wild Rose
2439 Ecstasy (4th Chakra)
2455 Expansion
2454 Let Go
5037 Joy
5695 Cherry Plum Fruit
5698 Cyclamen
5664 Healing Grief
5821 Healing Grief Spray
5704 Honesty
5708 Orange Wallflower
1645 Dampiera
1659 Illyarrie
1666 Mauve Melaleuca
1667 Menzies Banksia
1710 White Eremophila
1711 White Nymph Waterlily
5621 Loving Grace
1767 Arbutus
1846 Purple Crocus
1876 Starfish
1955 Chamomile
2006 Marie Pavié
2021 Pansy
5137 Hippopotamus
3832 Wild Horse

## 30. Grounding

3186 Azurite
3190 Brazilian Quartz
3193 Chrysoprase
1060 Comandra
1068 Cow Parsnip
3166 Fireweed Combo
1094 Green Bells Of Ireland
3201 Green Jasper
4134 Guardian
5121 Guardian Spray
3207 Malachite
1150 Pineapple Weed
1018 Rainbow Glacier
3224 Smoky Quartz
5461 Shock & Trauma
3505 Mediterranean Sage
3352 Sea Campion
1334 Thrift
2380 Alternanthera
2364 Angelica
2363 Clematis
2375 Field Scabious
4964 Giant Stropharia
4204 Greater Celandine
4963 Ground Elder
4205 Ground Ivy
2367 Mycena
2381 Purple Flower
2366 Red Poppy
2372 Terra
1368 Jacaranda
1383 Red Lily
1393 Sundew
3508 Balsam
2211 Bell Heather
2205 Daisy
2411 First Aid
4914 First Aid Gel
2208 Scottish Primrose
5211 Clairy Sage
5306 Master Yarrow
5233 Monkshood
5261 Wild Ginger
1513 Clematis
5853 Cedar
2436 Down To Earth (1st Chakra)
4920 Gulaga
4091 Rapa-Nui
2469 Sober Up
2460 Warrior
5713 Red Poppy
5602 Walking To The Earth's Rhythm
1819 Narcissus
1836 Pink Seaweed
2350 Sea Turtle
1882 Vanilla Leaf
1888 Windflower
1964 Curry
2015 Mushroom (Black)
2060 Viridiflora
3819 Bear
3818 Buffalo
5134 Elephant
5136 Giraffe
5137 Hippopotamus
3837 Robin
3831 Salamander
3822 Turtle
3811 Wolf

## 31. Guilt / Shame

3205 Kunzite
2737 Day Blooming Waterlily
2786 Wiliwili
2428 Assá
1340 Wood Anemone
2373 Evening Primrose
2377 Little Inky Cap
1346 Billy Goat Plum
1349 Boab
2226 Confid Essence
1359 Five Corners
1365 Hibbertia
1392 Sturt Desert Rose
3508 Balsam
3511 Iona Pennywort
2225 Rowan
5303 Healer
5223 Hyssop
1547 Pine
5853 Cedar
2448 Trust
5802 Crab Apple Fruit
5095 Forgiveness
5703 Gorse
5665 Original Innocence
5751 Original Innocence Spray
1781 Camellia
1949 Bougainvillea
2026 Pine
2058 Vanilla
2066 White Rose
5133 Chimpanzee
3824 Swan

## 32. Happiness / Joy

1052 Chiming Bells
3166 Fireweed Combo
1104 Harebell
1132 Moschatel
3212 Orange Calcite
1156 Prickly Wild Rose
1208 Tundra Rose
1228 Willow
4843 Empowerment Myst
5173 Blue Gel & Oil
2425 Celebração
5786 Floral Caju
2421 Jumping Child
5159 Marupiara
3885 Arizona Fir
1297 Bog Asphodel
1299 Bracken ( Aq. Extract)
1301 Buttercup
1303 Double Snowdrop
4972 Red Frangipani
2378 Borage
2383 Foxglove
4964 Giant Stropharia
2368 Red Henbit
2366 Red Poppy
2374 Yellow Star Tulip
1342 Alpine Mint Bush
1344 Banksia Robur
1348 Bluebell
1359 Five Corners
1371 Little Flannel Flower
1383 Red Lily
1394 Sunshine Wattle
2205 Daisy
2220 Elder
2206 Gorse
2412 Revelation
2223 Valerian
5325 Child Glow
5553 Exaltation & Joy
5301 Exaltation Of Flowers
5309 Summer Solstice
1497 Agrimony
1541 Mustard
1573 Wild Rose
2468 Champagne
2446 Children's Flower
2451 Happiness
4093 Pink Primula
5037 Joy
5694 Celandine
5698 Cyclamen
1638 Cape Bluebell
1659 Illyarrie
5467 Golden Radiance Spray
5415 Golden Radiance
5861 Happy Relief
5731 Happy Relief Spray
5621 Loving Grace
2355 Dolphin
1805 Hooker's Onion
1827 Nootka Rose
1871 Snowdrop
1970 Dianthus
1976 Fimbriata

1981 Gaillardia
4969 Regenerate
2041 Salad Burnet
2053 Sweet Annie
2067 Wild Oats
5133 Chimpanzee
3816 Dolphin
3815 Hummingbird
3821 Otter
3837 Robin
3840 Squirrel
3811 Wolf

## 33. Healing & Nurturing the Heart

1038 Blue Elf Viola
4132 Calling All Angels
5122 Calling All Angels Spray
1052 Chiming Bells
3192 Chrysocolla
3197 Emerald
1086 Foxglove
1096 Green Bog Orchid
1098 Green Fairy Orchid
3209 Montana Rhodochrosite
1140 Northern Twayblade
3216 Rhodochrosite
3218 Rose Quartz
1208 Tundra Rose
1210 Tundra Twayblade
2789 A'ali'i
2744 Jade Vine
2745 Kamani
2770 Passion Flower
2799 Streptocarpus
2784 Ulei
2424 Bromelia 2
2430 Seiva
3885 Arizona Fir
1301 Buttercup
1317 Milk Thistle
2383 Foxglove
4209 Love
2366 Red Poppy
2382 Snowdrop
1348 Bluebell
2236 Creative
1356 Dagger Hakea
3147 Freshwater Mangrove
1374 Mountain Devil
1384 Red Suva Frangipani
1385 Rough Bluebell
2206 Gorse
3510 Grass Of Parnassus
2216 Holy Thorn
2208 Scottish Primrose
5244 Rose Campion
5258 White Bleeding Heart
5259 White Foxglove
1529 Holly
2439 Ecstasy (4th Chakra)
2455 Expansion
4093 Pink Primula
4095 White Orchid
5710 Pink Cherry
5711 Pussy Willow
1667 Menzies Banksia
1675 Pink Everlasting
5467 Golden Radiance Aura Spray
5415 Golden Radiance
4116 Unveiling Affection
5538 White Beauty Aura Spray
5621 Loving Grace
2397 Alum Root
2355 Dolphin
1792 Fireweed
1803 Heart Spirit Essence
1805 Hooker's Onion
1808 Jellyfish
1812 Lily Of The Valley
1851 Salal
1869 Snowberry
1979 Foxglove
2031 Purple Garden Sage
2032 Rain Lily
2069 Wisteria
5133 Chimpanzee
3829 Dove
3832 Wild Horse

## 34. Inner Guidance / Intuition

3189 Brazilian Amethyst
1048 Cassandra
3194 Citrine
1084 Forget-Me-Not
1102 Hairy Butterwort
3203 Herkimer Diamond
1108 Icelandic Poppy
1122 Lamb's Quarters
3206 Lapis Lazuli
3208 Moldavite
3210 Moonstone
3220 Rutilated Quartz
1176 Shooting Star
3227 Sugalite
1208 Tundra Rose
1218 White Spruce
2747 Kou
2791 Lani Ali'i
2753 Mamane
2754 Mango
2757 Nana-Honua
2796 Papala Kepau
2774 Pua Melia (Plumeria)
5839 Spiritual Awakening Myst
5174 Magenta Gel & Oil
5159 Marupiara
2433 Revelação
4970 Almond
1299 Bracken ( Aq. Extract)
5588 Himalayan Blue Poppy
1315 Marigold
3340 Yin
2364 Angelica
2383 Foxglove
2381 Purple Flower
2384 Rue (Wijnruit)
2376 Tansy (Boerenwormkruid)
2374 Yellow Star Tulip
1343 Angelsword - New
3306 Autumn Leaves
1350 Boronia
1352 Bush Fuchsia
1354 Bush Iris
1362 Green Spider Orchid
1365 Hibertia
2229 Meditation Essence
1377 Paw Paw
1383 Red Lily
3421 Wise Action
3432 Reading Energy Fields
3433 Reveals Mystery Within
3798 My Heart Knows
3797 My Own Pure Light
3795 Unveiling Self
3923 Lucid Dreaming
5435 Meditative Mind
2219 Birch
2210 Broom
2415 Clear Light
3515 Rose Alba
2218 Scots Pine
5202 Angelica
5204 Bloodroot
5205 Blue Star
5227 Lavender
5229 Malva Zebrina
5230 Mauve Mullein
5233 Monkshood
5241 Purple Mullein
5274 Rose "Bonica"
5310 Vision Quest
1505 Cerato
4097 Astral Orchid
2452 Blue Dragon
2449 Chiron
2441 Clarity (6th Chakra)
2459 Gateway
5702 Goldenrod
5711 Pussy Willow
2084 Centering & Meditation
1629 Antiseptic Bush
5862 Active Serenity
5732 Active Serenity Spray
5851 Serendipity
5602 Walking to the Earth's Rhythm
5199 Clear Mind Aura Spray
5196 Clear Mind Essence
5816 Devata
1771 Barnacle
1773 Blue Camas
2404 Poplar
1884 Viburnum
2347 Whale
1947 Bluebonnet
1987 Indian Paintbrush
2036 Rod Malva
3819 Bear
3839 Canada Goose
3828 Crow
3816 Dolphin
3812 Eagle
5134 Elephant
3820 Owl
5139 Tiger
3842 Whale
3811 Wolf

## 35. Inner Strength / Willpower

2426 Embó Rudá
5787 Floral Orquidea
5788 Floral Soberania
2431 Ybá
2380 Alternanthera
4205 Ground Ivy
2371 Orchid
2379 Sensitive Weed
4207 Sneezewort
1370 Kapok Bush
1372 Macrocarpa
4554 Monga Waratah
1376 Old Man Banksia
1381 Red Grevillea
4938 Stepping Ahead Now
3430 Radiant Strength
5306 Master Yarrow
5237 Penstemon
1523 Gentian
1525 Gorse

1527 Heather
1533 Hornbeam
1543 Oak
1545 Olive
1551 Rock Rose
1398 Waratah
5032 Freedom
5522 Clearing The Way /Self Belief
5609 Core Of Being
5816 Devata
1777 Bluebell
1794 Forsythia
1878 Surfgrass
5138 Lion
3813 Mountain Lion
5139 Tiger

## 36. Insecurity

2432 Ararybá
2425 Celebração
4781 Kundalini
3352 Sea Campion
2380 Alternanthera
4205 Ground Ivy
2365 Moneyplant
2371 Orchid
2379 Sensitive Weed
2376 Tansy
1357 Dog Rose
2226 Confid
1395 Tall Mulla Mulla
2211 Bell Heather
2205 Daisy
3517 Sea Rocket
5326 Initiative
5306 Master Yarrow
5233 Monkshood
5559 Safe Boundaries
5853 Cedar
2438 Strength (3rd Chakra)
5647 Heart Of Peace
5648 Heart Of Peace Spray
5080 Light Anchor
5708 Orange Wallflower
1656 Happy Wanderer
1674 Pin Cushion Hakea
5522 Clearing the Way / Self Belief
5861 Happy Relief
5731 Happy Relief Aura Spray
2348 "Staghorn" Algae
1865 Urchin
1884 Viburnum
1888 Windflower
1944 Basil
1945 Begonia
1953 Catnip
2002 Madame Louis Levique
5135 Gazelle

## 37. Insensitivity

2745 Kamani
2799 Streptocarpus
2426 Embó Rudá
2373 Evening Primrose
2375 Field Scabious
1369 Kangaroo Paw
1385 Rough Bluebell
3434 Walking Out of Patterns
3508 Balsam
3510 Grass Of Parnassus
3513 Mallow
3519 Wild Pansy
2209 Willow Herb
5323 Boundaries
5250 Spiderwort
1511 Chicory
2437 Well Being (2nd Chakra)
5710 Pink Cherry
1719 Yellow Leschenaultia
4116 Unveiling Affection
1771 Barnacle
2023 Penta

## 38. Jealousy / Envy

2428 Assá
2424 Bromelia 2
2429 Moara
4963 Ground Elder
2374 Yellow Star Tulip
1374 Mountain Devil
1388 Slender Rice Flower
2216 Holy Thorn
2414 Karma Clear
2225 Rowan
1529 Holly
2439 Ecstasy (4th Chakra)
2443 Gratefulness
4095 White Orchid
5030 Harmony
5708 Orange Wallflower
1977 Fortunes Double Yellow

## 39. Life Purpose / Direction

3195 Covelite
1068 Cow Parsnip
3196 Diamond
1118 Ladies' Tresses
3221 Sapphire
3222 Sapphire/Ruby
1176 Shooting Star
3226 Star Sapphire
1232 Yellow Dryas
2790 Akia
2731 Bamboo Orchid
2791 Lani Ali'i
4848 Self Esteem Myst
2432 Ararybá
3353 Oribá
2433 Revelação
2380 Alternanthera
2370 Impatiens
2371 Orchid
2369 Rainbow
4207 Sneezewort
2376 Tansy
1345 Bauhinia
1349 Boab
1350 Boronia
1351 Bottlebrush
1370 Kapok Bush
1387 Silver Princess
1392 Sturt Desert Rose
3423 Purpose Flows
4938 Stepping Ahead Now
2215 Apple
2219 Birch
2415 Clear Light
3507 Hazel
2412 Revelation
2218 Scots Pine
3519 Wild Pansy
5229 Malva Zebrina
5310 Vision Quest
1571 Wild Oat
4920 Gulaga
5698 Cyclamen
5713 Red Poppy
3361 Hairy Yellow Pea
1679 Pink Trumpet Flower
1641 White Spider Orchid
5522 Clearing the Way / Self Belief
5602 Walking To The Earth's Rhythm
1783 Candystick
1838 Pipsissewa
1878 Surfgrass
1947 Bluebonnet
1951 Bronze Fennel
1997 Lilac
2068 Wild Wood Violets
3834 Beaver
3839 Canada Goose
3813 Mountain Lion
3836 Salmon
5139 Tiger

## 40. Loneliness / Isolation Alienation / Abandonment

3193 Chrysoprase
1176 Shooting Star
1178 Single Delight
1232 Yellow Dryas
2763 Noni (Indian Mulberry)
2425 Celebração
2421 Jumping Child
5158 Yatê
3526 Transition
2364 Angelica
2375 Field Scabious
4204 Greater Celandine
1360 Flannel Flower
1364 Gymea Lily
1366 Illawarra Flame Tree
1380 Pink Mulla Mulla
1395 Tall Mulla Mulla
1396 Tall Yellow Top
3508 Balsam
2216 Holy Thorn
2222 Lime
3515 Rose Alba
3516 Rose Water Lily
2202 Stonecrop
5871 Loved & Welcomed
5258 White Bleeding Heart
1497 Agrimony
1527 Heather
1559 Sweet Chestnut
1567 Water Violet
2441 Clarity (6th Chakra)
2439 Ecstasy (4th Chakra)
2442 Flight (7th Chakra)
2444 Hidden Splendor
2437 Well Being (2nd Chakra)
5708 Orange Wallflower
5086 Peace In A Storm
1653 Golden Glory Grevillea
1666 Mauve Melaleuca
1668 One-Sided Bottlebrush
1673 Parakeelya
1682 Purple Eremophila
1686 Queensland Bottlebrush
1703 Urchin Dryandra
1705 Veronica
1717 Yellow Flag Flower
5621 Loving Grace
1767 Arbutus
2355 Dolphin
2354 Hermit Crab
1827 Nootka Rose
1971 Dill
1990 Jasmine

1993 Lady Eubanksia
2016 Narcissus
5133 Chimpanzee
3837 Robin
3825 Spider
3832 Wild Horse
3811 Wolf
5140 Zebra

## 41. Love / Self Love / Self Acceptance

1028 Alpine Azalea
4132 Calling All Angels
5122 Calling All Angels Spray
1086 Foxglove
1096 Green Bog Orchid
1100 Grove Sandwort
1104 Harebell
3205 Kunzite
1012 Northern Lights
3218 Rose Quartz
1186 Sphagnum Moss
1208 Tundra Rose
1210 Tundra Twayblade
3231 Watermelon Tourmaline
2752 Macadamia
2760 Night-Blooming Waterlily
2769 Papaya
2770 Passion Flower
2428 Assá
5166 Clear Gel & Oil
2429 Moara
5168 Orange Gel & Oil
5170 Pink Gel & Oil
2433 Revelação
2430 Seiva
3885 Arizona Fir
1294 Bistort
1301 Buttercup
3330 Childhood
5461 Shock & Trauma
4973 Magnolia
1317 Milk Thistle
2373 Evening Primrose
4205 Ground Ivy
4209 Love
2379 Sensitive Weed
1346 Billy Goat Plum
1348 Bluebell
1356 Dagger Hakea
1357 Dog Rose
4821 Face Hand & Body Cream
1359 Five Corners
1360 Flannel Flower
1347 Freshwater Mangrove
1374 Mountain Devil
1379 Philotheca
1380 Pink Mulla Mulla
1385 Rough Bluebell
1388 Slender Rice Flower
4766 Sydney Rose
1396 Tall Yellow Top
5030 Opening the Heart Spray
3431 Centered Love
3796 Gossamer Steel / Enduring Love
4939 Heart to Heart
4936 I Like Being Me
3807 Internal Marriage
3508 Balsam
2220 Elder
4795 Eros
4913 Eros Gel
3510 Grass Of Parnassus
2361 Holy Grail
2216 Holy Thorn
3513 Mallow
2208 Scottish Primrose
5200 Agrimony
5228 Lovage
5871 Loved & Welcomed
5231 Money Plant
5232 Money Plant - White
5269 Rose "Cerise Bouquet"
5267 Rose "Mm Legras..."
5255 Tree Peony
1511 Chicory
1517 Crab Apple
1529 Holly
2439 Ecstasy (4th Chakra)
2443 Gratefulness
2458 Heart Of Tantra
2438 Strength (3rd Chakra)
2448 Trust
4095 White Orchid
5698 Cyclamen
5703 Gorse
5704 Honesty
5665 Original Innocence
5751 Original Innocence Spray
5710 Pink Cherry
5711 Pussy Willow
5655 Relationships
1642 Correa
1646 Fringed Lily Twiner
1666 Mauve Melaleuca
1684 Purple Nymph Waterlily
1691 Red Leschenaultia
1699 Snakebush
1703 Urchin Dryandra
1706 Violet Butterfly
1716 Yellow Cone Flower
5467 Golden Radiance Spray
5415 Golden Radiance
4660 Messenger of the Heart
4116 Unveiling Affection
5621 Loving Grace
2358 Diatoms
2398 Douglas Aster
1792 Fireweed
1802 Harvest Lily
1812 Lily Of The Valley
1827 Nootka Rose
2405 Pearly Everlasting
1882 Vanilla Leaf
1888 Windflower
1930 African Violet
2004 Magnolia
2034 Red Carnation
2043 Self-Image
5133 Chimpanzee
3816 Dolphin
3815 Hummingbird
3837 Robin
3830 Seal
3824 Swan

## 42. Masculine / Feminine Harmony & Balance

1098 Green Fairy Orchid
3231 Watermelon Tourmaline
2423 Bromelia 1
2424 Bromelia 2
2426 Embó Rudá
1299 Bracken ( Aqu.Extract)
1336 Tufted Vetch
3339 Yang
3340 Yin
2373 Evening Primrose
4204 Greater Celandine
2366 Red Poppy
2374 Yellow Star Tulip
1352 Bush Fuchsia
3807 Internal Marriage
3426 Balancing Extremes
2413 Spiritual Marriage
5210 Chive
5220 Ginseng
2461 Goddess
1631 Balga Blackboy
1652 Goddess Grasstree
1656 Happy Wanderer
1662 Macrozamia
1670 Orange Spiked Pea
5862 Active Serenity
5732 Active Serenity Spray
1768 Balancer Essence
1773 Blue Camas
2353 Rainbow Kelp
3829 Dove
5134 Elephant
5138 Lion
3833 Peacock
3825 Spider

## 43. Mental Focus / Learning / Memory

1046 Bunchberry
1190 Sticky Geranium
1232 Yellow Dryas
2757 Nana-Honua
2775 Poha
2798 Pua Kala
2432 Ararybá
2435 Obaiti
2434 Renascer
5162 Rudá
1309 Hairy Sedge
2363 Clematis
2375 Field Scabious
2383 Foxglove
2381 Purple Flower
2369 Rainbow
2376 Tansy
1352 Bush Fuchsia
4823 Calm & Clear Cream
4813 Calm & Clear Mist
2228 Cognis Essence
1367 Isopogon
1370 Kapok Bush
1377 Paw Paw
1383 Red Lily
1393 Sundew
1397 Turkey Bush
1402 Yellow Cowslip Orchid
4324 New Perceptions
2219 Birch
2210 Broom
2415 Clear Light
3512 Lady's Mantle
2218 Scots Pine
3519 Wild Pansy
5203 Blackberry
5213 Comfrey
1509 Chestnut Bud
1513 Clematis
1535 Impatiens
1557 Star Of Bethlehem
1569 White Chestnut
2452 Blue Dragon
2441 Clarity (6th Chakra)
5033 Focus

5696 Comfrey
5706 Lilac
5713 Red Poppy
2084 Concentration & Meditation
3361 Hairy Yellow Pea
1679 Pink Trumpet Flower
1681 Purple Enamel Orchid
1708 Star Of Bethlehem
1709 W. A. Smokebush
3479 Wattle
1715 Yellow Boronia
1719 Yellow Leschenaultia
5199 Clear Mind Aura Spray
5196 Clear Mind Essence
1773 Blue Camas
1775 Blue Lupin
1833 Periwinkle
1865 Urchin
1931 Alfredo De Damas
1946 Blue Danube Aster
1969 Delphinium
1988 Iris
2040 Rosemary
3834 Beaver
5132 Cheetah
3814 Deer
3820 Owl
5139 Tiger

## 44. Motivation / Apathy

1156 Prickly Wild Rose
1190 Sticky Geranium
1208 Tundra Rose
2732 Bougainvillea
2791 Lani Ali'i
3284 Milo
2773 Plumbago
2775 Poha
2776 Pua - Kenikeni
2777 Pua-Pilo
2778 Pukiawe
5787 Floral Orquidea
2431 Ybá
4964 Giant Stropharia
2369 Rainbow
1344 Banksia Robur
1359 Five Corners
1364 Gymea Lily
1370 Kapok Bush
1372 Macrocarpa
1376 Old Man Banksia
1387 Silver Princess
3423 Purpose Flows
4938 Stepping Ahead Now
2215 Apple
3509 Globe Thistle
2206 Gorse
3511 Iona Pennywort
3514 Monkeyflower
3515 Rose Alba
2207 Spotted Orchid
5768 Transformation
5203 Blackberry
5556 Motivation
5237 Penstemon
5254 Tomato
1533 Hornbeam
1573 Wild Rose
2449 Chiron
4920 Gulaga
2438 Strength (3rd Chakra)
5703 Gorse
5665 Original Innocence
5751 Original Innocence Spray
5804 The Rose (Mme Isaac Pereire)
3474 Giving Hands
1688 Red Beak Orchid
1697 Silver Princess Gum
5522 Clearing The Way / Self Belief
5816 Devata
1794 Forsythia
1878 Surfgrass
1942 Bachelor Button
2053 Sweet Annie
2057 Tiger's Jaw Cactus
2061 Wandering Jew
5132 Cheetah

## 45. Muscular Tension

1074 Dandelion
1184 Soapberry
2423 Bromelia 1
2422 Imbe
2431 Ybá
2368 Red Henbit
4206 Smooth Hawksbeard
1347 Black Eyed Susan
1355 Crowea
4823 Calm & Clear Cream
4812 Calm & Clear Essence
4813 Calm & Clear Mist
4820 Emergency Cream
1360 Flannel Flower
3519 Wild Pansy
5216 Dandelion
2454 Let Go
5803 Crimean Snowdrop
5699 Dandelion
3419 Body Bliss Lotion
1645 Dampiera
1665 Massage Lotion 2
1667 Menzies Banksia
2331 Pain Cream
1683 Purple Flag Flower
2333 Skin Lustre Cream
1704 Ursinia
1765 Anemone
1779 Brown Kelp
2346 Chiton
1796 Goatsbeard
1817 Mussel
2348 "Staghorn" Algae
1964 Curry
1986 Indian Hawthorn
1993 Lady Eubanksia
4858 Manage Pain
2018 Old Blush
2054 Tansy
5640 Animals To The Rescue
3829 Dove

## 46. Negative Thoughts / Negative Feelings

2424 Bromelia 2
5159 Marupiara
2430 Seiva
3493 Fears
2383 Foxglove
2381 Purple Flower
1349 Boab - New
1378 Peach Flowered Tea-Tree
1389 Southern Cross
1394 Sunshine Wattle
4936 I Like Being Me
3798 My Heart knows
3797 My Own Pure Light
5250 Spiderwort
1529 Holly
1547 Pine
1549 Red Chestnut
1573 Wild Rose
1575 Willow
5036 Courage
2083 Positivity
1712 Wild Violet
5522 Clearing The Way / Self Belief
5816 Devata
5467 Golden Radiance Spray
5415 Golden Radiance
5621 Loving Grace
5477 Renewing Life
5538 White Beauty Aura Spray
1785 Chickweed
1808 Jellyfish
1840 Plantain
1880 Twin Flower
3816 Dolphin
5137 Hippopotamus
3837 Robin

## 47. Nurturing & Support

1050 Cattail Pollen
1096 Green Bog Orchid
1100 Grove Sandwort
1132 Moschatel
1138 Northern Lady's Slipper
5834 Antitox Myst
5169 Yellow Gel & Oil
1294 Bistort
5461 Shock & Trauma
3505 Mediterranean Sage
3526 Transition
2375 Field Scabious
4209 Love
2374 Yellow Star Tulip
4821 Face Hand & Body Cream
1384 Red Suva Frangipani
5330 Artemis
5215 Crested Iris
5333 Demeter
5331 Hestia
1519 Elm
1559 Sweet Chestnut
2467 Renaissance
5036 Courage
5032 Freedom
5655 Relationships
5467 Golden Radiance Spray
5415 Golden Radiance
5538 White Beauty Aura Spray
5621 Loving Grace
1771 Barnacle
1819 Narcissus
2403 Red Huckleberry
1863 Sea Palm
3819 Bear
3834 Beaver
3817 Butterfly
3839 Canada Goose
5133 Chimpanzee
3816 Dolphin
3835 Fox
5135 Gazelle
5137 Hippopotamus
3815 Hummingbird
5138 Lion
3826 Rabbit
3837 Robin
3822 Turtle

## 48. Obsession

1112 Jacob's Ladder

2423 Bromelia 1
2422 Imbe
5157 Indaiá
1321 Obsession
1327 Scarlet Pimpernel
1350 Boronia
1351 Bottlebrush
1365 Hibbertia
1402 Yellow Cowslip Orchid
2219 Birch
2205 Daisy
3510 Grass Of Parnassus
3511 Iona Pennywort
3514 Monkeyflower
2212 Thistle
1507 Cherry Plum
1517 Crab Apple
1553 Rock Water
4098 Opium Poppy
5802 Crab Apple Fruit
1633 Blue China Orchid
1634 Blue Leschenaultia
1637 Brown Boronia
1771 Barnacle
1794 Forsythia
1819 Narcissus
1838 Pipsissewa
1865 Urchin
1991 Knotted Marjoram
2046 Silver Moon
2063 White Carnation
3821 Otter

## 49. Overly Sensitive

3187 Black Tourmaline
3195 Covelite
4134 Guardian
5121 Guardian Spray
1220 White Violet
1230 Yarrow
2432 Ararybá
5157 Indaiá
4781 Kundalini
2435 Obaiti
4107 Thini-A
1299 Bracken (Aqu. Extract)
2370 Impatiens
4208 Protection
2366 Red Poppy
2384 Rue
2379 Sensitive Weed
1358 Dog Rose of the Wild Forces
1361 Fringed Violet
1381 Red Grevillea
2219 Birch
3509 Globe Thistle
3510 Grass Of Parnassus
2208 Scottish Primrose
2223 Valerian
5227 Lavender
5306 Master Yarrow
5559 Safe Boundaries
5256 Valerian
1523 Gentian
1529 Holly
1539 Mimulus
1565 Walnut
1567 Water Violet
5853 Cedar
2437 Well Being (2nd Chakra)
5037 Joy
5803 Crimean Snowdrop
5700 Fleabane
5096 Light Heart Space
1658 Hybrid Pink Fairy
1641 White Spider Orchid
1800 Grass Widow
1865 Urchin
1932 Allergy
1994 Lantana
1996 Ligustrum
3822 Turtle

## 50. Panic / Emergencies / Trauma / Accidents / Shock

3188 Bloodstone
1050 Cattail Pollen
1066 Cotton Grass
1082 Fireweed
1114 Labrador Tea
1118 Ladies' Tresses
1138 Northern Lady's Slipper
3216 Rhodochrosite
3217 Rhodolite Garnet
1168 River Beauty
3218 Rose Quartz
1176 Shooting Star
3344 Soul Support
1210 Tundra Twayblade
1216 White Fireweed
1218 White Spruce
1230 Yarrow
4217 Aftershock
2770 Passion Flower
2780 Stenogyne Calaminthoides
2783 'Uala
5180 Emergency Plus Gel
5162 Rudá
1295 Blackthorn
3902 Depression & Despair
5461 Shock & Trauma
1308 Grief
3352 Sea Campion
5461 Shock & Trauma
2382 Snowdrop
2372 Terra
1355 Crowea
1358 Dog Rose of the Wild Forces
4820 Emergency Cream
2230 Emergency Essence
4814 Emergency Mist
1361 Fringed Violet
1375 Mulla Mulla
1398 Waratah
2211 Bell Heather
2205 Daisy
2411 First Aid
4914 First Aid Gel
3510 Grass of Parnassus
2225 Rowan
2208 Scottish Primrose
2212 Thistle
5212 Clematis "Ernest Markham"
5552 Emergency Relief
5234 Moonshine Yarrow
5245 Saint John's Wort
1499 Aspen
1521 Five Flower Remedy
1545 Olive
1551 Rock Rose
1557 Star Of Bethlehem
1559 Sweet Chestnut
2457 Vital Spark
5034 Relief Remedy
5695 Cherry Plum Fruit
5803 Crimean Snowdrop
5699 Dandelion
5647 Heart of Peace
5648 Heart of Peace Spray
5086 Peace In A Storm
5806 Peaceful Detachment
1643 Cowkicks
5776 Crisis Relief Drops
1649 Fuchsia Gum
1663 Many Headed Dryandra
1676 Pink Fairy Orchid
3476 Reed Trigger Plant
1692 Ribbon Pea
1706 Violet Butterfly
1709 W. A. Smokebush
5862 Active Serenity
5732 Active Serenity Spray
5861 Happy Relief
5731 Happy Relief Spray
5538 White Beauty Aura Spray
1768 Balancer Essence
1777 Bluebell
1792 Fireweed
1798 Grape Hyacinth
1865 Urchin
3001 Bouquet of Harmony
2064 White Hyacinth
3481 Angel Rejuvenation Spray
4600 Happy Pet
5840 Animals To The Rescue

## 51. Patience / Tolerance

1014 Polar Ice
2743 Impatiens
2426 Embó Rudá
4963 Ground Elder
2370 Impatiens
2377 Little Inky Cap
1347 Black Eyed Susan
4812 Calm & Clear
4823 Calm & Clear Cream
4813 Calm & Clear Mist
1368 Jacaranda
4936 I Like Being Me
4722 Infinite Patience
3509 Globe Thistle
2222 Lime
3513 Mallow
3515 Rose Alba
2207 Spotted Orchid
2209 Willow Herb
5225 Ivory Hollyhock
1501 Beech
1535 Impatiens
1547 Pine
2439 Ecstasy (4th Chakra)
2454 Let Go
2448 Trust
5696 Comfrey
5095 Forgiveness
5707 Manuka
5710 Pink Cherry
1636 Brachycome
3361 Hairy Yellow Pea
1669 Orange Leschenaultia
1718 Yellow & Green Kangaroo Paw
1719 Yellow Leschenaultia
1836 Pink Seaweed
2347 Whale
1977 Fortunes Double Yellow
1986 Indian Hawthorn
2045 Silver Lace
5132 Cheetah
3813 Mountain Lion

## 52. Protection / Boundaries

1046 Bunchberry
4132 Calling All Angels
5122 Calling All Angels Spray
3195 Covelite
1092 Grass Of Parnassus
4134 Guardian
5121 Guardian Spray
3202 Hematite
3769 Ladies' Mantle
1130 Monkshood
1142 One-Sided Wintergreen
3214 Peridot
1220 White Violet
1230 Yarrow
2745 Kamani
2771 Pa'u-O-Hi'iaka
3178 Protection
4846 Protection Myst
2782 Ti (or Ki)
2432 Araryba
5162 Rudá
5160 Tassi
5171 Violet Gel & Oil
5587 Black Locust
2364 Angelica
4962 Goldenrod
4963 Ground Elder
2377 Little Inky Cap
2367 Mycena
4208 Protection
2366 Red Poppy
2384 Rue
2379 Sensitive Weed
4207 Sneezewort
2372 Terra
1343 Angelsword
1361 Fringed Violet
2229 Meditation Essence
3508 Balsam
2205 Daisy
3509 Globe Thistle
3507 Hazel
3511 Iona Pennywort
3514 Monkeyflower
3515 Rose Alba
2202 Stonecrop
2221 Sycamore
5768 Transformation
3518 Watercress
5323 Boundaries
5306 Master Yarrow
5234 Moonshine Yarrow
5238 Pink Yarrow
5559 Safe Boundaries
5263 Yarrow
1503 Centaury

1565 Walnut
2446 Children's Flower
2437 Well Being (2nd Chakra)
4095 White Orchid
5700 Fleabane
5096 Light Heart Space
5713 Red Poppy
1629 Antiseptic Bush
1658 Hybrid Pink Fairy/Cowslip Orchid
1676 Pink Fairy Orchid
1696 Shy Blue Orchid
1865 Urchin
1953 Catnip
1954 Cécil Brünner
1980 French Lavender
1999 Lobelia
2010 Mexican Bush Sage
2047 Snapdragon
2058 Vanilla
2062 Weight
2066 White Rose
3822 Turtle
5140 Zebra

## 53. Recuperation / Convalescence

2751 Lotus
2794 Melastoma
2766 Ohi'a-Ai
2767 Panini-Awa'awa (Aloe)
2427 Pyatã
2372 Terra
1342 Alpine Mint Bush
1343 Angelsword
1344 Banksia Robur
4811 Electro Essence
1361 Fringed Violet
1372 Macrocarpa
1375 Mulla Mulla
1390 Spinifex
2220 Elder
3509 Globe Thistle
2206 Gorse
2096 Life Force
2217 Sea Pink
3517 Sea Rocket
2221 Sycamore
3518 Watercress
5215 Crested Iris
5333 Demeter
5315 Re-Enter Life
5243 Red Hollyhock
5247 Self Heal
5314 Trauma Ease
1517 Crab Apple

1533 Hornbeam
1545 Olive
2447 Healing
2457 Vital Spark
5697 Cowslip
5698 Cyclamen
5713 Red Poppy
1677 Pink Fountain Triggerplant
1709 Western Australian Smokebush
5477 Renewing Life
1796 Goatsbeard
1853 Salmonberry
1961 Country Marilou
1985 Iberis Candytuft
4693 Inner Strength
2041 Salad Burnet
2070 Yarrow
4796 Luce / Light Essence
4600 Happy Pet
3819 Bear
3837 Robin

## 54. Releasing the Past / Release

1032 Balsam Poplar
1066 Cotton Grass
1082 Fireweed
3166 Fireweed Combo
1118 Ladies' Tresses
1134 Mountain Wormwood
1138 Northern Lady's Slipper
1016 Portage Glacier
1156 Prickly Wild Rose
1180 Sitka Burnet
1202 Sweetgale
1204 Sweetgrass
1216 White Fireweed
2728 Amazon Swordplant
2730 Awapuhi-Melemele
2731 Bamboo Orchid
2737 Day Blooming Waterlily
2758 Nani-Ahiahi
2762 Noho-Malie
2435 Obaiti
2433 Revelação
2430 Seiva
1294 Bistort
3902 Depression & Despair
1304 Early Purple Orchid
1308 Grief
1313 Lilac
1318 Monk's Hood
1322 Oxalis
3526 Transition

1340 Wood Anemone
4964 Giant Stropharia
2377 Little Inky Cap
2384 Rue
4206 Smooth Hawksbeard
1349 Boab - New
1350 Boronia
1351 Bottlebrush
1361 Fringed Violet
1373 Mint Bush
1391 Sturt Desert Pea
1393 Sundew
3434 Walking out of Patterns
3507 Hazel
2412 Revelation
2225 Rowan
2202 Stonecrop
5221 Horseradish
5318 Prenatal Heal
5316 Release Trauma
5314 Trauma Ease
5327 Trauma Relief
1531 Honeysuckle
1565 Walnut
2455 Expansion
2454 Let Go
2456 Nirjara
4092 Nirjara 2
4098 Opium Poppy
2467 Renaissance
2457 Vital Spark
5803 Crimean Snowdrop
5707 Manuka
5665 Original Innocence
5751 Original Innocence Spray
3473 Candle Of Life
1638 Cape Bluebell
1667 Menzies Banksia
2083 Positivity
1707 Wallflower Donkey Orchid
5816 Devata
5477 Renewing Life
1785 Chickweed
1800 Grass Widow
1808 Jellyfish
1842 Poison Hemlock
1876 Starfish
2400 Yellow Pond Lily
1944 Basil
2026 Pine
2067 Wild Oats
3817 Butterfly

## 55. Resistance to Change / Flexibility / Moving On

1026 Alder
1042 Bog Blueberry
3198 Fluorite
1004 Full Moon Reflection
1006 Glacier River
1008 Greenland Icecap
1172 Round-Leaved Sundew
1188 Spiraea
1190 Sticky Geranium
1024 Tidal Forces
3788 Tourmalated Quartz
1224 Wild Rhubarb
1228 Willow
2729 Avocado
2752 Macadamia
2764 Ohai Ali'i
2777 Pua-Pilo
2423 Bromelia 1
2429 Moara
2435 Obaiti
2434 Renascer
3885 Arizona Fir
1304 Early Purple Orchid
1309 Hairy Sedge
1329 Single Snowdrop
4989 Spotted Orchid
5491 Stuck In A Rut
3526 Transition
2383 Foxglove
4205 Ground Ivy
2369 Rainbow
1345 Bauhinia
1351 Bottlebrush
3147 Freshwater Mangrove
1370 Kapok Bush
1373 Mint Bush
1381 Red Grevillea
1394 Sunshine Wattle
1400 Wild Potato Bush
4938 Stepping Ahead Now
3509 Globe Thistle
3507 Hazel
2414 Karma Clear
2412 Revelation
3515 Rose Alba
2202 Stonecrop
5304 Interesting Times
5555 Life's Transitions
5236 Pale Corydalis
5240 Purple Loosestrife
5257 Waterlily
1531 Honeysuckle
1553 Rock Water
1563 Vine
1573 Wild Rose
2454 Let Go
2437 Well Being (2nd Chakra)
5080 Light Anchor
5721 Light Anchor
5714 Rosebay Willowherb
1645 Dampiera
3474 Giving Hands
1655 Green Rose
1006 Shy Blue Orchid
5522 Clearing The Way / Self Belief
5851 Serendipity
5602 Walking To The Earth's Rhythm
1765 Anemone
1771 Barnacle
2399 Fairy Bell
1808 Jellyfish
1836 Pink Seaweed
1842 Poison Hemlock
1846 Purple Crocus
1863 Sea Palm
2402 Silver Birch
1869 Snowberry
1878 Surfgrass
1880 Twin Flower
1963 Crossandra
2013 Morning Glory
2015 Mushroom (Black)
3817 Butterfly
3836 Salmon
3823 Snake

## 56. Self Confidence / Self-Esteem / Independence

1028 Alpine Azalea
1040 Blueberry Pollen
1058 Columbine
3197 Emerald
3200 Gold
3202 Hematite
1116 Lace Flower
3215 Pyrite
1206 Tamarack
3228 Tiger's Eye
2736 Cup of Gold
2740 Hinahina-Ku-Kahakai
3284 Milo
4214 Self-Esteem
2425 Celebração
2426 Embó Rudá
5788 Floral Soberania
5172 Green Gel & Oil
5157 Indaiá
4781 Kundalini
2429 Moara
2430 Seiva
5160 Tassi
4107 Thini-A
5169 Yellow Gel & Oil
3330 Childhood
3902 Deptression & Despair
3493 Fears
1313 Lilac
4972 Red Frangipani
5468 Self Esteem
1332 Spring Squill
2364 Angelica
2373 Evening Primrose
4962 Goldenrod
4205 Ground Ivy
2371 Orchid
4208 Protection
4207 Sneezewort
2226 Confid Essence
1357 Dog Rose
1359 Five Corners
1365 Hibbertia
1366 Illawarra Flame Tree
1370 Kapok Bush
1387 Silver Princess
1389 Southern Cross
1392 Sturt Desert Rose
1397 Turkey Bush
1401 Wisteria
2211 Bell Heather
4795 Eros
4913 Eros Gel
3514 Monkeyflower
5768 Transformation
5207 Buttercup
5326 Initiative
5231 Money Plant
5232 Money Plant - White
5261 Wild Ginger
5328 Worthiness
5561 Worthiness
1505 Cerato
1517 Crab Apple
1523 Gentian
1527 Heather
1537 Larch
1567 Water Violet
2440 Authenticity (5th Chakra)
2444 Hidden Splendor
2438 Strength (3rd Chakra)
2460 Warrior
5031 Confidence
5702 Goldenrod
5703 Gorse
5708 Orange Wallflower
5087 Self Esteem
1642 Correa
1644 Cowslip Orchid
1651 Geraldton Wax
1653 Golden Glory Grevillea
1656 Happy Wanderer
1673 Parakeelya
1700 Snakevine
1703 Urchin Dryandra
1716 Yellow Cone Flower
5522 Clearing The Way
5010 Dovata
1790 Easter Lily
2406 Indian Pipe
1844 Polyanthus
1882 Vanilla Leaf
1965 Daffodil
2004 Magnolia
2016 Narcissus
2034 Red Carnation
2043 Self-Image
2053 Sweet Annie
3818 Buffalo
5133 Chimpanzee
3835 Fox
5135 Gazelle
5138 Lion
3813 Mountain Lion
3833 Peacock
3826 Rabbit
3830 Seal
3824 Swan
3832 Wild Horse

## 57. Selfishness / Care for Others / Compassion

2733 Chinese Violet
4210 Family Harmony
4844 Family Harmony Myst
2773 Plumbago
2428 Assá
2429 Moara
2375 Field Scabious
4963 Ground Elder
2371 Orchid
2381 Purple Flower
2374 Yellow Star Tulip
1348 Bluebell
1353 Bush Gardenia
1367 Isopogon
1364 Gymea Lily
1369 Kangaroo Paw
1382 Red Helmet Orchid
1385 Rough Bluebell - New
4766 Sydney Rose
3508 Balsam
2216 Holy Thorn
2414 Karma Clear

2208 Scottish Primrose
2204 Silverweed
2209 Willow Herb
5323 Boundaries
5250 Spiderwort
1511 Chicory
1527 Heather
2439 Ecstasy (4th Chakra)
2443 Gratefulness
4095 White Orchid
5710 Pink Cherry
5655 Relationships
1634 Blue Leschenaultia
1640 Christmas Tree
1644 Cowslip Orchid
1646 Fringed Lily Twiner
1661 Leafless Orchid
1669 Orange Leschenaultia
1675 Pink Everlasting
1680 Pixie Mops
1684 Purple Nymph Waterlily
3362 Spirit Faces (Banjine)
1641 White Spider Orchid
4116 Unveiling Affection
1792 Fireweed
1810 Kuan Yin
1851 Salal
2351 Sea Lettuce
1880 Twin Flower
1992 Kolanchoe
2023 Penta
2031 Purple Garden Sage
2049 Spike Lavender
2068 Wild Wood Violets
2069 Wisteria
3816 Dolphin
5134 Elephant
5136 Giraffe
3820 Owl
3837 Robin
5140 Zebra

## 58. Serenity / Inner Peace

3184 Aquamarine
4132 Calling All Angels
5122 Calling All Angels Spray
1048 Cassandra
1068 Cow Parsnip
1144 Opium Poppy
1148 Paper Birch
1202 Sweetgale
1212 Twinflower
2730 Awapuhi-Melemele
2746 Koa
2748 Kukui
2755 Mai'a (Banana)
2793 Mamaki
2762 Noho-Malie
2795 Pakalana
2785 Water Poppy
5173 Blue Gel & Oil
2423 Bromelia 1
2424 Bromelia 2
2425 Celebração
2422 Imbe
2429 Moara
5162 Rudá
4971 Cymbidium Orchid
3505 Mediterranean Sage
1321 Obsession
1331 Solomon's Seal
1335 Tranquility
4974 White Lotus
3339 Yang
3340 Yin
2375 Field Scabious
2370 Impatiens
2381 Purple Flower
2372 Terra
2374 Yellow Star Tulip
1347 Black Eyed Susan
1350 Boronia
1351 Bottlebrush
1355 Crowea
1358 Dog Rose of the Wild Forces
1363 Grey Spider Flower
1369 Kangaroo Paw
1373 Mint Bush
1377 Paw Paw
1384 Red Suva Frangipani
1393 Sundew
1383 Red Lily
2415 Clear Light
2411 First Aid
4914 First Aid Gel
3510 Grass of Parnassus
3516 Rose Water Lily
2208 Scottish Primrose
5207 Buttercup
5208 California Poppy
5225 Ivory Hollyhock
5228 Lovage
5233 Monkshood
5557 Relaxation
5246 Scarlet Pimpernel
1497 Agrimony
1507 Cherry Plum
1561 Vervain
1567 Water Violet
1569 White Chestnut
2442 Flight (7th Chakra)
2464 Lotus
2466 Morning Glory
4094 Rock Primula
2448 Trust
5030 Harmony
5647 Heart of Peace
5648 Heart of Peace Spray
5080 Light Anchor
5081 Light Anchor Spray
5721 Light Heart Anchor
5084 Light Heart Anchor Spray
1649 Fuchsia Gum
1657 Hops Bush
1658 Hybrid Pink Fairy
1670 Orange Spiked Pea Flower
1676 Pink Fairy Orchid
1682 Purple Eremophila
1693 Rose Cone Flower
1707 Wallflower Donkey Orchid
5862 Active Serenity
5732 Active Serenity Aura Spray
5602 Walking To The Earth's Rhythm
5538 White Beauty Aura Spray
5199 Clear Mind Aura Spray
5196 Clear Mind Essence
1768 Balancer Essence
2349 Sponge
1880 Twin Flower
1958 Christmas Cactus
2003 Maggie
2009 Meadow Sage
2046 Silver Moon
3002 Verbena
3818 Buffalo
3817 Butterfly
3814 Deer
3829 Dove
3827 Dragonfly
5139 Tiger
3842 Whale

## 59. Sexuality / Passion

1032 Balsam Poplar
3201 Green Jasper
2728 Amazon Swordplant
2729 Avocado
2737 Day Blooming Waterlily
2750 Lehua
2755 Mai'a (Banana)
2760 Night-Blooming Waterlily
2761 Niu (Coconut)
2769 Papaya
4211 Intimacy
5836 Intimacy Myst
2424 Bromelia 2
2426 Embó Rudá
2422 Imbe
5157 Indaiá
4781 Kundalini
5168 Orange Gel & Oil
3353 Oribá
2427 Pyatã
2431 Ybá
1336 Tufted Vetch
2373 Evening Primrose
2383 Foxglove
4209 Love
2368 Red Henbit
2366 Red Poppy
2374 Yellow Star Tulip
1347 Black Eyed Susan
1346 Billy Goat Plum
1353 Bush Gardenia
1355 Crowea
1357 Dog Rose
1360 Flannel Flower
1369 Kangaroo Paw
1371 Little Flannel Flower
1376 Old Man Banksia
1377 Paw Paw
4816 Sensuality Mist
2232 Sexuality Essence
1392 Sturt Desert Rose
1401 Wisteria
2215 Apple
3508 Balsam
4795 Eros
4913 Eros Gel
2206 Gorse
2216 Holy Thorn
3515 Rose Alba
2413 Spiritual Marriage
5334 Aphrodite
5211 Clairy Sage
5262 Wood Betony
2441 Clarity (6th Chakra)
2436 Down To Earth (1st Chakra)
2453 Golden Dawn
2458 Heart Of Tantra
2448 Trust
5038 Sexual Passion
5693 Blue Hibiscus
5705 Horse Chestnut
5712 Red Gladiolus
1631 Balga Blackboy
1652 Goddess Grasstree
1662 Macrozamia
1684 Purple Nymph Waterlily
1691 Red Leschenaultia
3479 Wattle
1711 White Nymph Waterlily
2355 Dolphin
1817 Mussel

1848 Purple Magnolia
2347 Whale
1952 Carrot
1970 Dianthus
1976 Fimbriata
1983 Gardenia
1084 Grüss An Aachen
2007 Marigold
2022 Passion
2069 Wisteria
3824 Swan

## 60. Skin Matters

2370 Impatiens
1346 Billy Goat Plum
1361 Fringed Violet
4810 Purification Essence
4821 Face Hand & Body Cream
1386 She Oak
1390 Spinifex
4822 Woman Cream
2204 Silverweed
2239 Five Flower Cream
1517 Crab Apple
2447 Healing
5802 Crab Apple Fruit
5665 Original Innocence
5751 Original Innocence Spray
5713 Red Poppy
3419 Body Bliss Lotion
1658 Hybrid Pink Fairy
1665 Body Sports Lotion
1666 Mauve Melaleuca
2331 Comfort Cream
2333 De-Stress Moisturizer
1767 Arbutus
1882 Vanilla Leaf
1938 Archduke Charles
1964 Curry
2010 Mexican Bush Sage
2012 Mexican Oregano

## 61. Sleep Patterns

1112 Jacob's Ladder
2762 Noho-Malie
2768 Pa-Nini-O-Ka
2423 Bromelia 1
2422 Imbe
3352 Sea Campion
4208 Protection
2366 Red Poppy
2372 Terra
1347 Bladk Eyed Susan
1350 Boronia
1354 Bush Iris
1355 Crowea
1357 Dog Rose
1362 Green Spider Orchid
1363 Grey Spider Flower
1372 Macrocarpa
1393 Sundew
3512 Lady's Mantle
2208 Scottish Primrose
5792 Sweet Dreams
2223 Valerian
5558 Restful Sleep
5245 Saint John's Wort
5872 Sweet Sleep
1499 Aspen
1551 Rock Rose
1569 White Chestnut
2466 Morning Glory
2462 Veil Of Dreams
5039 Serenity
5699 Dandelion
5700 Fleabane
1633 Blue China Orchid
1637 Brown Boronia
1657 Hops Bush
1677 Pink Fountain Triggerplant
1683 Purple Flag Flower
3476 Reed Trigger Plant
1706 Violet Butterfly
1710 White Eremophila
1716 Yellow Cone Flower
5504 Time Zone
1769 Balancer Oil
5421 Balancer Spray
5192 Heart Spirit Oil
5422 Heart Spirit Spray
1968 Deep Sleep
2046 Silver Moon
3002 Verbena
3827 Dragonfly

## 62. Space Clearing

3187 Black Tourmaline
5121 Guardian Spray
5120 Purification Spray
1204 Sweetgrass
2745 Kamani
4846 Protection Myst
2782 Ti (or Ki)
2378 Borage
4963 Ground Elder
2370 Impatiens
2377 Little Inky Cap
2371 Orchid
4208 Protection
2379 Sensitive Weed
1343 Angelsword
1349 Boab - New
4817 Space Clearing Mist
5163 Sanctuary Spray
5219 Garlic
5306 Master Yarrow
5559 Safe Boundaries
2445 Aura Cleaning
5803 Crimean Snowdrop
5098 Infinite Light
5096 Light Heart Space
5665 Original Innocence
5751 Original Innocence Spray
1676 Pink Fairy Orchid
5421 Balancer Spray
5422 Heart Spirit Spray
5740 Clearing Mist
2013 Morning Glory
2028 Pink Rose
3815 Hummingbird

## 63. Spinal Alignment & Movement

1120 Lady's Slipper
4781 Kundalini
2378 Borage
1351 Bottlebrush
1355 Crowea
1359 Five Corners
1364 Gymea Lily
1377 Paw Paw
1394 Sunshine Wattle
1389 Southern Cross
1396 Tall Yellow Top
1398 Waratah
3509 Globe Thistle
4091 Rapa-Nui
5696 Comfrey
5699 Dandelion
5702 Goldenrod
5706 Lilac
5711 Pussy Willow
2332 Arthritis Cream
1783 Candystick
2346 Chiton
1853 Salmonberry
2352 Sea Horse
1943 Bamboo
1959 Cinnamon Basil
1986 Indian Hawthorn
2015 Mushroom (Black)
2060 Viridiflora
3823 Snake

## 64. Spiritual Awakening / Meditation

1034 Black Spruce
3189 Brazilian Amethyst
1048 Cassandra
1092 Grass of Parnassus
1130 Monkshood
3223 Scepter Amethyst
1022 Solstice Sun
2741 'Ili' Ahi (Hawaiian Sandalwood)
2740 Koa
2751 Lotus
2754 Mango
4215 Spiritual Awakening
5839 Spiritual Awakening Myst
2432 Ararybá
2424 Bromelia 2
2422 Imbe
3353 Oribá
3904 Blue Pimpernel
4972 Red Frangipani
1331 Solomon's Seal
2364 Angelica
2363 Clematis
2375 Field Scabious
4962 Goldenrod
2365 Moneyplant
2381 Purple Flower
2374 Yellow Star Tulip
1343 Angelsword
1347 Black Eyed Susan
1348 Bluebell
1350 Boronia
1354 Bush Iris
1362 Green Spider Orchid
1364 Gymea Lily
2229 Meditation Essence
1373 Mint Bush
1383 Red Lily
3424 New Perceptions
2415 Clear Light
3509 Globe Thistle
3507 Hazel
3513 Mallow
2412 Revelation
2218 Scots Pine
5768 Transformation
5202 Angelica
5205 Blue Star
5218 Forget-Me-Not
5229 Malva Zebrina
5230 Mauve Mullein
5233 Monkshood
5235 Mugwort
5241 Purple Mullein
5264 Rose "Belle Story"
5273 Rose "Fruhlingsmorgen"
5272 Rose "Gertrude Jekyll"

5270 Rose "Konigin Von Danemark"
5266 Rose - Red Climbing
5246 Scarlet Pimpernel
5249 Snow Queen Iris
5310 Vision Quest
5260 White Mullein
2452 Blue Dragon
2449 Chiron
2441 Clarity (6th Chakra)
2442 Flight (7th Chakra)
2451 Happiness
2465 Isan
2464 Lotus
4096 Purple Orchid
4091 Rapa-Nui
5696 Comfrey
5701 Golden Daffodils
5097 Infinite Peace, Infinite Love
5080 Light Anchor
5721 Light Anchor
5083 Light Heart Anchor
5665 Original Innocence
5751 Original Innocence Spray
5714 Rosebay Willowherb
3473 Candle Of Life
2084 Centering & Meditation
1679 Pink Trumpet Flower
1684 Purple Nymph Waterlily
1687 Rabbit Orchid
1696 Shy Blue Orchid
3362 Spirit Faces
1711 White Nymph Waterlily
1715 Yellow Boronia
5467 Golden Radiance Aura Spray
5415 Golden Radiance
5477 Renewing Life
5851 Serendipity
5199 Clear Mind Aura Spray
5196 Clear Mind Essence
1767 Arbutus
1796 Goatsbeard
1802 Harvest Lily
2406 Indian Pipe
1815 Moon Snail
2404 Poplar
1884 Viburnum
2347 Whale
1930 African Violet
2048 Soapwort
2054 Tansy
3002 Verbena
3828 Crow
3816 Dolphin
3827 Dragonfly
3812 Eagle
5135 Gazelle
5136 Giraffe
5137 Hippopotamus
3836 Salmon
3824 Swan
5139 Tiger
3842 Whale
3811 Wolf

## 65. Stagnation / Blockages

5786 Floral Caju
2421 Jumping Child
2427 Pyatã
5158 Yatê
2378 Borage
4962 Goldenrod
2369 Rainbow
1345 Bauhinia
1349 Boab
1359 Five Corners
1370 Kapok Bush
1373 Mint Bush
1381 Red Grevillea
1394 Sunshine Wattle
1395 Tall Mulla Mulla
3429 Clearing Blockages
5203 Blackberry
5221 Horseradish
5254 Tomato
2082 Creativity
1713 Woolly Banksia
5522 Clearing The Way
5816 Devata
5851 Serendipity
1765 Anemone
2358 Diatoms
1805 Hooker's Onion
1808 Jellyfish
1840 Plantain
1842 Poison Hemlock
1851 Salal
5132 Cheetah
3813 Mountain Lion

## 66. Stress / Anxiety / Worry

1074 Dandelion
1102 Hairy Butterwort
1132 Moschatel
1148 Paper Birch
3344 Soul Support
2732 Bougainvillea
2735 Cotton
2738 Hau
2748 Kukui
2749 La'au'-Aila
2762 Noho-Malie
2795 Pakalana
2770 Passion Flower
2772 Pleomele Fragrans
3159 Stress Relief
5840 Stress Relief Myst
2785 Water Poppy
5180 Emergency Plus Gel
2429 Moara
2427 Pyatã
4107 Thini-A
2431 Ybá
1294 Bistort
1335 Tranquility
2378 Borage
2381 Purple Flower
1342 Alpine Mint Bush
1347 Black Eyed Susan
1345 Bauhinia
1350 Boronia
4823 Calm & Clear Crear
4812 Calm & Clear Essence
4813 Calm & Clear Mist
2228 Cognis
1355 Crowea
1357 Dog Rose
2230 Emergency Essence
4814 Emergency Mist
1368 Jacaranda
1370 Kapok Bush
1377 Paw Paw
1384 Red Suva Frangipani
1391 Sturt Desert Pea
2219 Birch
2220 Elder
2411 First Aid
4914 First Aid Gel
4972 First Aid Gel
2208 Scottish Primrose
2221 Sycamore
2223 Valerian
5324 Calm Time
5217 Dill
5227 Lavender
5308 Relaxation
5557 Relaxation
5268 Rose "English Elegance"
5275 Rose "Pink Heirloom"
5271 Rose - "Yellow Heirloom"
5256 Valerian
1497 Agrimony
1499 Aspen
1507 Cherry Plum
1519 Elm
1521 Five Flower Remedy
1527 Heather
1535 Impatiens
1539 Mimulus
1545 Olive
1549 Red Chestnut
1551 Rock Rose
1559 Sweet Chestnut
1561 Vervain
2436 Down To Earth (1st Chakra)
2454 Let Go
2457 Vital Spark
5036 Courage
5034 Relief Remedy
5039 Serenity
5700 Fleabane
5647 Heart Of Peace
5648 Heart Of Peace Spray
5711 Pussy Willow
3419 Body Bliss Lotion
1637 Brown Boronia
1645 Dampiera
1654 Golden Waitsia
1658 Hybrid Pink Fairy
1676 Pink Fairy Orchid
1683 Purple Flag Flower
3476 Reed Trigger Plant
2079 Relaxation
1692 Ribbon Pea
1693 Rose Cone Flower
2333 De-Stress Moisturiser
1709 W. A. Smokebush
1712 Wild Violet
1717 Yellow Flag Flower
5862 Active Serenity
5732 Active Serenity Aura Spray
5467 Golden Radiance Aura Spray
5415 Golden Radiance
5861 Happy Relief
5731 Happy Relief Aura Spray
5602 Walking To The Earth's Rhythm
5538 White Beauty Aura Spray
5199 Clear Mind Aura Spray
5196 Clear Mind Essence
5609 Core Of Being
1768 Balancer Essence
1777 Bluebell
1790 Easter Lily
1819 Narcissus
1833 Periwinkle
1838 Pipsissewa
1865 Urchin
1933 Amaryllis
3883 Reduce Stress
2040 Rosemary
3481 Angel Rejuventation Spray
5640 Animals To The Rescue
3818 Buffalo
3822 Turtle

## 67. Transitions / Change

1050 Cattail Pollen
1068 Cow Parsnip
1082 Fireweed
3166 Fireweed Combo
1008 Greenland Icecap
1102 Hairy Butterwort
3207 Malachite
1014 Polar Ice
1016 Portage Glacier
1156 Prickly Wild Rose
1178 Single Delight
1024 Tidal Forces
1210 Tundra Twayblade
2769 Papaya
2425 Celebração
5166 Clear Gel & Oil
5787 Floral Orquidea
2421 Jumping Child
2435 Obaiti
2434 Renascer
5158 Yatê
1294 Bistort
3902 Depression & Despair
1304 Early Purple Orchid
1329 Single Snowdrop
4989 Spotted Orchid
1332 Spring Squill
5491 Stuck In A Rut
3526 Transition
2369 Rainbow
1345 Bauhinia
1349 Boab
1350 Boronia
1351 Bottlebrush
3147 Freshwater Mangrove
1373 Mint Bush
1378 Peach Flowerered Tea-tree
1387 Silver Princess
1394 Sunshine Wattle
1400 Wild Potato Bush
2211 Bell Heather
3507 Hazel
2412 Revelation
2214 Snowdrop
2202 Stonecrop
5304 Interesting Times
5555 Life's Transitions
5306 Master Yarrow
5240 Purple Loosestrife
5559 Safe Boundaries
1531 Honeysuckle
1565 Walnut
2459 Gateway
4920 Gulaga
2456 Nirjara
2450 Pluto
5032 Freedom
5080 Light Anchor
5721 Light Anchor
5083 Light Heart Anchor
5711 Pussy Willow
5714 Rosebay Willowherb
1633 Blue China Orchid
1643 Cowkicks
5522 Clearing The Way / Self Belief
5851 Serendipity
5816 Devata
1787 Death Camas
1794 Forsythia
2407 Fuchsia
1800 Grass Widow
1829 Orange Honeysuckle
1842 Poison Hemlock
1963 Crossandra
1967 Day Lily
1984 Grüss An Aachen
4600 Happy Pet
3817 Butterfly
3841 Frog
3815 Hummingbird
3826 Rabbit
3838 Raccoon
3831 Salamander
3823 Snake

## 68. Travel Aids

1068 Cow Parsnip
3224 Smoky Quartz
3793 Travel Ease
5838 Protection Myst
2375 Field Scabious
2367 Mycena (Mushroom)
4208 Protection
1375 Mulla Mulla
2233 Solaris Essence
4825 Travel Cream
2235 Travel Essence
4815 Travel Mist
4817 Space Clearing Mist
5306 Master Yarrow
5243 Red Hollyhock
5559 Safe Boundaries
2457 Vital Spark
5647 Heart Of Peace
5648 Heart Of Peace Spray
5086 Peace In A Storm
1649 Fuchsia Gum
5504 Time Zone / Being In Time
1768 Balancer Essence
1769 Balancer Spray
1769 Balancer Oil
3001 Bouquet Of Harmony
1960 Cold & Flu
4968 Fatigue
4858 Manage Pain
3883 Reduce Stress
4600 Happy Pet
3839 Canada Goose
5134 Elephant
3815 Hummingbird

## 69. Trust

1044 Bog Rosemary
1102 Hairy Butterwort
1112 Jacob's Ladder
1172 Round-Leaved Sundew
3226 Star Sapphire
1220 White Violet
1222 Wild Iris
2731 Bamboo Orchid
5173 Blue Gel & Oil
2422 Imbe
5157 Indaiá
4107 Thini-A
1301 Buttercup
1314 Lily Of The Valley
2380 Alternanthera
2364 Angelica
2378 Borage
4962 Goldenrod
4205 Ground Ivy
2365 Moneyplant
2367 Mycena (Mushroom)
2371 Orchid
4208 Protection
2382 Snowdrop
2376 Tansy
2374 Yellow Star Tulip
1347 Black Eyed Susan
1348 Bluebell
1352 Bush Fuchsia
1354 Bush Iris
1360 Flannnel Flower
1363 Grey Spider Flower
1365 Hibbertia
1380 Pink Mulla Mulla - New
1389 Southern Cross
1390 Spinifex
1392 Sturt Desert Road
1395 Tall Mulla Mulla
1398 Waratah
2211 Bell Heather
3512 Lady's Mantle
5225 Ivory Hollyhock
5246 Scarlet Pimpernel
1499 Aspen
1505 Cerato
1523 Gentian
1529 Holly
1549 Red Chestnut
2439 Ecstasy (4th Chakra)
2454 Let Go
2448 Trust
5099 Infinite Abundance
5097 Infinito Peace, Infinite Love
5080 Light Anchor
5721 Light Anchor
1685 Purple & Red Kangaroo Paw
1691 Red Leschenaultia
1712 Wild Violet
5621 Loving Grace
2397 Alum Root
1765 Anemone
1771 Barnacle
1812 Lily of the Valley
1884 Viburnum
1886 Weigela
1930 African Violet
1939 Autumn Damask
2008 Marquise Bocella
2069 Wisteria
3817 Butterfly
3814 Deer
3841 Frog
3836 Salmon
3830 Seal

## 70. Understanding & Integration

1026 Alder
1028 Alpine Azalea
1034 Black Spruce
1038 Blue Elf Viola
1046 Bunchberry
1066 Cotton Grass
1074 Dandelion
1084 Forget-Me-Not
1086 Foxglove
1090 Golden Corydalis
1118 Ladies' Tresses
1142 One-Sided Wintergreen
3213 Pearl
1168 River Beauty
1180 Sitka Burnet
1218 White Spruce
2432 Ararybá
2424 Bromelia 2
5787 Floral Orquidea
5172 Green Gel & Oil
5159 Marupiara
2433 Revelação

5162 Rudá
5158 Yatê
1311 Leopardsbane
1318 Monk's Hood
2363 Clematis
4963 Ground Elder
2367 Mycena (Mushroom)
2371 Orchid
1390 Spinifex
2219 Birch
2210 Broom
2361 Holy Grail
3512 Lady's Mantle
2412 Revelation
2218 Scots Pine
2413 Spiritual Marriage
5204 Bloodroot
5230 Mauve Mullein
5239 Purple Bee Palm
5241 Purple Mullein
1509 Chestnut Bud
1529 Holly
1547 Pine
2465 Isan
4091 Rapa-Nui
5692 Blue Delphinium
5696 Comfrey
5706 Lilac
5804 The Rose (Mme Isaac Pereire)
1680 Pixie Mops
1685 Purple & Red Kangaroo Paw
1689 Red Feather Flower
1701 Southern Cross
1709 W. A. Smokebush
1714 Woolly Smokebush
1718 Yellow & Green Kangaroo Paw
5199 Clear Mind Aura Spray
5196 Clear Mind Essence
1765 Anemone
1779 Brown Kelp
1886 Weigela
2347 Whale
1956 Champneys Pink Cluster
1980 French Lavender
1983 Gardenia
1993 Lady Eubanksia
5137 Hippopotamus
3820 Owl
3838 Raccoon
3825 Spider
5140 Zebra

## 71. Victim Mentality

4205 Ground Ivy
2226 Confid Essence
1360 Flannel Flower

1379 Philothrca
1389 Southern Cross
1390 Spinifex
1392 Sturt Desert Rose
3510 Grass Of Parnassus
3514 Monkeyflower
2225 Rowan
3517 Sea Rocket
5768 Transformation
5221 Horseradish
2444 Hidden Splendor
2438 Strength (3rd Chakra)
5702 Goldenrod
5090 Integrity In Interaction
5413 Integrity In Interaction Spray
1703 Urchin Dryandra
1765 Anemone
1817 Mussel
1838 Pipsissewa
2349 Sponge
1989 Japanese Magnolia
2043 Self-Image
2072 Zinnia
3813 Mountain Lion

## 72. Winter Lows

3212 Orange Calcite
3225 Spectrolite
2378 Borage
2214 Snowdrop
5325 Child Glow
5243 Red Hollyhock
5245 Saint John's Wort
2451 Happiness
2457 Vital Spark
5694 Celandine
5080 Light Anchor
5467 Golden Radiance Spray
5415 Golden Radiance
2358 Diatoms
2355 Dolphin
2399 Fairy Bell
1798 Grape Hyacinth
1808 Jellyfish
1833 Periwinkle
2403 Red Huckleberry
1869 Snowberry
5640 Animals To The Rescue
3816 Dolphin
3815 Hummingbird
3821 Otter

## 73. Womanhood

3201 Green Jasper
2750 Lehua
2426 Embó Rudá
5786 Floral Caju
2427 Pyatã
2434 Renascer
2433 Revelação
2430 Seiva
2364 Angelica
2373 Evening Primrose
4209 Love
1351 Bottlebrush
1386 She Oak
4822 Woman Cream
3169 Woman Essence
3508 Balsam
2220 Elder
4795 Eros
4913 Eros Gel
3517 Sea Rocket
5334 Aphrodite
5330 Artemis
5332 Athena
5211 Clairy Sage
5333 Demeter
5331 Hestia
5222 Houseleek
5226 Lady's Mantle
5305 Lunar Intuition
1501 Beech
1541 Mustard
1565 Walnut
2461 Goddess
2453 Golden Dawn
5712 Red Gladiolus
1658 Hybrid Pink Fairy
1662 Macrozamia
2331 Pain Cream
1693 Rose Cone Flower
5816 Devata
1771 Barnacle
1783 Candystick
1790 Easter Lily
2402 Silver Birch
1975 Female Balance
1989 Japanese Magnolia
2007 Marigold
3824 Swan

## 74. Workaholic Tendencies

1132 Moschatel
1335 Tranquility
2381 Purple Flower
1347 Black Eyed Susan
4812 Calm & Clear
4823 Calm & Clear Cream
4813 Calm & Clear Mist
1358 Dog Rose of the Wild Forces
1368 Jacaranda
1376 Old Man Banksia
2215 Apple
3509 Globe Thistle
3507 Hazel
2221 Sycamore
2223 Valerian
5325 Child Glow
1519 Elm
1543 Oak
1545 Olive
2454 Let Go
2448 Trust
5698 Cyclamen
5665 Original Innocence
5751 Original Innocence Spray
5711 Pussy Willow
1681 Purple Enamel Orchid
5196 Clear Mind
5199 Clear Mind Aura Spray
5602 Walking to the Earth's Rhythm
1794 Forsythia
1863 Sea Palm
1865 Urchin
4968 Fatigue
2020 Orchid, Dancing Lady
3883 Reduce Stress
3821 Otter

# Index to the essences arranged by essence line

## Fox Mountain Singles



## Fox Mountain Goddesses



## Fox Mountain Kits



## Healing Herbs Bach



## Healing Herbs Bach Singles



## Himalayan Chakra Essences



## Himalayan Enhancers

## Pacific Combos



## Pacific Flower Singles



## Pacific Sea Singles



## Pacific Kits



## Petite Fleur Combos



## Petite Fleur Mists



## Petite Fleur Roses



## Petite Fleur Texans



## Petite Fleur Test Kit

# The following books are highly recommended for those that want to explore the field of flower essences in greater depth.

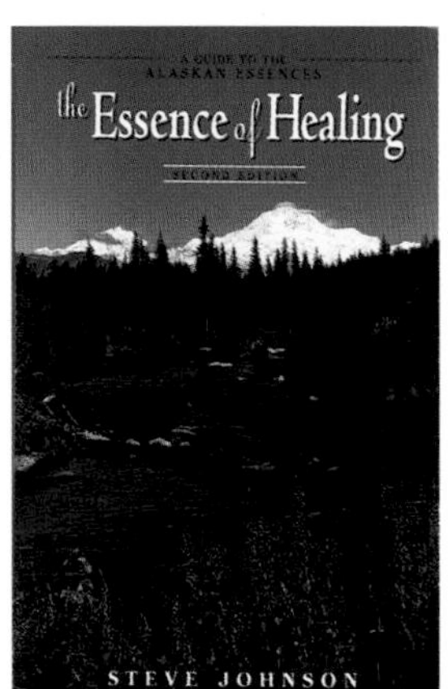


**THE ESSENCE OF HEALING**
*Steve Johnson*

Describes all three flower kits, Gem and Environmental kits, with application and use including animals and plants. 84 Full colour photos, showing all the 72 flower essences and 12 Environmental essences.

**THE BAILEY FLOWER ESSENCES HANDBOOK**
*Arthur Bailey*

Bailey Essences deal with Attitudes of Mind. Distinct from the Bach essences, Arthur describes their action, selection, preparation and descriptions of each flower essence.

**ANYONE CAN DOWSE FOR BETTER HEALTH**
*Arthur Bailey*

Helpful hints and tips on how everyone can learn to dowse, with occasions for use.

**AUSTRALIAN BUSH FLOWER REMEDIES BOOKLET**
*Ian White*

A booklet giving brief descriptions of Ian's original individual and combination essences including negative and positive indicators.

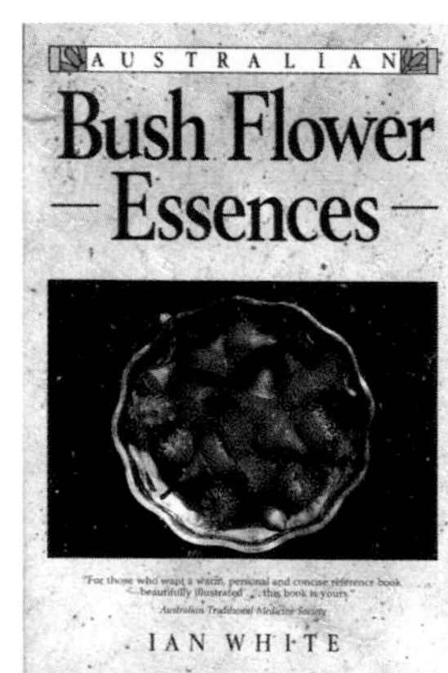


**AUSTRALIAN BUSH FLOWER ESSENCES**
*Ian White*

Describes the history and purpose of essences, how they work and how to use them with Numerology and Kinesiology. Explains negatives and positives and detail for each flower.

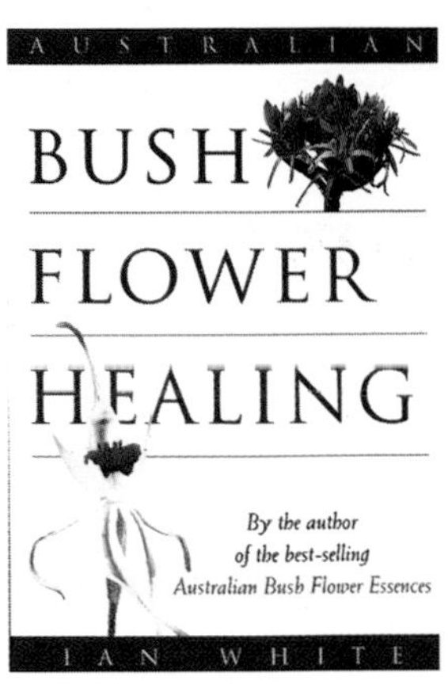


**BUSH FLOWER HEALING**
*Ian White*

A companion to the first book, includes updated analyses and new essences. Also contains sections on Kinesiology and Iridology.

**THE HEALING HERBS OF EDWARD BACH**
*Julian & Martine Barnard*

Introduces the interrelationship of humankind to plants, flowers and the natural environment, then details the 38 remedies, indications and preparation methods.

**THE MANA OF FLOWERS**
*Penny Medeiros*

Analyses each of the flowers including identity, overview, Devic analysis and Affirmation. Also describes preparing and making essences, diagnosis and case studies.

**THE COLLECTED WRITINGS OF EDWARD BACH**
*Julian Barnard, editor*

The writings of Dr Bach, including his early papers on bacteriology and homeopathy and all his writings on the flower remedies. Contains lectures, letters and papers from 1920 to 1936.

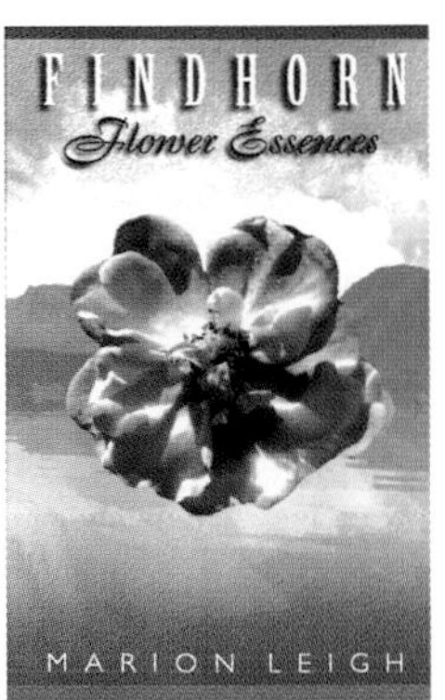


**FINDHORN FLOWER ESSENCES**
*Marion Leigh*

Explains how flower essences aid transformation. Contains keynotes and attributes of each remedy and how to choose and make essences

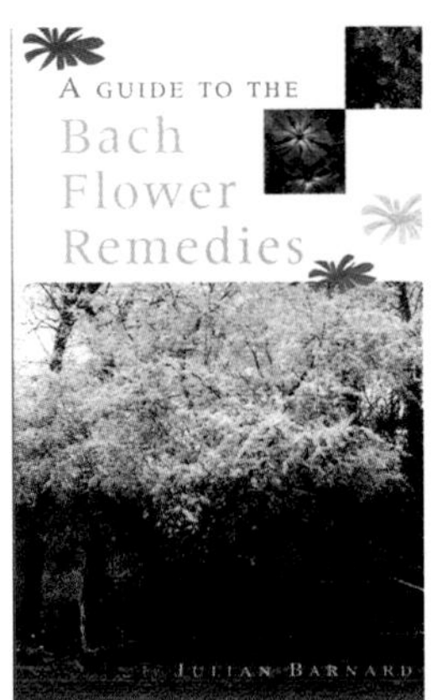


**A GUIDE TO THE BACH FLOWER REMEDIES**
*Julian Barnard*

Introduces Dr Bach, explaining how he discovered and made his remedies in the 1930's. It describes how they work, what happens when we take a remedy, diagnosis and prescription.

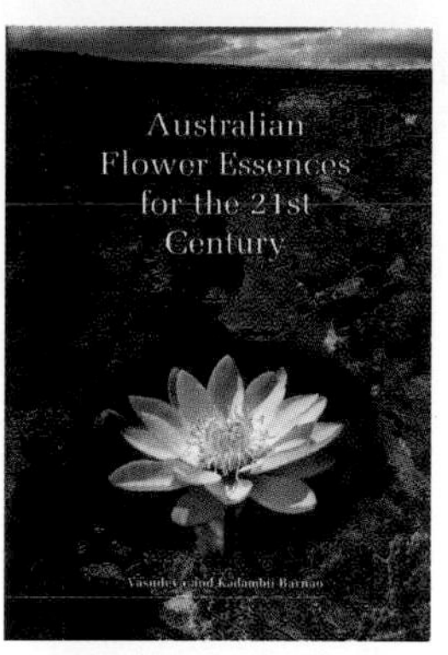


**AUSTRALIAN FLOWER ESSENCES FOR THE 21st CENTURY**
*Vasudeva & Kadambii Barnao*

Contains an introduction to the history of wild flowers used by the native Australian community. Describes key qualities and use of each essence, including use of flower essences on acu-pressure points on the ear.

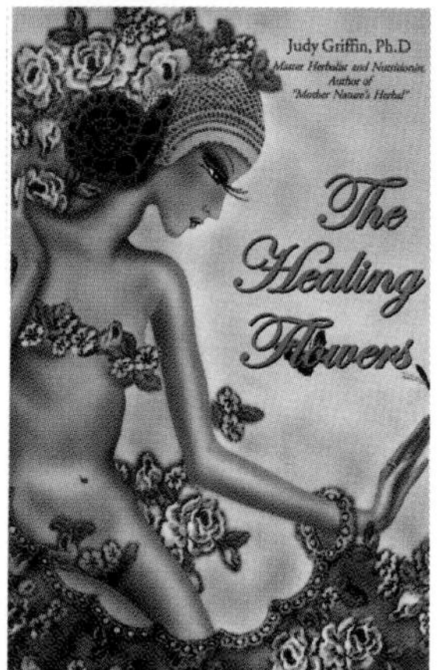


**THE HEALING FLOWERS**
*Judy Griffin, PhD*

Details The Original Petites, the Masters, Native Texans, Antique Roses and Combinations.

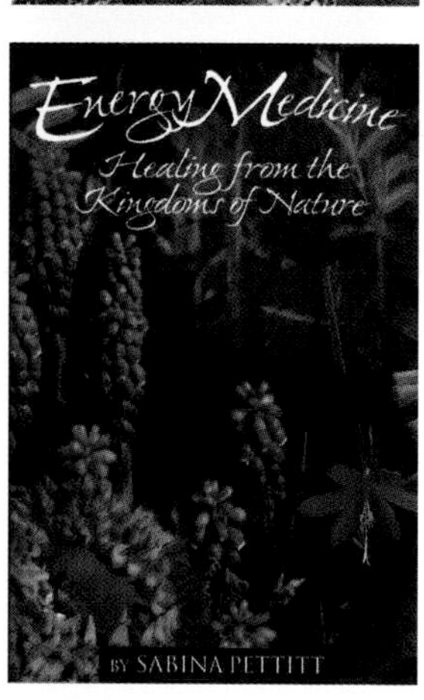


**ENERGY MEDICINE**
*Sabina Pettitt*

Here Sabina matches flower and sea essences to the body's meridian channels and chakras, showing how they interact with us to achieve health and well being. Includes use with other therapies.

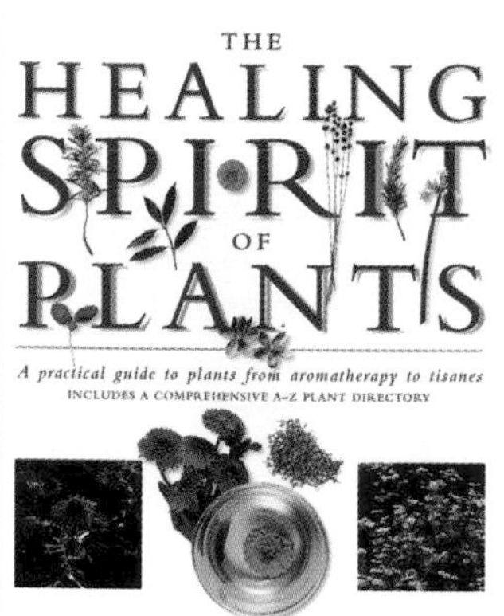


**HEALING SPIRIT OF PLANTS**
*Clare Harvey & A Cochrane*

Practical information and ancient lore explaining the significance of plant/flower spirits. Describes the chakras, meridians, and subtle anatomy.

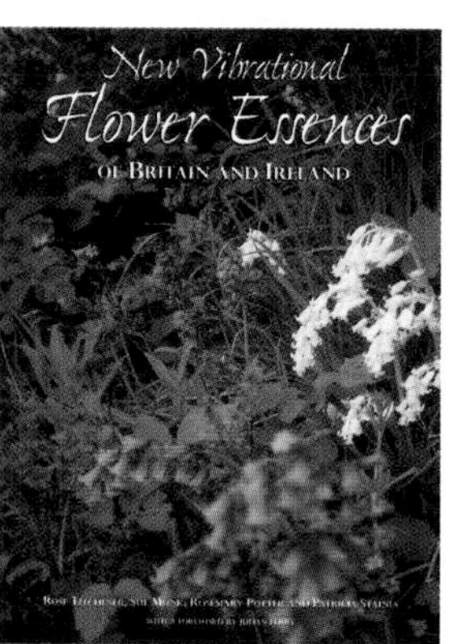


**NEW VIBRATIONAL FLOWER ESSENCES OF BRITAIN & IRELAND**
*Titchiner, Monk, Potter & Staines*

A comprehensive handbook of the new vibrational flower essences researched and developed in the British Isles and Ireland since the 1930's

**BACH FLOWER REMEDIES FOR ANIMALS**
*Helen Graham & Gregory Vlamis*

Describes relationship of flower essences to homeopathy, the various emotional states of pets and how essences can restore harmony and balance to an animal's true nature.

**FLOWER ESSENCES FOR RELATIONSHIPS**
*Martin J Scott*
*& Gael Mariani*

Covers major relationship stages in our lives - looking for love, romance, setting down, children, rifts, relationships ending and moving on - and appropriate essences for treatment.

**PATTERNS OF LIFE FORCE**
*Julian Barnard*

Reviews the life and work of Dr Edward Bach and his discovery of the Remedies, placing his method of healing in a wider context to show its effectiveness and future implications.

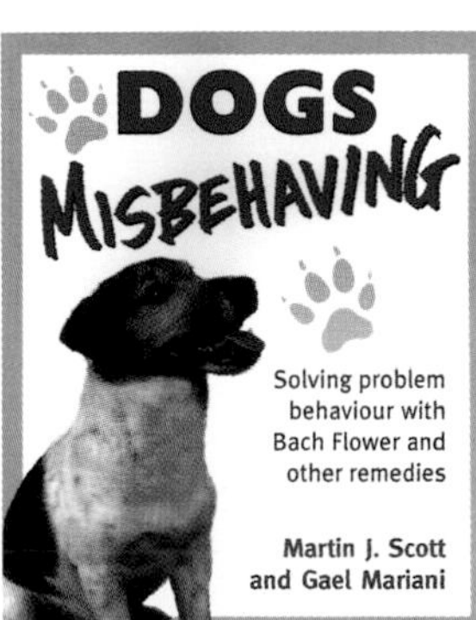


**DOGS MISBEHAVING**
*Martin J Scott*
*& Gael Mariani*
Explains how to tackle your dogs problems i.e trauma , aggression, barking, travel sickness, destructiveness , nervousness and anxiety - using Flower Remedies with practical dog training methods.

## FURTHER USEFUL INFORMATION

For in-depth training courses/workshops:

IFVM
Middle Piccadilly Natural Healing Centre
Holwell
Sherborne
Dorset DT9 5LW
Tel/fax: 01305 849 379
email: info@vibrationalmedicine.net

The following shops in the UK carry or will special order the products described in this book:

The Nutri Centre
7, Park Crescent
London W1B 1PF
Tel; 020 7436 5122
email: enq@nutricentre.com
Web: www.nutricentre.com

Revital Health
(three London shops,
also Beaconsfield & Stratford-upon-Avon)
Tel: 0800 252 875
Email: enquire@revital.com
Web: www.revital.com

Napiers Dispensary
(Edinburgh & Glasgow)
Tel: 0131 225 5542
email: napierspr@talk21.com
Web: www.napiers.net

Fresh & Wild
(six shops in London)
Tel: 0800 9 175 175
email: shop@freshandwild.com
Website: www.freshandwild.com

Neal's Yard Remedies
(21 shops across the UK)
For Bush Essences Only
Tel: 020 7627 1949 (Customer services)

The Cosmic Trader
76, Gillygate
York YO31 7EQ
Tel: 01 904 622 706

IFER supplies over 300 retail outlets in the UK. To find your local stockist please contact the International Flower Essence Repertoire.

IFER also runs weekend seminars at intervals throughout the year. For information please feel free to contact us to be on our mailing list for such events.

IFER
The Living Tree
Milland
Near Liphook
Hampshire GU30 7JS
Tel: 01 428 741 572
Fax: 01 428 741 679
email: flower@atlas.co.uk

# Acknowledgements

We wish to thank all the flower essence producers for their dedication and integrity in offering to the public some of the finest quality of essences available, without which this book would not have been possible. We would like to thank all the staff at IFER for their loyalty and hard work above and beyond the call of duty. Their support would be hard to overstate, or to thank adequately.

Savio Joannes of the Nutri-Centre for providing much of the idea for the inspiration for this book. Raj Vora of Revital Health for his clear early support throughout IFER's early years. Susan Curtis and Romy Fraser of Neals Yard Remedies for their care, interest and support.

Our thanks to John Breese of Red Box Design, and for the all-nighter to get this book finished on time! And our continuing gratitude to David Jenkins of Bonner & Jenkins Printing.

We must also thank all of the professional therapists who, as customers and as friends over the years, have helped nurture IFER in its growth. Their research and feedback has and will always be invaluable to us and to the flower essence makers.

Without Margaret Gallier's extraordinary support IFER would not be where it is today.

Belinda Usmar's help and laughter also contributed enormously, and we miss her as well.

Reid & Peggy Dennis, whose support of their son's interest in photography enabled the photographs of the cover to come into being. And for much else besides.

Peter Tadd has enabled IFER to work to higher standards of selection of our products than would otherwise have been possible; and in the course of the years has contributed deeply and significantly to our understanding of the nature of the essences. His friendship and humour and patience have continually enriched the life of all here at The Living Tree.

Sharon Heaver, for continually coming up with terrific ideas, such as the colour-coding of the reference section of this book. How many more ideas do you have?

Gail Shaw has provided assistance with such skill and generosity that it has been truly a pleasure to work with her over the years since IFER was founded; and her remarkable daughters Francine and Natalie have each been greatly helpful and supportive.

For the laughter and cheer she brings each day to the office, Helen Johnson is our own office lighting. Her generosity, and interest in the essences shines forth for us all.

Angela Priddle so deftly handles the phones and despite the odds manages to organize our office! You are a star.

Barbara Lord has brought her delightful spirit and integrity and compassion to The Living Tree each week, to the benefit of all who have contact with her.

And Janette Ross, we'll miss you & your help, but know you'll be greatly enjoying New Zealand.

Lizzie Staples helps us all simply with her smiling eyes, and her friendship over the years is cherished by us all.

Rob Findlay has been a constant friend and help, and has enabled our workshops to flow more smoothly.

To Maria, welcome!

Without Julia Crangle's constant, tremendous, and untiring support over the weeks of the preparation of this book, this Compendium would almost certainly not have seen the light of day. Thank you, Julia.

Suzanne, for keeping the ship on course each day. What good fortune to have your help!

And Gwen. Words cannot express our thanks and our love.

Don Dennis Clare G. Harvey

We wish to thank each of the developers for their kind permission to use their photographs.

A special thank you to Carson Barnes for the photos of the Dancing Light Orchids. (Heart Wings photo on page 59 by Don Dennis.)

Mark Titchiner for the photograph of Rose Titchiner's hands on the title page.

Cover photographs and Living Tree Orchid photographs by Don Dennis.

Front Cover photo: Devata *Comparetia speciosa*. See description on page 100.
Back Cover photo: Angelic Canopy *Lailiocattleya Angel Love*. See description on page 100.

Prints of other orchid photographs are available from The Living Tree, please feel free to contact us for details.